A WO
WITH
JESUS

*A year book of daily readings
of the sayings of Jesus*

with questions for individuals
and group discussions

Paul Rosier

LOXWOOD PRESS

ISBN 978-1-908113-63-4

The music and complete words of the song extracts
can be found in *Mission Praise*, published
by Marshall Morgan & Scott

Printed by Kenads Printers

Loxwood Press, 50 Loxwood Avenue, Worthing,
West Sussex BN14 7RA

Introduction

SOME books are good for the time it takes to read them, and then lie forgotten on a shelf. Others are started, but never finished, or even opened! There are books, however, which are lifelong friends, offering comfort, insight and encouragement on each visit. This could be such a companion. It is offered in the prayerful hope that it will help you encounter the words of Jesus with a freshness and faithfulness to inspire you to read more and heed more the wisdom and life-changing power of the Saviour. Although offered as a personal journal for spending a year in the company of Luke as he records the sayings of Jesus, it also offers small group material for discussion and reflection. Read carefully and prayerfully, listening intently to the words of Jesus and the heart behind the truths. The Gospels are full of the stories of people who were changed by their encounter with Him – it is my prayer that we will be changed too.

Paul Rosier
2021

How to use this book

● As a personal journal for daily reading. Each day's text comes with a reference to the host passage, and it is essential to read this wider "Key passage" to grasp the context of the day's reading.
● As a personal reflection, giving time to think about the issues raised.
● As a personal prayer guide, using the prayer each day to promote further prayer.
● As a corporate guide to study, using the "Key Questions" as discussion starters. These are identified by the key logo.

JANUARY 1

"Why were you searching for me...?"
Luke 2:49   Key passage: Luke 2:41-52

We all do it...lose things! We can't remember where we left the items, when we last saw them, where they might possibly be - and when we find the item (where it was all along!) we are relieved. The item was not "lost" – our memory of where it might be was "lost".

Luke uniquely records these first words of the boy Jesus to his anxious parents. They had travelled together with large numbers of fellow-worshippers, content in their security. But when they could not find their son, they retraced their steps, to find Him in the Jerusalem temple courts, sitting at the feet of the teachers. The indignant expression of their anxiety is met with a loving but positive assertion – "Why were you searching for me...?"

How many days have you travelled until you realise you are missing the presence of Jesus? What anxieties have gnawed away at you until you have discovered the need to go back and find Him where He has always been? What drives you to search for Him when life seems tough?

Lord, thank You that You are never far from me, even when I have wandered far from You. You know my longing to find You. Thank You that You are always wanting to find me.

Where were you when you found Jesus? Where was He when He found you? How long did it take you to find Him? At the start of a new year, what would you like to "forget" from last year? What do you need to "remember"?

January 2

"Didn't you know…?"
Luke 2:49   Key passage: Luke 2:41-52

We call them "lightbulb moments" – when we discover something new, come to a fresh realisation, work something out…and then find out that other people already knew! Knowledge is rarely "new" – often it's just "rediscovered".

Jesus is nonplussed by the concern of His parents at his apparent "disappearance" – surely they knew where they would find him, but for them that entailed a journey in reverse, back to Jerusalem and the temple. Sometimes the journey of our life slips into reverse gear – and we find ourselves reverting to childhood pleasures, reliving simpler experiences.

Maybe we need to rediscover the thrill of knowing Jesus personally as if for the first time, the newness of God's grace in Christ, the wonder of being forgiven and loved by Him. Didn't you know this for yourself as a wonder and work in your life?

Jesus, thank you for the thrill of knowing we are loved by You, saved by You, and kept secure in Your grace. May I know You personally in my life today.

January 3

"I had to be in my Father's house…"
Luke 2:49   Key passage: Luke 2:41-52

"Home – where they know the worst about us and love us the best". But where is "home"… a particular building, a location, a family, the place of your birth or childhood?

Jesus assures His parents that whilst He needs to "go home" with them to Nazareth, He has another "home" – the temple of His Father – where His presence is necessary. Home is a place of necessity, of familiarity, of reassurance. It is the place of reflection, of learning, of completeness. It is the place which offers security, certainty, solitude. It is also the place of origin, and the place of return. For some, home can be a welcoming place. For others it is a lonely place, shadowed by memories of what is now lost, a reminder of blessings now past.

But home is above all *our* place – somewhere unique to us. For Jesus, His words echo with authority. Where else could He be, but in His Father's house? For Him, this is not just a matter of location, but also of calling. He knows where He belongs, and to whom He belongs. What about you?

God, may I know that I belong to You, and may I find security in Your presence today.

What's the difference between a "house" and "home"? Where and how do you experience the presence of God? How can "church" be "home"? How can your "home" be "church"?

January 4

"It is written…"
Luke 4:4   Key passage: Luke 4:1-13

Rules, rules, rules. We can't live without them, but we often can't live with them. Rules are fine when we are on the right side of them, when they benefit us, when they are easy to obey. But how is it when they curtail us, challenge us, cost us? Is it ever OK to bend them, ignore them, disobey them?

The response of Jesus to the temptation of the devil is to remind him of the rules. "It is written…". The devil proposes bending the rules, since apparently this will not matter much. After all, isn't Jesus hungry for food, respect and power? What the devil has to offer does not seem unreasonable, except that none of these things are his to give in any case!

"It is written…" – let's be clear about the rules. God's Word is God's Word for a reason…He speaks with authority, power and relevance. To ignore God's Word is to ignore the word of life itself. To misrepresent God's Word is to seek to bend the will of God to our will for our benefit. It is written with all clarity, compulsion and conviction - and demands our full obedience.

Thank you, Lord, for Your Word which speaks with such power and persuasion. May this Word speak to me today, and may I respond with joyful obedience.

January 5

"Man does not live on bread alone…"
Luke 4:4   Key passage: Luke 4:1-13

We are creatures of habit – and not all habits are helpful or healthy. There is however a difference between a habit and a necessity. A necessity by definition is essential to the support of life and wellbeing. A habit may not be a necessity but may become a need – and a necessity in our opinion. "I can't do without…" whatever it is.

The devil presumes that the hunger of Jesus presents an opportunity to tempt Him into submission to the devil's power. It seems only a small matter, and perfectly reasonable, that Jesus might use His power to meet His own needs. "You've got to look after yourself". But when that conflicts with the needs of others, there are choices to be made…

…and Jesus chooses, not Himself, but you and me! When the pressure was on, He set His face to the task of salvation, to the road that would lead to Calvary, to the cross, to resurrection and hope. He who was to speak of Himself as "the bread of life" yields not to His own needs, but to the needs of a hungry and wanting world.

Thank you Jesus that You set Your love for me above all things, and You meet my needs in every way, body, mind and soul. Bless You for your faithfulness.

What gets in the way of you spending time with God? What do you find difficult in concentrating on in your personal devotions? How can you help encourage others in the devotional life?

January 6

"Worship the Lord your God and serve him only"
Luke 4:8   Key passage: Luke 4:1-13

Sometimes, there's nothing for it…but to start all over again. The computer document which mysteriously disappears, the DIY task which goes wrong, the conversation which gets misunderstood – it's back to the beginning and get it right.

Ask many people what the Ten Commandments are, and the chances are they will quote the "popular" ones: "Do not commit adultery", "Do not kill". The first commandment gets forgotten – "You shall have no other gods before me". God repeatedly had to remind people of this simple principle of His pre-eminence based on the proof of what He had done for them. "Fear the Lord your God, serve him only…" (Deut. 6.13) for "…(He) brought you out of Egypt, out of the land of slavery" (Deut. 6.12).

The devil tempts Jesus to overlook the uniqueness of God and bow down to him instead. Jesus will not be fooled. How often are we cowed into forgetting that God is above all things, and that all things are in His hands? When the issues of life today become too knotty, go back to the beginning!

Forgive me Lord when I forget that my life truly finds its meaning and purpose in who You are.

January 7

"Do not put the Lord your God to the test"
Luke 4:12   Key passage: Luke 4:1-13

"Does what it says on the tin" – a catchy way of selling your product. After all, honesty appeals to us. We know where we are. When the product fails to live up to its promise, we are not just disappointed – we may begin to doubt the integrity of the manufacturer.

When the devil tempts Jesus to prove the promises of God, Jesus responds with the powerful assertion of the reliability of God… "Do not put the Lord your God to the test…" Quite simply, if God is God, then it goes without saying that He keeps His promises. Any doubt about the capability of God is doubt about the culpability of God – He cannot be who He claims to be. Jesus asserts that His knowledge of the Father God is absolute and compelling – and for this reason God is not to be tested. He will keep His word.

If only we would keep our word and trust Him in all things!

Help me, Lord, to trust You completely in all circumstances, and especially when the going is tough.

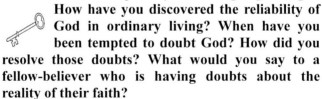 **How have you discovered the reliability of God in ordinary living? When have you been tempted to doubt God? How did you resolve those doubts? What would you say to a fellow-believer who is having doubts about the reality of their faith?**

January 8

"Today this scripture is fulfilled in your hearing"
Luke 4:21   Key passage: Luke 4:14-21

I has always wanted to play the triangle with an orchestra…and when I retired a kind friend made it possible for me, even supplying me with my own triangle! The technique is important, but the timing even more so. It was only one strike of the instrument, but it really mattered when I did it! One false move, and the whole effort of the rest of the orchestra would have been spoiled.

Moments matter – and in the synagogue at Nazareth Jesus takes the moment to declare from the reading that the time of God's favour is now… He is not just the means of delivering God's good news – He *is* the good news. The moment is now – the long-awaited coming of God's salvation is here, the One who ushers in the Jubilee, who comes to redeem the helpless and hopeless…He is here in the person of Jesus of Nazareth.

"Salvation is found in no-one else, for there is no other name under heaven given to men by which we must be saved" (Acts 4.12). Don't miss the moment!

Jesus, I acknowledge You as the Saviour, my Saviour, here and now this day. Thank You.

January 9

"No prophet is accepted in his home town"
Luke 4:24   Key passage: Luke 4:20-30

Some things are viewed best at a distance – a mighty mountain, the rolling ocean, the billowing clouds. Too close, and we miss the scale, the beauty, the wonder. Important moments can only be appreciated sometime later, when the impact has been felt and impressions gained. Stand back, mind the gap and understand!

There were those in the synagogue at Nazareth that day who heard Jesus read the Isaiah scroll and were pleased – "(they) spoke well of him and were amazed…" because he was one of them, a "local lad" – "Isn't this Joseph's son?" But in their closeness and clamour they missed the import of what He was saying. That's why Jesus declared "No prophet is accepted in his home town". He knew that before long they would be questioning His very person.

Beware of familiarity – we all know where that leads! Listen carefully to the words of Jesus, understand what He is saying, who He is addressing, and what He is saying. It may just be that He is speaking to you!

Lord, may I never take Your word for granted, but help me listen attentively, act obediently and honour you eternally.

"Sermons are not for listening to – they are for acting on." When has God's Word had a direct impact on you? What was it that touched or challenged you? What did you do about it? Share passages of Scripture that have been particularly important to you at times in your life.

January 10

Be quiet...!"
Luke 4:35   Key passage: Luke 4:31-37

In this age of digital technology, everyone is talking. 24/7/365…endless communication. Wall-to-wall television, rolling news, limitless opinion, e-mails in industrial quantities. Screaming headlines, angry customers, demanding consumers. People glued to their phones, social media clashing, a veritable Babel of words, words, words…and often proclaiming the blindingly obvious.

Jesus the living Word demands attention – and when confronted by the evil spirit possessing this man, a spirit convulsing in recognition of the divine power and authority of Christ, He demands "Be quiet…!" After all, the spirit is only declaring the obvious, that Jesus is the One with true power over all conditions, who can bring wholeness to the sick and suffering.

"Be quiet…!" The command is short and shocking – but is absolutely necessary. Without the silence, the truth of Jesus' dynamic power will not be heard. At times of crisis, the world's response is a crescendo of noise. When your life is in crisis, be quiet and listen to who this Jesus is…He has the power to bring healing, wholeness and help.

Lord, forgive me when I have so much to say, and so little desire to listen. Teach me to listen to who You are.

January 11

"Come out of him!"
Luke 4:35   Key passage: Luke 4:31-37

Choice. You have choice. From waking moment to the blessing of sleep, it's choice, choice, choice – what to wear, where to go, what to do. Who to see, to speak to, to like and love. Choice is the token of life, the necessity of the age. A world without choice is hard to imagine…

…but sometimes there is no choice. Compelled by authority to follow, we can only respond. Authority does not come with trumpeting clarity but quiet conviction, not overbearing burden but overwhelming wholeness. We recognise true authority when we encounter it.

Jesus encounters the man with the evil spirit, and it is the evil spirit speaks first, reacting to the divine authority of Christ before a word is spoken. The words of lies that are the norm for the spirit can only become words of truth in the presence of Jesus – "I know who you are". Authority (Gk: *exousia*) at heart means "that which comes out". The *exousia* of Jesus which comes from Him can only demand the spirit to come out from the demoniac. The presence of Jesus is dynamically challenging – "Come out!"

"Majesty, kingdom authority flows from his throne…"
(Jack Hayford). Jesus, the One with true authority over all things, I worship You.

Think of "authority figures in our society – how does the authority of Jesus compare or differ? What happens if we ignore "society" authority figures? What happens if we ignore Jesus? Why do we struggle with authority?

January 12

"I must preach…to the other towns also…"
Luke 4:43   Key passage: Luke 4:38-44

"See you later…!" How many times has a shop assistant said that to you, when the likelihood of it actually happening is nil? It's an attempt to appear friendly and "customer-focussed"…but sadly often has no impact..

Jesus is pursued by the people who want to hear what He has to say and see what He has to do. The presence of Jesus is comforting, encouraging, inspiring. But Jesus knows that there are many others who need to hear the good news. He cannot stay.

How many times have you wished to "stay in the moment" – but we must move on? How many times have you been thrilled by the word of Jesus, but forgotten that it's a word for others too? We can often talk about the imperative to share the good news, but never actually get round to doing it.

Where would God want you to be today? It may be just where you are, in the home, the office, the school. It may be somewhere else, in a situation of need or despair. Make sure you are in the right place today!

Lord, thank You that You will guide me today to the right place and the right moment. May I be Your good news to others today.

January 13

"Put out into deep water…"
Luke 5:4   Key passage: Luke 5:1-11

Learning to swim is one of life's greatest challenges. The earlier children are introduced to water, the easier they find it to trust themselves to the science – that the human body will float! It's one thing knowing this as a truth – quite another matter proving it!

It's the letting go that we find so difficult – and allowing ourselves to be carried by other forces. The disciples have been up all night fishing, with little to show for all their efforts. How often have we reflected on a day's effort and wondered what we achieved?

Then comes the word of Jesus "Put out into deep water…". That demands effort, energy, enthusiasm. Surely we've tried? Maybe there was a moment, a place, an opportunity we missed. But we would rather be in the shallow water, the place of safety and comfort, the place of familiarity. Does Jesus know what we do not?

Where would Jesus have you be today or tomorrow? Where would you want to be?

Grant me courage, Lord, to hear Your call to the "deep water" and to go today where You would have me be.

 Where might be the "deep water" for you? Is it always a difficult place or a challenging context? How can you work out whether God is genuinely calling you to involvement in a specific situation, or whether it is your own aspirations? What are the dangers of "deep water"?

January 14

"Let down the nets for a catch…"
Luke 5:4   Key passage: Luke 5:1-11

The world is full of experts – and in a crisis they all have an opinion on the matter. It's not always clear how you become an "expert", but it's very clear that others will listen! Not all experts will agree on the matter, so in the end it's up to you who you believe…

When Jesus encounters Simon standing on the shore washing his nets, he commands the experienced but frustrated fisherman "…let down the nets for a catch". Does this Jesus know anything about fishing? Does he understand that we've just been doing that all night (without success)? Doesn't he know that it's the wrong time of day to be going out again? Who's the expert here…?

"Because you say so, I will…" Simon may be dubious, but he's not so dumb as to ignore the command. And the result?

How many "catches" have we missed because we were in the wrong place, at the wrong time, listening to the wrong impulse, and expecting the wrong outcome…? And all because we doubt the word of Jesus.

Lord, thank you that you know me intimately. Forgive my doubting mind and heart, and help me to be obedient to your call on my life today.

When have you had to admit that you did not "know best"? Why do we find humility hard to exhibit? Who has shaped your thinking about specific areas of your life and experience? Who do you tend to "listen to"?

January 15

"…From now on you will catch men".
Luke 5:10   Key passage: Luke 5:1-11

A university education is a wonderful thing – but not always a preparation for the life that follows. A school friend read the sciences and is now a car salesman, and one of my sons qualified as an Occupational Therapist and now plans maintenance works for Network Rail. Skills gained in one field are occasionally useful in another…

Jesus' encounter with Simon was dramatic and life-changing. We are not told what happened to the fishing nets and boats when Simon left to follow Jesus. The call of Jesus is, however, compelling – "You will catch men". Jesus does not always call a disciple to leave everything just like that. He calls a disciple to put all their skills and energy to the service of the kingdom. Simon (Peter) would soon demonstrate he was not always best equipped for the task and often made a complete mess of things – but he was first to declare the messiahship of Jesus, and it was he who spoke on the Day of Pentecost of the coming of the Spirit.

Do you hear the call of the King?

Hear the call of the Kingdom to reach out to the lost,
With the Father's compassion in the wonder of the
cross,
Bringing peace and forgiveness, and a hope yet to
come;
Let the nations put their trust in Him.
King of Heaven, we will answer the call,
We will follow, bringing hope to the world,
Filled with passion, filled with power to proclaim
Salvation in Jesus' name.

(Stuart Townend)

January 16

"I am willing"
Luke 5.13   Key passage: Luke 5:12-16

Feelings – the battlefield of every Monday morning, every dull day, every difficult decision. We don't feel like doing something, going somewhere, being something that challenges us, costs us. We readily expect others to respond and comply, but when it comes to us, the rules change!

Jesus encounters a man with leprosy, the most repugnant member of society – he didn't look good, he didn't feel good, and he certainly wasn't expecting any goodness from anyone else. "If you are willing, you can make me clean…" His cry was one of despair mixed with demand. Jesus' response is solid – "I am willing…" Jesus responds with compassion – but his statement is not one of pure emotional persuasion. God does not bend to our demands according to the earnestness of our prayers or the emotions of our hearts. He responds because that is His very nature, to bring healing and wholeness. "I am willing…" speaks of the very heart of the Saviour, whose will is to do the will of his Father, and look with compassion on the heartfelt prayers of His children.

Today He is willing to hear you…

Lord Jesus, if you are indeed willing, hear my prayer today for those in need of Your healing and redeeming touch. Amen.

 How do doubts impact our prayers? How do we pray in full assurance of God's willingness to hear us without being over-confident or under-committed? How do we discover God's will?

January 17

"Be clean!"
Luke 5:13   Key passage: Luke 5:12-16

How much is "enough"? How much money do you need to be "rich"? What temperature does the oven have to be to be "hot"? How much scrubbing is necessary to make the dishes "clean"?

Jesus' command to the leper "Be clean!" rings with authority, for Luke records that "immediately the leprosy left him". That was the visible, public bit. What we cannot see is what happened to the soul of the leper. He came asking for physical relief; he left with something greater.

How do we know this? Because Luke, in recording the words of Jesus, intimates that the cleansing was of body, mind and spirit. With the belief that illness was a sign of God's judgment upon the sin of an individual or a forebear, the man carried the visible stigma with him every moment. There was no escape – but then there was no hope. Now there is something remarkable – Jesus' command "Be clean" is not just direct, it is also demanding. It addresses the physical scar and the spiritual problem. The healing is instantaneous, the effect incredible – "the leprosy left him". "Be…" – don't just experience something; be it!

Lord, show me what You want me to "Be" – if that be healed, whole, compassionate, loving, understanding, or just to "be" You to a hurting world.

January 18

"Go…show…"
Luke 5:14   Key passage: Luke 5:12-16

"Would you like a test drive…?" The salesman knows that by this point you are highly likely to purchase the car. It's just a question of time. You play cool, trying to ask intelligent questions and nodding and humming as you count the tyres and gaze under the bonnet…The decision has already been made.

As Jesus heals the leper, His command is curious – "Don't tell anyone, but go…show…" Surely people would see the man, now completely recovered, and wonder. Let others work it out! The priests needed to verify the healing and give thanks to God, fulfilling the ancient requirements of sacrifice. What was this man before, and what is he now? It's one thing telling people a reality, quite another letting them see it for themselves.

Who are the people who have made a deep impression on you in your life? Do you remember what they said, or what they were? What made the difference?

"I hear and I forget, I see and I remember, I do and I understand". Lord, help me to not just speak of You, but to show You in all I am and do. Amen.

 Share stories of those who have modelled Christian living for you. What was it or is it about that them that has been so powerful? Why is personal example often more powerful than persistent exhortation?

January 19

"Friend, your sins are forgiven…"
Luke 5:20   Key passage: Luke 5:17-26

Ah…the smell of freshly-baked bread as you step inside the supermarket. The bakery is often at the furthest point from the door, ensuring that you pass by other offers and bargains *en route* to that crusty loaf. Supermarket layout is a science of its own, and they know how to get you! How often have you just "popped in for a pint of milk" and come out clutching other good things?

This paralytic cannot get to see Jesus, but he has friends! So desperate are they to get their man to Him that they resort to making a hole in the roof and letting him down gently. Luke does not tell us what they were hoping for, but if they had to extract their man by the same route theirs would have been the embarrassment. For Jesus, physical challenge and spiritual change go hand-in-hand. "Friend, your sins are forgiven…" is a staggering statement. How often does an encounter with the Master result in something greater than the hope expressed. What dare you ask Jesus for today, and what do you believe He wants to do for you?

Lord, help me to believe that You are more than equal to my needs today, and grant me the faith to trust You.

January 20

"Why are you thinking these things…"
Luke 5:22   Key passage: Luke 5:17-26

Some people are difficult to please! They always give a polite answer when all you want is a straight one. They ask a question, but you instinctively know that another issue lies behind their words. They profess gratitude when you sense the opposite may be true. O to be able to read the mind of others…!

When Jesus healed the paralytic, onlookers from the ruling classes said nothing but gave away everything – and Jesus knew what they were thinking! "Who is this man?" "What right does he have to do what he's just done?" "How dare he make such claims!" Jesus knows the human mind – he has just witnessed the intentions of the paralytic's friends and rewarded their faith (Luke 5.20). Now he witnesses the suspicions of the "professionals" – the religious leaders. The very people who should speak out the truth can only harbour doubts in their minds – and the Saviour exposes them in public! There's nothing intrinsically wrong with doubt – but when we give it too much room, we become caught in its grip and reveal our lack of trust. May we be open in our words and actions.

Teach me, Lord, to be open and honest, to express my doubts but seek your truth in all I am and do today. Amen.

Some Christians think that doubting is negative. How can expressing doubts help us or hinder us in our daily walk with Jesus? Where do we find help in dealing with our doubts? How would you help a fellow believer who is struggling with their doubts?

January 21

"...take your mat and go home..."
Luke 5:24   Key passage: Luke 5:17-26

Our trains only have two seats – those facing forward and those facing backwards. Some people like to travel seeing where they are going. Others prefer to see where they have just come from. That's life!

The paralytic, now healed, is discharged by Jesus with the instruction "...take your mat and go home...". He had a future to look forward to right now! No longer would he be an outcast, dependent on the kindness of others or despondent at the curtness of strangers. He would be able to support himself and be a useful member of the community. He would be welcome at the synagogue worship and share in the blessing.

Yet Jesus requires him to take his mat with him. The very reminder of his curse, that which had been his anchor and weight for so long has now become his release. He does not need it any more. It could have been left behind there and then – but it goes with him. Sometimes we struggle to leave behind our weights because they have become part of us. For him, it was a reminder of that which was gone...for ever!

Lord Jesus, thank you that You have taken the very things that have weighed me down and brought me release and freedom. Help me to let go and be reminded daily of the freedom You have won for me. Amen.

January 22

"Follow me…"
Luke 5:27   Key passage: Luke 5:27-32

Membership has its benefits! Yet the organisations that have grown the fastest in recent years are those that make few demands of their members – the National Trust, the AA, and (curiously) the Freemasons. You pay your subscription fee and enjoy the benefits…often without having to do anything else by way of commitment.

When Jesus calls Levi the invitation is direct and compelling – "follow me". He does not ask him if he'd like to, or explain the potential benefits of the deal. He calls him, there and then. It's not just a logistical invitation – "come here" – or an intellectual proposition – "do what I'm doing" – but a whole life compulsion. The word of Jesus implies total submission to His ways, irrespective of the cost. For Levi, that would be critical – a sudden and complete loss of income, alongside the disdain of his neighbours who would suspect him of becoming involved in some other grubby money-making venture. When Jesus calls, the invitation is personal, powerful and profound. No excuse, no delay, no short-termism. When Jesus called you to follow him, what was your response – and what is your response today? Don't just "belong" – be "long"!

Jesus, help me to hear your call to me today, and give me the courage to "be long" with You!

 How has life changed since you first followed Jesus? What would you say to someone who is thinking of following Jesus? What difference does it make to you... and to other people?

January 23

"It is not the healthy who need a doctor…"
Luke 5:31   Key passage: Luke 5:27-32

It seems there are two sorts of people in the world – those who talk and those who listen! Some people expect to be heard, and dominate the conversation to the exclusion of anyone else. Their view is paramount, and of course always correct! It's almost impossible to interject, and you do so at your peril.

When Jesus calls Levi to follow him, the Pharisees and teachers of the law start grumbling again. They expect to be heard, because that is their station in life. They are professional complainers, and command a loyal following of listeners. After all, don't they sound like they know what they're talking about? The problem is, they are so wrapped up in their own opinions, they don't realise there's a different slant on life. Jesus' words are enigmatic but engaging – "it is not the healthy who need a doctor…". Beware of thinking that the problem always lies with someone else. Take a look at yourself. Jesus knows your need, and waits to minister to you. All it needs is the realisation of your need of Him. It's time to stop talking…and start listening.

Jesus, show me my need of You, and grant me humility to receive your gracious intervention in my life this day. Amen.

January 24

"I have…come to call…sinners to repentance"
Luke 5:32   Key passage: Luke 5:27-32

Every organisation and company has its strapline to express its mission. Our local police force declares "Our priority is you". I've never been quite sure what that means, or why they should think it necessary to say such a thing.

Jesus declares "I have come to call sinners to repentance". True, but these words are spoken to people who can't see that it applies to them. If it's not relevant, why should I bother? If you think that life is OK, that there's not too much amiss with the way you are living, that there's very little you personally need to amend, then the words of Jesus may be safely and quietly ignored. But if you are honest and humble, then listen. He holds the possibility of a signal difference, of real peace of mind and heart, and the promise of a terrific future. Jesus knows that His mission purpose is to bring wholeness to the missing and marginalised, to the needy and the seedy. They are the ones who know they need a change, and are ready to make it. Do you get it? Jesus' priority is you!

"He comes the broken hearts to heal, the prisoners to free; The deaf shall hear, the lame shall dance, the blind shall see…Make way!" (Graham Kendrick)

Why does it often seem that the church is full of nice people? How often do we hear the stories of people and the difference Jesus as made to them? Share stories of what Jesus has done for you, and what He has done for others.

January 25

"Can you make the guests…fast?"
Luke 5:34 Key passage: Luke 5:33-39

The world is full of experts! Even in the middle of a global pandemic, which is constantly described as "unprecedented", the experts continue to offer their opinions as to what ought to be done, when the plain truth is that no one knows. The world is continually bombarded by the bleatings of the naysayers – those complaining about something, about someone not obeying the rules. Rules need to be obeyed, but for a reason…

Jesus encounters the Pharisees and expert law-teachers complaining that His disciples have not been obeying the rules of fasting. Jesus is well aware of the rules, but has to question the rationale of such rules. What is the point of doing something when the people have forgotten why they do it? "Can you make the guests of the bridegroom fast while he is with them?" Of course not – no one attends a wedding breakfast then declines to eat! This is the time for celebration. The time for fasting will come soon enough. Open your eyes, see the moment and seize the moment. Today is the day of God's opportunity for you – take it and live it!

Help me, Lord, to seize today and its opportunities, and to see Your presence in every moment and situation.

January 26

"No one tears a patch from a new garment…"
Luke 5:36   Key passage: Luke 5:33-39

"There's a hole in my bucket…" – a much-loved hit of Harry Belafonte illustrating the impossible dilemma faced by the unfortunate Henry and the wise Liza as he tries to work out how to mend the hole – without needing the bucket itself. Some problems in life are just not solvable…

Jesus is frustrated with the Pharisees over their apparent inability to see the folly of their religion, and He employs a parable to challenge them. Who in their right mind would ever look at their ragged coat and decide to buy a new one, only to cut a patch from the new one to cover up the old…? Result – two ragged coats. When you buy something new, you discard the old one…right? Or do we hang on to the old one "just in case"…?

Do we cherish old habits because they give us security? Do we find new things threatening? What about the call of Jesus challenging us to discard former behaviours to follow His ways? Why are we always more comfortable in "what we know"? Why is the new "never a patch on the old"?

"From the old I travel to the new, Keep me travelling along with you" (Sidney Carter)

Why do we find change so challenging? Which elements of "church" give us security? When is it right to embrace change, and when is it wrong? What do we need to leave behind personally or collectively to be true to the call of Jesus?

January 27

"No one pours new wine into old wineskins"
Luke 5:37   Key passage: Luke 5:33-39

We love "Pirate Santa" at Christmas – the opportunity to give presents anonymously to those we love with humour and meaning. Sometimes the bigger the box, the more ridiculous the contents! As participants choose a gift from the pile, some cannot resist the larger offerings…not always to their benefit…

You can't always tell the worth of something from the box. Centuries before, the Lord said of the young David "Man looks at the outward appearance, but God looks at the heart" (1 Samuel 16.7). How often have you judged someone by their appearance, age or attitude? Jesus reproves the Pharisees for their judgement of His disciples and their actions without understanding the reason for their behaviour. "No one pours new wine into old wineskins". The "wine" of the Pharisees is "old" – what Jesus has to offer is "new" and not welcomed by those who do not understand. The "new" wine needs "new" wineskins – the people who will hear, believe and respond to the call of the kingdom. Those people are the poor, the needy, the rejected, the powerless. Never mind the box – it's what's inside that matters!

Thank You, Lord, that You know each of us inside and out. Bless You that you choose to call those who are the least in human terms to share in the blessings of Your kingdom. Help me to see others as You do, and to love them with Your love.

January 28

"No one after drinking old wine wants the new…"
Luke 5:39   Key passage: Luke 5:33-39

"How many men does it take to change a lightbulb?" The jokes are plenteous…but the sharpest riposte is "Change…?" Change is challenging, costly…and crucial.

Jesus is challenged by the Pharisees concerning the apparently careless behaviour of the disciples. The Pharisees are all about conservatism – why change the accepted norms of religion? Keep things as they are – we know what's what, and it gives satisfaction and security. The Pharisees cannot grasp that Jesus has come to challenge the self-delusion of the religious classes. Their religion is all well and good, but leads nowhere. Jesus has come to lead His people to a better place, a place of forgiveness, of hope, of fulness. It's easy to drink the "old wine" and think there's nothing better – it's challenging to leave behind the security of what we know and step out in faith…

... yet how often have you been challenged to do that? What may God be saying to you right now about trusting Him for tomorrow, for a new situation, a new location, a new relationship? This may be God's moment for you.

"Father, I place into Your hands the way that I should go, For I know I always can trust you." (Jenny Hewer)

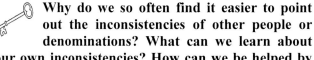 **Why do we so often find it easier to point out the inconsistencies of other people or denominations? What can we learn about our own inconsistencies? How can we be helped by other people? Share experiences of having a spiritual mentor to walk alongside you.**

January 29

"The Son of Man is Lord of the Sabbath"
Luke 6:5   Key passage: Luke 6:1-11

We love playing games with our grandchildren…and hopefully they enjoy playing with us. But we notice that sometimes the rules of the game change depending on who's winning! Of course, as adults we wouldn't dream of adapting the rules to our advantage, would we…?

We have rules for a reason – so that everyone can participate fairly. When Jesus encounters the Pharisees watching His every move, He is prompted to challenge their understanding of the rules. "Have you never read…what David did…?" Clearly the Pharisees were more interested in the mechanical observance of the rules than the rationale for the rules. The Sabbath was God's gift to His children for their enjoyment and enlightenment. But by their rigid observance, the Pharisees had lost the plot. Their one concern was what everyone else was doing…or not. "Man's chief end is to worship God and enjoy Him for ever". The worship of God is not a duty – it is a delight. Jesus asserts that the Sabbath is not to drive us to despair, but to deliver us to wonder.

Lord, release me from the burdens of duty and drudgery and renew me in worship and wonder.

What does the Sabbath mean to you? How do you determine how you spend your Sabbath? What is good to do on the Sabbath...and what is to be avoided? How can we help get a right focus and emphasis on the worship of God on a Sunday?

January 30

"Get up and stand in front of everyone"
Luke 6:8   Key passage: Luke 6:1-11

Do you remember the words of Bob Monkhouse? "People laughed when I said I wanted to be a comedian – well, they're not laughing now!" It takes something extraordinary to stand before an audience, whether you are a singer, entertainer, actor, teacher or preacher. You become someone else for that moment – or display another side of your character which may not be seen very frequently.

The man with the deformed hand was used to people staring at him…or not. For some, he was a figure of curiosity and curse - how could he cope with a hand like that? For others he would not be regarded, a figure of disgust and God's judgment. And then Jesus healed him…

…and challenged him "Get up and stand in front of everyone". Not for the man's sake – he was used to public exposure – but for the crowd's sake…you see the withered hand? Now whole and wholesome, as beautiful, effective and useful as the day he was born…

...and all the crowd could do was condemn the healer – the healer who himself was to hang on a cross to public disregard and disdain.

"Bearing shame and scoffing rude, in my place condemned He stood,
Sealed my pardon with His blood, Hallelujah! What a Saviour!" (Philipp Bliss)

January 31

"Stretch out your hand"
Luke 6:10   Key passage: Luke 6:1-11

One of our favourite pictures at home shows an elephant dancing through the bush. It's not the normal sort of picture we'd go for, and certainly not our usual style of art. So why do we have it? Because the elephant isn't an elephant at all – it's made from the paint handprint of one of our grandchildren adapted to be the pachyderm - clever stuff!

The human hand is a wonderfully adaptive tool. Just think what your hand has done today – to greet and eat, mend and tend, care and share. The hand is powerful – to grip and rip, hold and fold, hire and fire. The hand is personal – to lead and plead, seek and speak, yield and wield…

…and Jesus commanded the man "Stretch out your hand". The Pharisees were stretching out their hands to accuse Jesus of Sabbath impropriety. Their hands were challenging, threatening, confrontational. What of the man's hand? It was "completely restored"! The healing had come through the One whose hands were soon to be stretched out in mercy on the cross. Isn't that an "elephant in the room" worth sharing?

"Hands that flung stars into space…to cruel nails surrendered…This is our God, the Servant King." *(Graham Kendrick)*

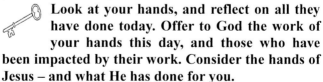 **Look at your hands, and reflect on all they have done today. Offer to God the work of your hands this day, and those who have been impacted by their work. Consider the hands of Jesus – and what He has done for you.**

FEBRUARY 1

"Blessed are you who are poor…"
Luke 6:20   Key passage: Luke 6:17-22

Oh, the delusion of the television quiz show, when you get a question right…and the experts don't! Somehow you feel far more intelligent than "them" and the world seems an unfair place....

…and it is! If there's one life lesson we need to learn, it's just that – a lot of things in life are not fair. The Psalmist spent a lifetime musing on why the wicked should prosper, and ever since the garden of Eden, we have had to accept that some things just aren't fair…

But wait a moment! It doesn't have to be like that! The words of Jesus here – the so-called "Blessings" or "Beatitudes" – indicate that in God's economy things are very different. Jesus signals a special blessing for "the poor" – by contrast (Luke 6.24) the rich "have already received (their) comfort". But for the poor a greater blessing awaits – the inheritance of "the kingdom of God" and the realisation that the goods of this world are useless in the light of eternity, and all we shall need for eternity is found in Jesus.

"What can I give Him, poor as I am? If I were a shepherd, I would bring a lamb;
If I were a wise man, I would do my part; yet what I can I give Him – give my heart"
                    (Christina Rossetti)

February 2

"Yours is the kingdom of heaven"
Luke 6:20   Key passage: Luke 6:17-22

To be economical and save the planet, our family regularly recycles wrapping paper. The only drawback is when you find someone else's name from a previous gift written on it…sometimes going back several years! Of course "it's the thought that counts", but the wrapping paper does help!

It's always special to see your name on a gift. Someone has thought about you, spent time and money to give you something special, and gone to some bother to present it to you. Jesus tells His disciples of a special gift for those who are His people – the gift of "the kingdom of heaven". That kingdom, Jesus taught is not visible but is "within you", "around you", "among you". That kingdom exists in the authority of who Jesus is as Son of God. That kingdom authority is yours to claim and yours to keep. When you confront life's challenges today, meet them head-on with the authority of the kingdom of heaven – knowing that there is power in the name of Jesus. Today is the present – a gift from God. Welcome it, with all its trials, and thank the Giver.

"Majesty, kingdom authority, flows from His throne unto His own, His anthem raise!" (Jack Hayford). Thank you, Lord, for Your gift of the present, and the present of Your gift…to be part of Your kingdom today!

What does it mean to you to be "part of the kingdom"? How would you describe your relationship with Jesus today, and your relationship with others who follow Jesus? How does the authority of Jesus empower you for daily living?

February 3

"Blessed are you who hunger now…"
Luke 6:21   Key passage: Luke 6:17-22

"It's only words and words are all I have to take your heart away…" (Bee Gees). Words are plentiful and cheap…but vital. If a word is the expression of a thought, the thought counts. Jesus declared to His disciples "Blessed are you who hunger now…". The disciples heard one thing, but Jesus spoke of something else. The disciples naturally had to eat and drink because "the inner man" matters.

But notice Jesus' choice of words – He did not speak of being "hungry" – but of those who "hunger". Mere words – or something profound? Being hungry demands external action – food! Having "hunger" speaks of internal longing – fulfilment. The hunger of which Jesus speaks is a hunger for the things of "righteousness" – the knowledge of God, of His love in Christ, of peace through forgiveness, of wholeness of mind, of hope, of eternal reassurance. How often do we hear the word of Jesus but only hear what we *want* to hear, not what we *need* to hear. Listen carefully to the Lord today – it's more than words!

"Open our ears, Lord, and help us to listen" (Robert Cull). Lord, instil in me a hunger for You and Your word.

February 4

"You will be satisfied"
Luke 6:21   Key passage: Luke 6:17-22

"More?? You want…more?" The well-known riposte to the plaintive Oliver for more food in Charles Dickens' *Nicholas Nickleby.* Child hunger should be a thing of history but clearly is far from so. We are told that there is enough food to feed the world, but two-thirds of the world go to bed hungry every night.

But it is more than physical food that Jesus speaks of here…and it is more than physical fulness that He implies. Those who seek Him "will be satisfied". Sometimes we encounter people who speak of a personal "religious experience" at some time, but that is now history. They have "moved on". Something did not satisfy…and there is so much that may "put us off" church, life, or other people. The word Jesus uses of "being satisfied" is the word farmers use of fattening their stock, of providing good wholesome pasture, succulent grass for grazing. The stock is not left to find it – that is the farmer's task. The task of the animal is to feed on it…and be satisfied. The Psalmist knew this – "The Lord is my shepherd…I shall not be in want".

Lord, teach me contentment in following and serving You today.

How has Christian faith "satisfied" you in your life...and where do you still feel "hungry"? Why are so many always feeling dissatisfied with life? What can we do as churches to "feed" God's people properly? What resources have you found helpful in feeding on God's Word?

February 5

"Blessed are you who weep now"
Luke 6:21   Key passage: Luke 6:17-22

"I'm sorry…" Words that should melt the heart – but they are words that are heard in the judicial context so often…and you are left wondering whether the perpetrator is sorry for what they have done, or sorry for getting caught…? It was thought that crocodiles shed tears as they consumed their victims (although the "tears" are simply the crocodile lubricating their eyes when out of water) leading to a display of false sympathy.

Yet Jesus has something powerful to say about the blessedness of weeping. There's nothing wrong with tears – in fact there's something very right. If the Lord of creation should weep at the death of a friend (see John 11.35) before raising him to life again, then your tears may bring healing and blessing too. Weeping was often accompanied by wailing – the physical expression of the spiritual agony of sorrow. Jesus had cause to rebuke the professional wailers, but He commends the humble penitent. "Weeping may remain for a night, but rejoicing comes in the morning" (Psalm 30.5). Tears are the expression of the present – pain, shock, anger, regret. May they be tears of Jesus for you too.

"For the tears that flow in secret in the broken times…for this I have Jesus!" (Graham Kendrick)

February 6

"You will laugh"
Luke 6:21   Key passage: Luke 6:17-22

The interview was not going well; the questioning was intense. The candidate was nervous, and sensed we were not impressed. Then I asked a different question: "And what makes you laugh?" She was not expecting the question, but suddenly her face lit up, and she became animated as she spoke of what brought a smile to her…and we saw a completely different individual.

  Jesus assures those who find themselves in the direst of circumstances that in His kingdom wrongs will be put to right – and tears will be transformed to laughter. He does not speak of tears being converted to smiles, or gladness or happiness…but actual laughter! Laughter in the face of adversity, of pain, of trial…laughter that is not disdainful or disrespectful, but laughter that is supremely joyous. There will be laughter in heaven, for it is promised that in the presence of the Lamb "there will be no more tears, or crying or pain". Laughter may be furthest from you right now…but Jesus assures us the day is coming when all our sadness is turned to laughter. Does that bring a smile to your face?

Lord Jesus, take my angst, tears and pain and help me to experience Your promise of laughter today.

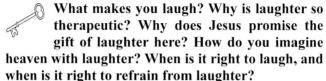 **What makes you laugh? Why is laughter so therapeutic? Why does Jesus promise the gift of laughter here? How do you imagine heaven with laughter? When is it right to laugh, and when is it right to refrain from laughter?**

February 7

"Blessed are you when men hate you…"
Luke 6:22   Key passage: Luke 6:17-22

"If it's sounds too good to be true, it is…!" How many people have been lured by the promise of a deal, something special just for them, only to discover it wasn't quite what they thought…? We do well to test everything, asking of its genuineness and real worth, and the intentions of the giver. I must confess that when I receive an offer of a "free gift" for something, I immediately work out how it is that I'm paying for it another way!

Jesus tells His followers that in this world they will not be universally liked. Bearers of "good news" or "free gifts" rarely are. Many people will remain indifferent to the gospel and those who proclaim it. Some will be openly hostile. The word Jesus uses for "hate" describes being regarded with less affection or diminished esteem. It's the kind of grudging sentiment expressed when it was said of the early Christians "See how much they love each other!" We are not to invite such hatred by our actions – our love must be genuine – but we are to stand firm in the face of society's disdain.

"Stand up! Stand up for Jesus! You soldiers of the cross" (George Duffield). Lord, give me the courage to stand up for You when I hear your name misused and your people abused for their faith.

February 8

"Leap for joy...for great is your reward in heaven"
Luke 6:23   Key passage: Luke 6:23-26

We have a painting at home which my wife's grandfather bought at auction. The artist is unknown, and the subject obscure...but we like it for what it is. I harbour a hope that it's a "missing Great Master" and worth a fortune...probably not!

Being a follower of Jesus may not appear very rewarding. In fact, Jesus promised that discipleship would come with a price tag. For some, that means unpopularity, disregard and disdain. For many Christians, the cost is enormous – rejection by family and society, accusations, imprisonment, torture, even martyrdom. For Christians in the West, such things are unimaginable, but they are nevertheless real. We may regard the promise of heaven as a bit of a luxury after the joys of our index-linked life – but when you have nothing, then heaven is everything. That's why Jesus is able to tell His followers to "leap for joy...for great is your reward in heaven". What is the real value of all you have in this world, when Jesus offers something priceless in the next?

"Onward we go...till, at the last, with joy we'll Jesus in glorious majesty; live with Him through eternity – reigning Lord!" (James Seddon)

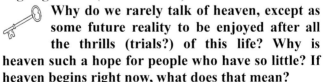 **Why do we rarely talk of heaven, except as some future reality to be enjoyed after all the thrills (trials?) of this life? Why is heaven such a hope for people who have so little? If heaven begins right now, what does that mean?**

February 9

"Woe to you…"

Luke 6:24   Key passage: Luke 6:23-26

Many of us may be conversant with the Sermon on the Mount – but few are aware of the Sermon on the Plain! The words of Jesus recorded by Matthew and Luke correspond at many points, but uniquely Luke records the contrast to the "Blesseds" – the "Woes"! The word Jesus uses for "woe" is a Scrabble dream – *ouai* – not worth many points but it does use up your spare vowels! It is not threatening, just reflective of the fact that for every blessing there will also be a burden.

That burden is the realisation that "you're on your own". Sinatra's mantra "I did it my way" is repeated at funerals in an effort to reflect the independent spirit of the departed. Jesus has something to say in these verses about the human spirit and qualities that are held as being desirable and praiseworthy – to be rich, well-off, popular, humorous, well-regarded…Such things are admirable, but easily deny us the possibility of discovering the sufficiency of God for now and for eternity. The regret expressed is not just ours – God Himself is full of woe for each one who wants to say "I did it my way".

Lord, may I never just live life in my way – teach me to live in Your way.

 Why do we value independence of spirit so highly? Why might following Jesus appear unattractive to some people? How has the church contributed to the idea that Christianity is marginal and irrelevant? What can we do to change that perception?

February 10

"Love your enemies"
Luke 6:27   Key passage: Luke 6:27-36

Good friends visited the Holy Land and came home with several souvenirs, including a scroll written in Hebrew. I admired the item they had so carefully framed and hung on their wall, but something wasn't right – it was upside down!

What Jesus has to say in these verses seems upside down, especially to a people living under hated Roman rule. As we discover in times of national crisis, there is strength in coming together to face the challenge of a foe whether seen or unseen. Surely we should stand tall and oppose the enemy by whatever means – but is that not to give in to the very evil that confronts us? The way of Jesus is the way of love. Love cannot be selective – we are to love all people. That is not namby-pamby love. That's tough, hard-edged, telling, challenging love.

We may not feel we have particular "enemies" – but anyone who challenges our thinking, whose lifestyle is different, whose values clash with ours can easily be our "enemy". We are to love them…without having to love their values or actions. Jesus showed us how. Get the picture up the right way!

"With shield of faith and belt of truth, we'll stand against the devil's lies; an army bold, whose battle cry is love, reaching out to those in darkness". (Stuart Townend/Keith Getty)

February 11

"Do good to those who hate you"
Luke 6:27   Key passage: Luke 6:27-36

One look was always enough. We knew not to mess with the teacher. Some people have "got it" and others haven't…and Mr. Beaumont had it! Sometimes words are not just inadequate – they are also unnecessary.

Jesus urges His followers to find a new way of discipleship…"Do good to those who hate you". The very idea of it! Surely the mighty Romans, whose very presence on the streets spelled oppression and resentment, should be hated in the measure in which they exercise the politics of hate. We still live in an age of "hate" – where any opinion contrary to the perceived norm is labelled as hateful – and tolerance has become the god of the age (strangely the only thing we will not tolerate is intolerance…). Doing "good" is disarming. The proverb of King Solomon (quoted by Paul in Romans 12.20) is telling: "If your enemy is hungry, give him food to eat; if he is thirsty, give him water to drink. In doing this, you will heap burning coals on his head…".

"Take my hands and let them move at the impulse of Your love". (Frances Havergal)

How is Christianity meant to be counter-cultural? Think of ways in which this actually happens. Are we counter-cultural in a desire to be different or a desire to have an impact? Who or what are the "enemies" of the faith? How are we to respond to them?

February 12

"Bless those who curse you"
Luke 6:28   Key passage: Luke 6:27-36

"Sticks and stone may break my bones but words will never hurt me" – really? An African saying from 1862, clearly meant to suggest that words are powerless against the human spirit. But why do so many of us take umbrage at things said to us, or about us? We easily feel offended, and our natural reaction is to retaliate, in word or thought if not in action. In this current generation, every reaction is magnified – people are always "angry", every disagreement is now a "row", and everyone has an opinion on everything, constantly belittling the efforts of others.

What would Jesus say? "Bless those who curse you…" Retaliation only increases the anger. This does not mean that Christians are to be soft in their response to anger, but we are to be resolute. After all, Solomon knew a thing or two about wisdom – and he urged "A gentle answer turns away wrath, but a harsh word stirs up anger" (Proverbs 15.1). Mind your language today!

"May the words of my mouth and the meditation of my heart be pleasing to you, Oh Lord, my rock and my redeemer." (Psalm 19:14)

How are words so hurtful? Why is social media such a difficult medium to use well? How are we to treat fellow believers with grace and love? What is a proper response to "those who curse you"?

February 13

"Pray for those who ill-treat you"
Luke 6:28   Key passage: Luke 6:27-36

Ombromanie – you did it as child! – made shadow shapes on the wall with your hands. A shadow needs imagination, but is all too real. Have you ever tried to escape your shadow – without success! For many people the past is a shadow from which they would love to escape.

Jesus urges His disciples "Pray for those who ill-treat you". "Ill-treat" means "insult" or "harass". The impact of the behaviour of others is not always direct or obvious. Sometimes it comes from surprising sources – the colleague who takes the name of Jesus lightly, the friend who teases about faith, the family member who asks where God is in a particular circumstance. By themselves few of these behaviours are "ill-treatment" – but they can leave us feeling worthless and derided. Similarly, things from the past may haunt us. Jesus urges us "pray for (them)…" Prayer is amazingly healing as we give to God the experiences and the people who shadow us. The Jesus way is the way of love – for God loves the faithful and faithless alike. And over us is the shadow of the cross – the proof of the power of love.

"Do thy friends despise, forsake thee? Take it to the Lord in prayer! In His arms He'll take and shield Thee, Thou wilt find a solace there" (Joseph Scriven)

 Why do past experiences sometimes haunt us? How can we escape the hurtful shadow of the past? How can friends so easily "insult" or "harass" us?

February 14

"Do to others what you would have them do to you"
Luke 6:31   Key passage: Luke 6:27-36

In 1993, news presenter Martyn Lewis insisted television should broadcast more "good news". Although he later suggested he was misunderstood, the point was important. Any alien tuning into News at Ten might wonder what planet they had come to! Death, disaster, destruction, disease, disagreement, dispute – it's all there!

Jesus sums up His teaching in this passage in the saying "Do to others what you would have them do to you". This was an ancient maxim, but had always been expressed negatively – Hillel the prominent Rabbi taught "What is hateful to you, do not do to your neighbour". He insisted this was the sum of the Law "and the rest of it is commentary thereon". "He never did anyone any harm" is frequently said in a tribute to someone – but the issue is not about "doing harm" – Jesus calls us to "do good". In times of crisis, it's positive acts of kindness that are telling – the phone call, the encouragement, the gift, the smile, the coffee. This is not just human kindness – it's kingdom kindness too! What might you do today to make good news?

Lord, teach me to be positive in all I say and do, and in days of personal and national crisis, may I radiate your positive love and grace.

What can we do to radiate the love of Christ to others today? Share the ordinary things you do, maybe without thinking about them, that help other people. How can your paid work impact others with God's grace? How does your behaviour impact your neighbours?

February 15

"Be merciful…"
Luke 6:36   Key passage: Luke 6:27-36

I reclined in the dentist's chair as he uttered "This won't hurt…". Who was he trying to convince? How many times have you caught yourself saying to someone "I know how you feel…?" when in all probability you don't. The careful parent soothes their child's sobs with some gentle rubbing and strategic diversion, but we may hear ourselves urging compassion on others when our genuineness may be in doubt.

Compassion is a tough call – and Jesus urges His disciples "Be merciful". The word literally means "have compassion on, exercise grace or favour towards" and speaks of kindness expressed in the relief of sorrow or want. The point is that mercy must be genuine, and not forced. True mercy springs from a heart of love for God and His children. "The quality of mercy is not strained. It droppeth as the gentle rain from heaven" (Portia – *The Merchant of Venice*). Jesus adds "…just as your Father is merciful". As in all things, Jesus doesn't just give us the rule, He gives us the example as well. God's mercy extends to all – irrespective of their regard for Him – from the cross.

"Soften my heart, Lord…from all indifference set me apart; to feel Your compassion, to weep with Your tears – come soften my heart, O Lord…!" (Graham Kendrick)

February 16

"Do not judge…"
Luke 6:37   Key passage: Luke 6:37-42

When I was a child, my mother used to check the label in my pullover wasn't hanging out – we didn't people to know where the garment came from! Then in the 1970's "designer" labels became popular, and we all wanted people to know whose brand of sweatshirt we wore – the name said something about us!

Whose name do we "wear"? Jesus has something powerful to say here about image and importance. We automatically judge other people – by their appearance, apparel or aptitude. We subconsciously need to know where we fit in the pecking order – as long as it's superior to other people! Remember the Pharisee in Luke 18.12 who declared "God, I thank you that I am not like other men…". We don't imagine that we have such an attitude, but we often do! The danger is that if we judge others, they will judge us – but the greater danger is that we also face the judgement of God Himself. Our judgements are often sadly so faulty and unwise, but God's judgments are true and wise. God's grace will change us to be forgiving. "Forgiven and forgiving" – wear those words with gratitude!

"No condemnation now I dread; Jesus, and all in Him, is mine! Alive in Him, my living Head, and clothed in righteousness divine…" (Charles Wesley)

 How do we judge other people? What's the difference between "summing them up" and judging? When have you been proved wrong in your assessment of someone? How did that impact you? On what basis does God judge us?

February 17

"Do not condemn…"
Luke 6:37   Key passage: Luke 6:37-42

How amazing that in any crisis, so many "experts" appear! People who, like the rest of us, have never experienced this situation before, but nonetheless seem to know exactly what to do…or rather, they seem to know that what everyone else is doing is wrong! Individuals and governments make mistakes, but for some there seems no room for error.

Jesus reinforces His kingdom teaching by restating the behaviour that is to be the hallmark of disciples – "Do not condemn…". We pass judgment on others so easily, on their actions, behaviour, personality, abilities, motivation – and leave no room for the possibility of change, that we might be awry in our view. It's not just politicians that we treat in this way – we do it to neighbours, colleagues, family members, and fellow church members! So many churches are thwarted by historic situations of condemnation. I once had cause to visit two church families who were also neighbours but never spoke to each other – the reason for the impasse went back two generations, and should by now be forgotten, but was still very much alive. When we condemn others, we stand condemned ourselves. Grace given is grace received!

"Spirit of the living God, fall afresh on me…break me, melt me, mould me, fill me…" (Daniel Iverson)

February 18

"Forgive…!"
Luke 6:37   Key passage: Luke 6:37-42

How to test a new bed? Two minutes on it in the showroom is hardly adequate. When a salesman invites us to spend twenty minutes testing a particular model, we need to get it right because we'll spend a third of our life on it...

Jesus urges His disciples to learn the art of forgiveness – the quality of showing understanding, mercy and kindness in the way that God has forgiven us. It can take time, not just two minutes. Forgiveness is an art, an attitude of heart. It is something we need to face the trials of life, for without it we shall become wearied and wearisome. Forgiveness demands hard work – it will not just "happen". Forgiveness is personal and private – each of us have situations needing forgiveness that only we can tackle. Forgiveness takes time – we may have issues to work through to achieve it. No wonder then that Jesus' call to forgiveness is challenging! What do you need to ask the Lord's help for today? You may spend time deciding…!

Show me, Lord, where my attitudes and behaviours are unforgiving, and do not reflect You and Your mercy to me. "Forgive, as God in Christ has forgiven you". (Ephesians 4.32)

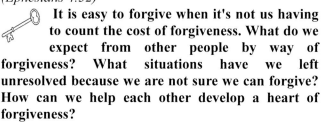 **It is easy to forgive when it's not us having to count the cost of forgiveness. What do we expect from other people by way of forgiveness? What situations have we left unresolved because we are not sure we can forgive? How can we help each other develop a heart of forgiveness?**

February 19

"Give, and it will be given to you"
Luke 6:38   Key passage: Luke 6:37-42

I've never quite understood the science of fund-raising. Someone bakes a cake, then sells it for a cause. Very commendable, but in terms of money expended, it's more cost-effective to donate the cost of the ingredients. It's all about giving…and some of us find the concept hard.

Giving challenges us, because deep down we like to ask "What's in it for me?". The idea of giving without repayment confronts our sense of importance. God never intended our giving should be a drudge – "God loves a cheerful giver". It's no accident that "fund" raising starts with "**fun**-raising" – but fun should never be a substitute for serious commitment in our giving. The fun comes from blessing others without expecting anything in return. Jesus speaks these words, however, not in the context of finance, but in the concept of forgiveness. The more generous we are to others, the more generously we receive in blessing from God and others. It's all about heart-attitude, not hard cash, but the principle holds good for our finances as well. May our generosity not be half-baked, but full…and free, just like God's generosity.

Lord, open my mind to understand Your generosity to me, open my heart to be generous to others, and open my hands to share all your love in every way possible.

February 20

"Pressed down, shaken together and running over…"
Luke 6:38   Key passage: Luke 6:37-42

Marie Kondo has made a fortune out of other people's misfortune – helping organise those who are disorganised. Her methods of storing items from clothes to photographs have become widely known and copied. Many of us think that the important thing in life is to pack in as much as possible – whether that's in a wardrobe or a weekend. But we give little thought to what it is that we are packing in, and how we do it. Not surprising, then, that many of us are exhausted, overwhelmed, and frankly confused about life…

The promise of Jesus here is all about God's blessing. Whilst God is generous, He is not reckless. His generosity pours from His heart, but it is amplified by the generosity of our hearts. For many people, the maxim of life is "What can I get?" God calls us to have a heart which asks "What can I give?", recognising that all that we have is not ours, and is certainly not some kind of measure of our success in life. God's blessing will be given to us "pressed down, shaken together and running over…" Now that's generosity!

"May the love of Jesus fill me as the waters fill the sea…" (Kate Wilkinson)

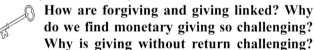 **How are forgiving and giving linked? Why do we find monetary giving so challenging? Why is giving without return challenging? How does the generosity of God challenge our attitudes?**

February 21

"Look at the speck…"
Luke 6:41   Key passage: Luke 6:37-42

I sat in the optician's chair as he said to me "Read the bottom line of letters on the screen". "D..E..L..L.." I offered. "Impressive" he replied "but that's the make of the computer – try again…"

Jesus had something that sounded ridiculous to His disciples about specks and planks. Who can see a speck of dust when it's in someone else' eye? We know when it's in our eye – it hurts, it pricks, it annoys. We marvel that something so tiny can cause so much distress and discomfort. But when it's in another's eye, it is equally annoying. It may not annoy them, but it certainly annoys us! We find the foibles of other people so irritating, the behaviour of others intimidating, the success of others isolating. Why should they have all the plunder, the promotion, the popularity? Admiration soon turns to envy, envy to jealousy, and jealousy to hatred. That's why Jesus urges us to refrain from judging others because you may not always get the right picture! Read others carefully – you may not be on the right lines!

Lord, help me today to see other people with Your eyes, and not with my own skewed sight. Thank you that You see me with eyes of love and mercy.

February 22

"Brother, let me take the speck out…"
Luke 6:42   Key passage: Luke 6:37-42

Pareidolia is an ability you may not have heard of, but it's the ability to perceive things that don't really exist, such as seeing shapes in clouds or faces in inanimate objects. It's quite normal and imaginative to see such things…until it becomes an obsession! Worryingly someone opened up their jar of Marmite recently and found an image of the face of Jesus in the residue stuck to the inside of the lid…

One of life's most important lessons to grasp is that we are all different, but made in the image of God. Thankfully not everyone is like us! Not everyone will like us! The words of Jesus to those who would point out the shortcomings of others challenge us to refrain from unfair and unfettered judgment of others. The religious people of Jesus' day were particularly good at condemning those who fell short of their own standards. We easily pass judgment on those who do not own the name of Jesus…and in so doing bring judgment on ourselves. It is not our task to judge the world – God has already done that, and He sent Jesus!

Thank you, Father, that You looked into my eyes, saw the real problem, and sent Jesus to redeem me.

 There is a reason people are like they are.. when has your view of someone changed when you understood their background? How do you think people see you... and how would you like them to see you? How might our fellowship be changed by greater understanding and less criticism?

February 23

"No good tree bears bad fruit"
Luke 6:43   Key passage: Luke 6:43-45

One of life's mysteries is how two parents can produce children who may be so different to each other. You may have a sibling with whom you share few likenesses, yet you are brother or sister! Whatever may differ, you share the same essential genes. Why the differences is a whole other science…

Jesus is clear that it's what's inside a person that will define them. Nothing can mask the essential character. It is no accident that the words of Jesus here come immediately after His teaching on eyes – it was often thought that the eye is the window of the soul. Look in – and you may need to look out! No good tree bears bad fruit, nor does a bad tree bear good fruit. We may try to pretend otherwise, and want to be well-regarded by others, but somewhere our true nature will show. We may be painfully aware of those parts of our nature we would rather deny – the jealousy, disdain, selfishness, pride – but we cannot hide them from the seeing God. Yet He can change us from the inside, and He has.

"Spirit of the living God, fall afresh on me; Break me, melt me, mould me, fill me…" (Daniel Iverson)

February 24

"Out of the overflow of (the) heart (the) mouth speaks…"
Luke 6:45   Key passage: Luke 6:43-45

"They come not back – the sped arrow, the spoken word…" (Aiki Flinthart). Oops! I shouldn't have said that! You knew the moment the words left your lips that it was wrong…but it was too late. There's only one thing worse, and that's not realising your mistake. Mumbled apologies, cheerily trying to carry on like nothing's happened…we've all done it!

The teaching of Jesus here is incisive. Words are easy and cheap, but real heart attitude is deep and costly. Each day many of us speak thousands of words, most of them forgotten and forgettable. Yet each word is a window to our souls, a revelation of what really matters to us, what we really think or desire. Jesus speaks about real Kingdom living in these verses, starting with a check on our tongues. Guard today what you say, and to whom you say it. The spoken word cannot be taken back.

"May the words of my mouth and the meditation of my heart be pleasing in your sight, O Lord, my Rock and my Redeemer." (Psalm 19.14)

When have you regretted saying something, and what were the consequences? When is it right to speak and right to keep silent> How can we guard our language?

February 25

"Why do you call me "Lord, Lord"...
Luke 6:46   Key passage: Luke 6:46-49

I'm tired of bad mathematics. How often we hear somebody telling us that they've given "110%" to a task in hand. What do they really mean – that they've gone beyond the call of duty or their level of ability to get something done? But you cannot give more than 100%! The problem is that most of the time we are reluctant to give anything 100% in any case.

Jesus prefaces his story of the two house builders with words of direct challenge – "Why do you call me "Lord, Lord"..." then don't do what He asks us? Our words belie our lack of commitment or understanding. Jesus has some stinging criticism for those who would follow Him but only on their terms. The two house builders are uncomfortably like us. We can "talk the talk" but find it much harder to "walk the walk". When we decide to follow Jesus, there's not an options menu for us to choose when or how – He calls us total obedience and true commitment.

"Make us to be what we profess to be; let prayer be prayer and praise be heartfelt praise; From unreality, O set us free, and let our words be echoed by our ways." (Henry Twells)

What does it mean to own Jesus as "Lord"? What does that look like in daily living? How do you see that worked out in other people? Who has shown you the grace of humble Christian obedience?

February 26

"I will show you what he is like..."
Luke 6:47   Key passage: Luke 6:46-49

When Bonnie Prince Charlie's 1745 attempt to take the English throne ended in ignominy at Culloden, he escaped to the Scottish isles pursued by the English. Followers took to drinking a daily toast to him, but since it was illegal to possess his image, they resorted to a clever invention – a board on which paint resembling an artist's palette would seem to have been smeared. When a silver goblet was placed in the centre of the board, his image miraculously appeared in reflection!

   Jesus speaks of revealing the true image of the disciple. He can do this because he knows the heart of each person. All our words, intentions and actions find their true form in Him. Jesus commends the one who comes to Him, "hears my words and puts them into action". The secret of true fulfilment of life with Jesus is foundational obedience. Don't just listen to the words of Jesus, don't just read them, don't just know them, don't just agree with them...do them, Sermons aren't for listening to, they are for acting on. In Jesus, life then makes sense. Do you get the picture?

Lord, may others see Jesus in me, through me and with me today.

February 27

"...like a man who dug down deep..."
Luke 6:48   Key passage: Luke 6:46-49

We once employed a builder to erect an extension to our house. We were worried when he turned up on the first morning and asked "Where do you want it?" The architect's drawings (which he had forgotten) provided the answer – in the ground! His foreman dug the footings (in the right place) and it's still standing.

Jesus knows all about foundations, for He commends the man who roots his life deep. The unseen foundations matter, giving strength and security. To dig deep, you must ignore the debris and detritus of former times, the rubble of previous edifices, taking time and expending effort in the process. Why does this matter? No one will see your toil when the edifice is finished? What counts is what impresses…

…but the builder has an eye to the future. It's hard to think of tomorrow when today beckons us. It's hard to think of eternity when life is pressing. But dig deep, deep into Jesus and who He is, and what He has done and waits to do for you. But don't live life without the architect's plans in your hand!

" 'I know the plans I have for you…plans to give you hope and a future' says the Lord" (Jeremiah 29.11)

What are the foundations on which your life exists? Who gave you those foundations – parents, friends, family, Scripture? What foundations can we give our children and young people? When have foundations mattered?

February 28

"…a man who laid the foundation on rock…"
Luke 6:48   Key passage: Luke 6:46-49

I shall always remember the most comfortable car I ever owned. Its seats were sumptuous, and it was the most reliable of vehicles…it would never start in the morning! Day after day it was a challenge…but at least it was comfortable!

Reliability is a rare commodity. It all depends what we are looking for. Jesus commends the man who builds on the reliable foundation of rock, as compared to the life-builder who sits lightly to such unseen preparations. After all, what does it matter? But when change comes, who will be able to endure?

Change can come suddenly, and often unexpectedly. We seek reliability, certainty, sureness in the things around us. Jesus asked Peter the searching question "Who do you say I am?" and despite his vacillations Peter replies "You are the Christ!" (Matthew 16.16). Jesus, in a master-stroke, declares "You are Peter ("Rocky") and on this rock I will build my church". It was no accident that this happened at Caesarea Philippi, the location of the temple of Pan, the god of all things. In the face of "anything goes", Jesus is the rock par excellence.

"Faithful One, so unchanging, Ageless One, You're my rock of peace". (Brian Doerksen) Thank you, Lord, that in You and who You are I find my certainty.

MARCH 1

"I have not found such great faith even in Israel"
Luke 7:9   Key passage: Luke 7:1-10

"If…" – What a small word with a big impact! "If only I'd made a different choice", "If I hadn't been there at that moment", "If only they'd kept their promise" – if, if, if. Kipling turned the word into a poem as a tribute to a revolutionary whose failed coup precipitated the Boer War. If one small thing had changed, world history might have been a different story.

Jesus encounters a Roman Centurion whose servant is dying. Despite his Roman credentials, he is well-regarded by the Jews who plead for Jesus to intervene. The Centurion's faith is exemplary – "Say the word, and my servant will be healed". No condescension, no wavering, no doubt – his faith is simple and absolute. He recognises in Jesus the one who has authority to heal, and for him that's enough. That is the essence of faith – knowing simply that Jesus is sufficient for our need. That is why Jesus commends his faith, in sharp contrast to the complicated religiosity of those around Him. Keep faith simple – and keep simple faith. No ifs, no buts…

"In Christ alone my hope is found…" (Keith Getty)

If faith is simple, why and how do we make it so complicated? How do our circumstances complicate our expectations of Jesus? How are we challenged by the simple faith of others who have little to lose in this world?

March 2

"Don't cry"
Luke 7:13   Key passage: Luke 7:11-17

"Individually, we are one drop. Together, we are an ocean" (*Ryunosuke Satoro*). We may be forgiven for thinking when we hear inspirational quotes of "We're all in this together" that some are more "in" than others! But when Jesus encountered the widow of Nain about to bury her only son, Luke records that "his heart went out to her…" There's a word used to describe what Jesus felt – it's a bit earthy and challenging…Jesus' "bowels churned inside Him". You'll not hear that translation too often, but it's what it means!

It's knowing of the need of another, the pain of their plight, the tragedy of their turmoil. When Jesus said to her "Don't cry" these were not words of forlorn comfort, designed to cheer her up (if such was possible right now). The reason for Jesus' words is hidden in what Luke recorded in this verse – "When the LORD saw her…". This is the first time Luke uses the name of the LORD. He is the Lord of life and death. When Jesus the Lord is present, tears of pain may turn to tears of joy.

"O give Him all your tears and sadness, give him all your years of pain, and you'll enter into life in Jesus' name." (John Wimber)

 Why do we find it difficult to grasp that Jesus does not just know our "todays", but also our "tomorrows"? How do you respond to the idea that "there is a man in heaven, the man Christ Jesus, who intercedes for us"? What does that mean for you? How does that change the difficulties you face?

March 3

"Young man…get up!"
Luke 7:14   Key passage: Luke 7:11-17

Some time ago we organised a "flash mob" in our local supermarket on Easter Saturday – the song of choice had to be "You raise me up" – and it took the store by storm! Some customers were even reduced to tears…for good reasons, we hope! It's amazing how, when we do something together, we "lift our game".

The encounter of Jesus with the widow from Nain is the first Lucan-recorded miracle of resurrection. Jesus' "heart went out to her" because all her future was gone, and she was now entirely vulnerable. As a doctor, Luke may have been intrigued by the medical details, but his account is straightforward. Jesus touched the coffin (rather than taking the dead man by the hand) and addressed death directly. "Young man…get up!" His command to resurrection implies "Come on – there is something far better!" It's the word used of encouragement to greater effort and improvement, shouted from a thousand touchlines every Saturday, the word uttered by a parent to their child as new skills are learned and practised. It's the word of life that Jesus speaks to us today in our struggles – "You raise me up!"

"You raise me up so that I can stand on mountains" (Brendan Graham)

March 4

"Go back…report…what you have seen and heard"
Luke 7:22   Key passage: Luke 7:18-23

My wife and I love long-distance walking, and have done some remarkable paths in our time. When walking a coastal path, it's relatively easy – as long as you have the sea one side of you. Sometimes, you become aware that you are not where you think you ought to be, and there's nothing for it but to go back to a point you recognise and start again.

John is in prison, so he cannot ask the question directly himself. He has been proclaiming Jesus as the Powerful One, expecting that Jesus would do something dramatic to prove Himself – and when his hopes seem to have come to nothing, he sends envoys to ask the question.: "Is Jesus the one who was to come…or should they expect someone else?" Jesus' response is challenging – "look at the evidence": people healed, the dead raised, and the good news proclaimed. Look at the evidence…and read the map! Go back to the beginning– Jesus is here with us!

"Be Thou my soul's shelter, Thou my high tower…"
Lord, thank you that in the middle of each crisis, we can come back to You and learn again You are the Promised One, our Saviour!

 What evidence can we produce concerning the Lordship of Jesus? How might we be part of that evidence? What will convince the doubter of the truth of Jesus Christ? What evidence can your small group share of the power of Jesus at work?

March 5

"Blessed is the man who does not fall away…"
Luke 7:23   Key passage: Luke 7:18-23

The media is full of it…dramatic stories of the rich and famous. Often the "scoop" is nothing more than an attempt to dramatize the mundane, but it "sells papers" and engages the internet trawlers. "Star has corn flakes for breakfast" – now that's a story you didn't think would attract attention!

Yet we love the "gossip", we are fascinated by the cult of "celebrity". What other people say and think matters. When John sends envoys to ask of Jesus' credentials, Jesus' reply is searching: "Blessed is the man who does not fall away on account of me…" "Falling away" means being embarrassed by, being scandalised (that's the actual word Jesus used). Being identified as a follower of Jesus is the challenge – are we proud to be so, or just so slightly awkward? Will other people think less of us? Will they disregard us? Jesus never promised that discipleship would make us popular. He does commend those who are faithful and steadfast in the face of difficulties and disdain. Be resolute in faith, humble in heart and loving in spirit. What others say and think is irrelevant in the face of the love of Jesus for you today.

When do you shy away from acknowledging that you are a follower of Jesus? We are called to be "as wise as serpents, and as harmless as doves" (Matthew 10.16). When is it wise to be silent, and when is it good to speak?

March 6

"What did you go out into the desert to see?"
Luke 7:24   Key passage: Luke 7:24-28

We live on the North Sea coast, with vast areas of marshland superb for bird-watching. In normal times you see the bird watchers in their green coats with enormous telescopes slung over their shoulders, all seeking that elusive creature… Sometimes something really rare flies in, followed by the "twitchers" in their droves. Often we secretly wonder "Just what are they looking at…?"

Jesus asked the followers of John "What did you go out into the desert to see…?" Doubtless there were some who had little idea what they were pursuing, but a crowd draws a crowd…The man became more interesting than the message he was conveying. Jesus points out, however, that John, as the messenger, was of no account; it was his message that was important. Yet so often we imbue our messengers with an importance way beyond their reality. The cult of the "superstar" preacher or speaker is a dangerous one, and stands in danger of us not hearing the message. When people thank me for my sermon, I frequently (and I hope graciously) reply "So what are you going to do about it, then?"

"Do not merely listen to the word, and so deceive yourselves. Do what it says…" (James 1.22)

Think of a memorable sermon you have heard. What was it that spoke to you and what did you do about it as a result? Think of a passage of Scripture that has moved you at some time. What was the situation it addressed for you, and what did you do about it?

March 7

"The one who is least in the kingdom of God is greater than he"
Luke 7:28   Key passage: Luke 7:24-28

I have a friend who "collects" degrees – every communication from him is headed by his name followed by a jumble of letters of degrees, certificates, and qualifications most of us have never heard of. I'm not really sure what he is trying to prove…

…but then some people are impressed by status. Other people play down their achievements, and often we are surprised to learn of their skills and standing. In his encounter with the crowd, Jesus is keen to acknowledge the importance of John in announcing the coming kingdom, but He is urgent to focus on the kingdom and the possibility of being part of it. John is indeed afforded the role of prophet, but a prophet is no more and no less than a messenger of something or someone greater. In Jesus' words, the greater person is the one who is part of the kingdom of God because the greatest thing is to know God and belong to Him. Today that is you, for Jesus makes it possible. Your greatest "qualification" is to know Jesus and follow Him!

"The greatest thing in all my life is knowing You…" (Mark Prendergras). Teach me, Lord, to know You, love you and serve You humbly this day.

March 8

"To what then can I compare the people of this generation?"
Luke 7:31   Key passage: Luke 7:31-35

Who'd be a politician? Derided, ignored, envied, abused, we do not have a good track record in regarding our leaders. We complain when they don't do something, and moan when they do. We elect them with enthusiasm and sack them with greater enthusiasm. There is no shortage of people wanting to do the job, although most of us wouldn't dream of it…

…but then some people are difficult to please. It's always the politician's fault (and sometimes it is) but never ours…Jesus has tough words about the people who reject both John and Himself for entirely opposite reasons. They thought John was too dull and heavy, and that Jesus was too serious – mediocrity was what was needed! We are devotees of the mediocre – "neither hot nor cold" – and the rhyme that Jesus quotes says it all…like children who will not be appeased or pleased. We are so strong in our mediocrity, it's scary! The problem is, where Jesus is concerned, you cannot be mediocre and He said "He who is not with me is against me" (Luke 11.23). Today is the day to be bold!

Lord, may I never be weak in my commitment to You. Teach me to be strong and decisive in following You this day.

What is appealing about mediocrity? Why are we often content with the mediocre? What does this say about the level of our commitment to Jesus? What does this say about the level of our spiritual maturity? How can we learn to become strong and decisive in our discipleship?

March 9

"Wisdom is proved right by all her children"
Luke 7:35   Key passage: Luke 7:31-35

Dad's Army is one of the great British sitcoms, a gem of writing and finely drawn characterisations. There is the bumbling but ultimately triumphant Captain Mainwaring and his dreamy Sergeant Arthur Wilson, who finds Mainwaring insufferable but endearing – Wilson's permanent retort to Mainwaring's bold plans is the telling phrase "Do you think that's wise, sir?". For Mainwaring, it's not about wisdom, but necessity…

The people's response to John the Baptist and Jesus is rather similar. They thought John too ascetic, and Jesus too populist. They could not cope with John's lifestyle – the locusts, wild honey and no wine. Neither could they cope with Jesus – "a glutton and a drunkard, a friend of tax collectors and sinners". They could not dream of keeping such company…surely that was not "wise". Yet Paul later asserts "the foolishness of God is wiser than man's wisdom…" (1 Corinthians 1.25). The really wise see the wisdom of God in Jesus. He is God in human flesh, come for us. Now do you think that's wise?

Show me Jesus in all His glory as the Saviour of the world – and grant me grace to acknowledge my own poor judgement and lack of faith.

March 10

"…I have something to tell you…"
Luke 7:40   Key passage: Luke 7:36-50

We like a good story, especially when it appeals to our sense of wonder, humour or entertainment. Publishers are a different matter – how many "best-sellers" have been rejected multiple times because they'll "never catch on"? When Jesus says to Simon the Pharisee "I have something to tell you" Simon is spooked – has Jesus somehow read his mind about the matter of this sinful woman who has been getting rather intimate with him? It's one thing reading a book – quite another when someone else reads us like a book!

What Jesus has to tell is a story of justice and grace that would challenge the mores of a Pharisee – why should anyone forego the dues of a debtor? Simon gives the politically correct answer, but would have been appalled at the very question. He had invited Jesus to dine with him, but his intentions were questionable – interested probably in what this might do for his own kudos. And now this man seems to know exactly what he is thinking and feeling! When you entertain Jesus, know that the story will be gripping – and it'll be a story of justice and grace!

Thank you, Lord, that You know all about me…and still love me!

 Imagine you have invited Jesus for a meal. How do you think the conversation might go? What would you want to talk about and what do you think He would want to talk about?

March 11

"...which of them will love him more?..."
Luke 7:42   Key passage: Luke 7:36-50

We feel clever when we can answer questions on General Knowledge – especially when the "experts" on TV fail! It is noticeable that when there is a "celebrity" version of a quiz, the questions are somewhat easier...but sometimes the "celebrities" still get them wrong!

Jesus asked Simon the Pharisee a question which was apparently a "no-brainer" – which of the two forgiven debtors would be more grateful? Simon's reply is telling: "The one who had the bigger debt cancelled...I suppose". He seemed dubious even then, but is engaged by the question. Where is Jesus going with this? What's the point of this story? What has this got to do with me? We may feel suspicious when stopped in the street or called on the phone by someone whose first words are "I'm not selling anything...!" What are they doing, then? Yet the question Jesus asks Simon is the same as He will ask the disciple Simon Peter "Do you love me?" He asks the question of us too today and every day – "Do you love me...?" The question always demands an answer – make sure we get it right!

"I love You, Lord, and I lift my voice to worship You...take joy, my King, in what You hear" (Laurie Klein)

March 12

"Do you see this woman?"
Luke 7:44 Key passage: Luke 7:36-50

We once had tickets for a visit to a stately home near where we live. Arriving at the grand front door, which seemed to be shut, we rang the bell, the door creaked open, and we were greeted by an ageing gentleman in rather shabby clothes whom we took to be the caretaker. When we enquired, he welcomed us in personally and proceeded to give us "the tour" – to our astonishment he was the lord of the manor, a descendant of Britain's first Prime Minister! How easily we make assumptions about people by their appearance!

   Jesus challenges Simon the Pharisee – "Do you see this woman?" We are not told how the woman came to be in Simon's house, except that he was entertaining Jesus, and bystanders may have gathered. What is certain is that by her actions of devotion to Jesus, Simon is rattled. He had disregarded her, even found her presence and actions annoying and insulting, but Jesus commends her. "Do you **see** her?" Not just notice her – **see** her? Look carefully, for the Saviour sees beyond the obvious, the reputation, the social regard. He **sees** the heart and commends her.

Thank you Lord that You see me, not just as I am, but also as I can be by Your transforming grace. Grant me to see others with Your eyes of love and mercy.

What do you imagine Jesus saw in you that He should call you to be a follower? How do you think you have changed since you became a follower? What do you think Jesus still needs to change in you?

March 13

"Her many sins have been forgiven – for she loved much"
Luke 7:47   Key passage: Luke 7:36-50

Having reached the end of a long and arduous walk of 630 miles (over seven years!) my wife and I turned to each other and said "What do we do now?" The expected sense of elation was overtaken by a sense of anti-climax. We knew we should feel good, but just at that moment we didn't…

The woman who anoints Jesus in Simon's house had "lived a sinful life", but what now? She certainly didn't feel good, but she knew that she stood forgiven by Jesus. God's grace is equal to any and all her sins. She was not forgiven by her act of devotion in anointing Jesus, nor was she forgiven through the lavishness of her actions. God's forgiveness is never dependent on the scale of our deeds, the vigour of our worship and praying, or the enthusiasm of our work. Her extravagant ministry to Jesus was a sign of her understanding of the active grace of God for her. Simon didn't get it…make sure you do. By faith in Jesus, you are forgiven.

"There is now no condemnation for those who are in Christ Jesus" (Romans 8.1) "I'm accepted, I'm forgiven…There's no guilt or fear as I draw near to the Saviour and Creator of the world" (Rob Hayward)

March 14

"He who has been forgiven little loves little"
Luke 7:47   Key passage: Luke 7:36-50

We once volunteered for aircraft evacuation trials. We were paid for attending, and each time we were in the first 50% of passengers to escape we earned extra! Rationally we said to ourselves "This isn't real…in a real emergency I wouldn't behave like this…or would I?" When it's life and death anything goes…

   Simon the Pharisee was trying to evacuate this difficult situation with this sinful woman. Astonishingly Jesus proclaims her forgiveness, but Simon is stumped, for the words of Jesus, gracious as they are, are also challenging. He had taken the bother to invite Jesus to dine with him and Jesus has engaged in conversation, but this gate-crashing brazen woman… Surely Jesus can see through this, can't He…? He can, and He does, for He reveals the truth that love is a true reaction to grace, and knows no bounds. Simon has been seeking authentication for his status – the woman receives absolution for her sins.

What is the difference between worship that is a duty and worship that is a delight? How does knowing you are loved and forgiven by God change the way you worship?

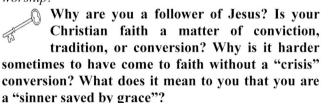 **Why are you a follower of Jesus? Is your Christian faith a matter of conviction, tradition, or conversion? Why is it harder sometimes to have come to faith without a "crisis" conversion? What does it mean to you that you are a "sinner saved by grace"?**

March 15

"A farmer went out to sow"
Luke 8:5   Key passage: Luke 8:4-15

It's a dangerous business being a preacher! Dangerous because you might stumble and stutter, forget your point or fudge the truth, ram your point home and then realise that it's you that needs to hear it! The polite folk who "thank you for the sermon" sometimes haven't grasped the truth – but they are matched by those who thank you for something you've said when you have little recollection of saying it!

Farming is what farmers they do, but it's not always successful. Jesus tells this parable of the farmer who scatters the seed because every harvest begins with a sowing. Surely that's not difficult, is it? All you have to do is distribute the seed. Responsibility for the resting place of the seed doesn't lie with the sower – he cannot possibly know or direct where it might end up. Today you are the "sower" of seed. Stop fretting about the effectiveness of your witness – just get on with the sowing! God may yet surprise you!

Thank You, Lord, that all You ask of me is to be a faithful witness to You.
"Take from our souls the strain and stress, and let our ordered lives confess the beauty of Your peace" (John Whittier)

How careful should the farmer be in the sowing of the seed? Whose responsibility is the growth? Who is responsible for the harvesting? How does this parable address our understanding of personal evangelism? What does it teach us about corporate evangelism?

March 16

"Some fell along the path"
Luke 8:5   Key passage: Luke 8:4-15

A colleague once asked his congregation their impressions of how many hours their pastor spent doing particular tasks in an average week. One respondent duly returned her form indicating that she thought the pastor worked 180 hours, although there are only 168 hours in a week. Perhaps she had an over-optimistic impression of what pastors do.

It's a great temptation to give the idea that busyness is a measure of importance. The problem is that we mistake activity for actuality. The farmer of whom Jesus speaks may seem busy in his task of sowing, but he is so busy he seems indifferent to the location of the seed – "some fell along the path". We are not told whose feet trample on it – the farmer's or someone else's – but trampled it is. Just when it should go deep into the soil, it lies vulnerable and is picked off by the birds. It starts the day as seed – but ends as supper. Jesus's explanation is that there are some who hear the word but never get to making a response. May we not be guilty of trampling on anyone's fledging faith!

"Encourage one another and build each other up…" (1 Thessalonians 5.11) What can you do to encourage those who are young in the faith?

 How does fledgling Christian faith get trampled on? What do we do as individuals and churches to nurture young believers? How do we encourage those who are more mature in the faith?

March 17

"Some fell on rock"
Luke 8:6   Key passage: Luke 8:4-15

"How did we do?" Feedback is important, but sometimes it seems to take precedence over service. Companies and individuals are desperate for 5 stars – anything else will just not do! Were we to rate the actions of the farmer of whom Jesus speaks, he may not get good feedback on his sowing skills. Surely any farmer with any agricultural nous looks carefully where he is spreading the seed – a "hit rate" of just 25% is just not impressive. But read the story carefully – who is responsible for the outcomes?

The suggestion is it's certainly not the farmer – he gives equal opportunity to all of the seed. The problem seems to lie with the seed itself and its response to the challenges of its environment. Some seed fell on rock; it germinated fine, but then began to wither because of a distinct lack of moisture. Blame the farmer? Blame the rock? Blame the weather? Blame the government…? Have you ever discovered plants and weeds that have found a home in a crevice, and hung on to flourish? Dig deep, send out roots, endure…don't let the time of testing be the time of ending.

Lord, I'm in a rocky place right now, and the going is tough. Help me to hang on to You as You have promised to hold on to me.

What are the "roots" of faith that need nurturing? Where do we receive our nurturing? Reflect on how you think you have grown in the faith. Who or what was vital to your growth as a Christian? What are the "rocks" that make faith difficult?

March 18

"Other seed fell among thorns"
Luke 8:7   Key passage: Luke 8:4-15

One of the strange things of living through a pandemic has been the wearing of face masks – we have often failed to recognise people in the street, but then maybe they haven't realised it was us greeting them! Masks are functional…but not exactly pretty. That hasn't stopped some people having "designer" masks, in an attempt to appear more presentable. To them, image matters.

Jesus spoke of the seed that fell among thorns. Apparently there was nothing wrong with the soil in which this seed was sown – but the environment was something else. It choked the young plants. Step by step, inch by inch, day by day the "thorns" of anxiety, responsibility and self-satisfaction matched the growth of the plant until they took over. The plant stood no chance, and withered. Just how do you keep faith when there's so much to challenge it? The problem with thorns is they grow faster than anything else! There's only one way to deal with thorns, and that is to uproot them – pruning merely encourages faster growth. What is it that challenges your faith…and how do you recognize it and deal with it? Don't mask the problem!

"The dearest idol I have known, whate'er that idol be, help me to tear it from Thy throne, and worship only Thee" (William Cowper)

How do you tell the difference between "weeds" and "thorns"? How are each to be dealt with? What are the pressures that younger Christians in particular face? How can older believers help them deal with them?

March 19

"Other seed fell on good soil"
Luke 8:8   Key passage: Luke 8:4-15

Leaving home is one of life's signal moments. At whatever age you take the plunge, the realisation of a wider world out there is sometimes a shock, more often a revelation. Mark Twain reportedly said "When I was a boy of 14, my father was so ignorant I could hardly stand to have the old man around. But when I got to be 21, I was astonished at how much the old man had learned in seven years."

There's only one environment in Jesus' parable which gets commended – the good soil which receives the seed and nourishes it to full harvest. The seed does what it is designed to do – germinate and flourish. The ground does what it is meant to do – host the seed and nurture it. But notice Jesus' warning – it takes perseverance! Growth doesn't just happen – it takes time, effort and resolution. God sends His word to us, but we must receive it and work at understanding it, reflecting on it, and responding to it. Grow up into His word, and He will grow it in you.

"Show me the truth concealed within Your word, and in Your book revealed I see You, Lord" (Mary Lathbury)

What have you learned in the last year about the importance of your faith? How do you think you have grown as a Christian in that time? What does it take to grow in faith? How important is the reading and understanding of Scripture to personal spiritual growth?

March 20

"He who has ears to hear, let him hear"
Luke 8:8 Key passage: Luke 8:4-15

"I hear what you're saying…" is one of the most annoying phrases possible since it probably means that the person speaking it has not heard what you are saying, and may well have dismissed your concerns/understanding/point of view without further consideration. There is a world of difference between hearing and listening! In an age of constant communication, it feels like everyone's talking, but few people are actually listening.

As Jesus concludes his explanation of the parable of the sower, his closing words resonate directly – "if you have ears, then hear!" Listen to the words of the Master. What Jesus has to say really matters – this is the word of life! Don't just dabble with His words – believe them and respond to them! In the 1890's Mark Barraud owned a dog called Nipper, and when Mark died, the dog was inherited by his brother Francis, along with a phonograph on which Francis played recordings of Mark speaking. The dog would sit spellbound by his master's voice…and was encapsulated in the famous HMV trademark. Say to the Lord today "I hear what you're saying."

"Do not merely listen to the word…do what it says"
James 1.22

March 21

"The knowledge of the secrets of the kingdom of God has been given to you"
Luke 8:10   Key passage: Luke 8:4-15

You may not have heard of John Stith Pemberton, but you will have heard of his invention. Wounded by a sabre in battle in 1865, Pemberton became addicted to morphine to control the pain. As a biochemist, he experimented with painkillers resulting in the creation of what became Coca Cola. Today the recipe remains a closely-guarded secret…but someone must know what's actually in it!

By definition, a secret is something that is not generally known – and cannot be known except by a few. In reply to the disciples' enquiry as to the meaning of the parable of the sower, Jesus enigmatically suggests that the disciples have received the truth of the kingdom whereas for others it remains a mystery. This does not mean that God is in the business of deliberately hiding the truth – rather, He is in the business of revealing truth, and they are the early recipients of that truth. The secret of the kingdom is invested in His disciples…if only they would recognise it! Today God reveals that same secret in you – share it; the secret is out.

"God has chosen to make known…the riches of this mystery, which is Christ in you, the hope of glory" (Colossians 1.27). Thank you, Lord, for opening up this mystery to me, and for opening me up to the power of this mystery.

 How would you describe the "mystery" of faith? What does it mean to you to be a recipient of this "secret"? What does "the hope of glory" look like?

March 22

"This is the meaning of the parable…"
Luke 8:11   Key passage: Luke 8:4-15

We were on a guided tour of the Hermitage in St. Petersburg – the vast museum of Russian art and culture in the former capital. Our guide spoke excellent English, and was so enthusiastic about every painting and artefact…but after about four hours we were exhausted. He wasn't – one question from one of the more enthusiastic members of our group, and he was off again. We slept very well that night.

Knowing what you are looking at is a great help, but it can take huge effort and concentration to engage with the subject. Doubtless we viewed so many world masterpieces, but the memory suffers overload. The disciples similarly dared ask a question as to the meaning of the parable, but were not prepared for the answer. Parables both uncover and hide truth. Some people hear the story, but their understanding stops there. Others engage with the underlying truth. The irony is the disciples belonged to the latter group, but were content to remain in the former! The mystery of God in Christ is of His revealing, not our own comprehension. Let God speak to you. Stand back and see the picture!

Lord, open my eyes to the truth of Your word; open my mind to the power of Your truth; open my heart to the impact of Your power. Amen.

March 23

"There is nothing hidden that will not be disclosed"
Luke 8:17   Key passage: Luke 8:16-18

We live on the coast and can see the lighthouse on the cliff nearby. At night its light shines into our house, and it is strangely comforting. While we sleep safely, the light does its job warning those at sea of the dangers of rocks and cliffs underneath. The light was never designed for our satisfaction but for the safety of mariners. By its repetition sailors can discover their location as well defend their lives.

Jesus speaks frankly to His disciples about His divine purpose – He has come to bring light to a dark world. He has come to bring truth to a people in darkness. He has come to bring salvation to a people in despair. He who is the light declares "No one lights a lamp and hides it…". Rather, the light is placed on a stand – literally "set on a solid foundation" – from where it illuminates all around. The disciples will be the beacons of this light, which will show all men the truth of God in Christ and their need of Him. This is your task and mine – to reflect Him.

"May others see Jesus in me? For how will the lost know of Jesus if they cannot see Him in me?" (Leonard Voke)

How come we may talk a lot about "mission", but so very little about Jesus? What can we do by way of training or encouragement to help each other speak positively about Jesus and what it means to follow Him? What have you found helpful in aiding your personal witness to Him?

March 24

"Consider carefully how you listen"
Luke 8:18   Key passage: Luke 8:16-18

"People who live in glass houses shouldn't put all their eggs in one basket". You know you shouldn't mix your metaphors, but we often do it. As Jesus addresses His disciples in the defining image of this Sermon on the Plain, the mixed metaphor may be overlooked – literally "See how you listen!" In any audience, there are different kinds of listeners. An actor friend revealed that after a theatre performance, whilst the audience are discussing the performance of the cast, the cast are discussing the performance of the audience!

Similarly, Jesus urges His disciples to look carefully at their listening. He has revealed truths of the kingdom to them, but as so often it may not have registered. He warns that if the light of God's truth and grace does not penetrate their hard hearts, they will remain in darkness, but if they hear God's word and respond to it voluntarily, then they will grow in their knowledge of Him. What sort of listener are you – reluctant or responsive? The power of God's word is never dependant on the skill of the preacher, but on the submissiveness of the listener.

"Lord, open my eyes that I may see wonderful things in your law" (Psalm 119.18)

March 25

"My mother and brothers are those who hear God's word…"
Luke 8:21   Key passage: Luke 8:19-21

"All animals are equal, but some are more equal than others" (George Orwell "Animal Farm"). Never has it been truer that "we're all in this together" especially at a time of national crisis – but even in crisis some people cannot let go of the instinct for priority – "You've got to look after yourself, haven't you?"

The words of Jesus at the arrival of his mother and brothers might sound harsh. Jesus does not dismiss his family, but He makes the point there are priorities. That does not mean some things or relationships are lessened – simply that sometimes other things have a greater importance. "My mother and brothers are those who hear God's word and put it into practice…" The emphasis is on the doing. Duty is paramount – duty to God and the kingdom. That duty is not a drudge, but a delight, never a burden but a blessing. To be in the family of God means to be in the way of serving Him and His kingdom. Do not ask "What must I do?" Ask "What may God ask of me today?"

"Teach us, good Lord, to serve You as you deserve…to labour and to ask for no reward save that of knowing that we do Your will through Jesus Christ our Lord". (Ignatius Loyola)

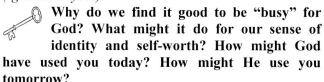 **Why do we find it good to be "busy" for God? What might it do for our sense of identity and self-worth? How might God have used you today? How might He use you tomorrow?**

March 26

"Let's go over to the other side…"
Luke 8:22   Key passage: Luke 8:22-25

It's all very friendly really (apparently), but the "derby" match between our local football teams is the most heavily policed game in the country! It seems that what really matters is beating the other team – nothing else has any importance.

Jesus suggests to His disciples they take a boat trip and they are eager, full of faith and enthusiasm. This is fun! Little do they know what is just around the corner… "Let's go over to the other side…" What could possibly go wrong? The storm comes, and the recumbent Jesus has to be awoken to deal with the situation, since they were suddenly full of fear. How quickly their emotions change.

"Let's go over to the other side…" How many Monday mornings have we thought the "grass must be greener on the other side"? How often have we wished to be somewhere else, doing something else, even being someone else? Surely it's better on "the other side". Fear of failure, of shame, of death paralyzes us. "Lord, we're drowning…!" What about the Saviour who has been to "the other side" and now demands our trust – is He in the boat with us?

Thank You, Jesus, that You have been "to the other side" for me and won the victory! Keep me safe in the knowledge of Your love today.

Why is "the other side" often so attractive? If you could be somewhere else today, where and how would it be? What worries you about "the other side"? How does knowing Jesus bring comfort and hope?

March 27

"Where is your faith?"
Luke 8:25   Key passage: Luke 8:22-25

In a Tony Hancock sketch, Kenneth Williams plays a rogue aircraft engineer who finds himself hanging onto the wing of the plane as it soars into the sky. "Where's that stiff upper lip?" the petrified Williams is asked. "Above this flabby lower one…" he replies.

The disciples must have thought something similar as the squall appeared from nowhere and threatened to sink their boat. What to do now? Didn't they see it coming? Hadn't any of them dealt with something like this before? Who's in charge? Who's to blame?...They wake Jesus. How could He possibly be asleep with all this going on? Doesn't He know, doesn't He care?

"Where is your faith?" He asks them gently but directly. It's a difficult question to answer just at that moment – we don't need faith, we need something practical.. But Jesus had already stilled the storm. The only limits of faith are the ones we impose. The ability to trust in the wisdom and power of God when in the eye of the storm is challenging. The strength to hang on when all else has failed – now that's faith!

"Those who hope in the Lord will renew their strength…they will soar on wings like eagles" (Isaiah 40.31)

 What challenges are you facing today? What do you believe God can do for you in the problems you experience?

March 28

"What is your name?"
Luke 8:30   Key passage: Luke 8:26-39

We can't help it - my wife and I were both teachers; when it comes to the naming of children, certain names provoke particular memories…

Names originally identified people's place of origin, role in a community, or their particular skill. Other names seem completely random. Jesus asks the demoniac his name. "Legion" is the forlorn reply. What could he say? He was what he had become – possessed by a veritable army of spirits. Everything about this man is tragic – homeless, helpless, naked, nothing…bound and broken, possessed and pursued. Yet something brings him to Jesus' feet. His desire for release is matched by the demons' desire for revenge. The presence of Jesus affronts them. The Name that Saves versus the Name that Seizes. The man may have suffered cruelty at the hands of the invading Romans – his ascription "Legion" simply suggests that his demons were many and mighty. The legion was the professional, elite part of the Roman army. His problems were overwhelming, but at the gracious invitation of Jesus, he was transformed "dressed and in his right mind". The name would provoke memories…but they are now in the past.

"See, I have engraved you on the palms of my hands" (Isaiah 49.16). What does it mean for you today that your name is known to God?

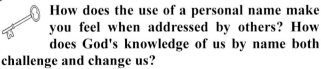 **How does the use of a personal name make you feel when addressed by others? How does God's knowledge of us by name both challenge and change us?**

March 29

"Return home and tell how much God has done for you"
Luke 8:39   Key passage: Luke 8:26-39

"You turn if you want to – the Lady's not for turning". Famous words of Margaret Thatcher when accused of a political U-turn. U-turns are usually dangerous things, politically and traffically!

Jesus commands the demoniac "Return home…". The word of command is literally "apostrophe". This is not a full stop, the end of the story for the man now made whole – rather it is a "joining point", a moment to draw breath then continue with the narrative. Up to this moment the man's life had been punctuated by question marks ("who is he?"), exclamation marks ("you'd think he'd make himself scarce!") and parentheses ("we don't welcome people like him"). Now in this moment of change in his encounter with Jesus, he is made whole and commanded to "tell how much God has done…". He would have gone with Jesus, but is sent on his own path. The sharing of the good news begins at home, the place where often it's the hardest but probably the most needed. It's easy to be a Christian in church – home can be more of a challenge.

Lord, help me to be obedient to Your call to discipleship beginning in my home, in my daily living, my recreation, my work, my relationship, my family, my friends. Help me to not turn from Your way.

March 30

"Who touched me?"
Luke 8:45   Key passage: Luke 8:40-56

"I promise to tell the truth, the whole truth and nothing but the truth…"– words of the affirmation spoken daily in law courts across the land – but what do they mean? What is truth? Truth is what you understand, how you perceive an event, an action, a statement. Someone else has to work out where the truth lies in competing statements.

In the jostling crowd, Jesus asks, "Who touched me?" Peter, ever helpful, points out the blindingly obvious – "the people are crowding and pressing against you". Several people must have touched Jesus, but one person has done so from need, not necessity. Peter could not see that, but Jesus sensed it – "power has gone out from me". Jesus did not mean that His power was diminished, rather that the healing in another has been enhanced. You cannot encounter Jesus and do so secretly! The truth will out…

"Your touch still has its ancient power, no word from You can fruitless fall; hear, in this solemn evening hour, and in your mercy heal us all". (Henry Twells)

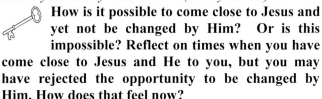 **How is it possible to come close to Jesus and yet not be changed by Him? Or is this impossible? Reflect on times when you have come close to Jesus and He to you, but you may have rejected the opportunity to be changed by Him. How does that feel now?**

March 31

"I know that power has gone out from me"
Luke 8:46   Key passage: Luke 8:40-56

Today our telephone and internet broke down. "No problem" I assured my wife "I'll report it…" That's when the trouble started! Where is the telephone supplier's number? Online, of course… Sometimes you are just helpless…

The helpless woman in this episode touched the tassel of Jesus' cloak, and in that moment she was healed. "Who touched me?" Jesus asked. He knew full well who it was, but He asked the question to enable her to be a witness to the doubters around. He wanted her to be fully restored to her family and community, and above all He wanted her to know the power of God's grace in her life. He also wanted it known that her healing had come, not through the "superstitious" touching of his garment, but through faith. In great anxiety she comes to the feet of Jesus to confess all…but all she needs to confess is Jesus Himself. The One who subjected Himself in weakness to the cross is the One who offers Himself in power to us.

"He left His father's throne above – so free, so infinite His grace – 'tis mercy all, immense and free; for, O my God, it found out me!" (Charles Wesley)

APRIL 1

"Don't be afraid; just believe, and she will be healed…"
Luke 8:50   Key passage: Luke 8:40-56

I boarded the bus and showed my ticket to the driver. Before I sat down he said to me "Can you help me? Which way do we go now?" It was his first day on the route! We assume the people driving us know what they're doing…

Jesus is diverted from His encounter with Jairus by the unclean woman, and by the time he is back on the route, it seems too late – the girl has died. Jesus knows where He is going. "Don't be afraid – just believe." Remarkably the words "Don't be afraid" or "Fear not" occur 365 times in the Scriptures – one for each day of the year! We recoil when someone tells us "Don't panic" – that instantly becomes our default response! But when those words come from the lips of the Saviour, we must take note. This is not bravery in the face of impossible odds, but a call to faith. "Just believe." Say to the Saviour, "Where do we go now?"

"Lord, I believe, help my unbelief" (Mark 9.24). Lord, show me where we need to go today, and grant me faith to trust in You.

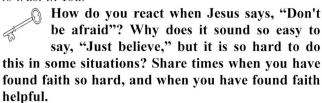 **How do you react when Jesus says, "Don't be afraid"? Why does it sound so easy to say, "Just believe," but it is so hard to do this in some situations? Share times when you have found faith so hard, and when you have found faith helpful.**

April 2

"Stop wailing…"
Luke 8:52   Key passage: Luke 8:40-56

Legend suggests that crocodiles shed tears whilst consuming their prey – a theory shown to be false; they are simply lubricating their eyes when out of the water – but the phrase has passed into folklore.

In Jesus' time, professional mourners would be employed to help the bereaved mourn their loss. Their cries and moans were real enough – their sentiments less convincing. Jesus reprimands them when he arrives at Jairus's house. You know what they say about "empty vessels"? Jesus boldly states, "She is not dead but asleep…"

That was just too much for the mourners – "they laughed at him", from mourning to merriment. For Jesus death is no more than sleep, and with it comes the possibility of waking to a new day, a new reality. That is the essence of resurrection and the Christian hope. No more crocodile tears, and no more hopelessness! In Jesus the new day has dawned.

"I will turn (your) mourning into gladness; I will give (you) comfort and joy instead of sorrow" (Jeremiah 31.13). What do you need to turn over to God today?

April 3

"My child, get up!"
Luke 8:54   Key passage: Luke 8:40-56

Some words stay with you. Many still remember the stirring words of Churchill, "We will never surrender" or Neil Armstrong's, "That's one small step for man…". Scripture has its own highlights: "Jesus wept", "He is not here, He is risen!" alongside the words of Jesus here. Luke chooses to record them in Greek, but Mark in his parallel account has them in the original Aramaic – *Talitha cum* – "little girl, arise!"

It would be easy to eulogize Jesus' invitation to Jairus' daughter as if there was some dramatic mood music playing in the background – but the context is challenging and terse. The professional mourners are disdainful of Jesus' word of promise "She is not dead but asleep". There is tension in the air, not relieved by their sarcastic laughter at the very suggestion that death has not visited this household. Yet Jesus is insistent – and leaving the crowd outside, He goes in to the room where the young girl is laid, and calls her to life. The words are powerful, intimate and compelling. And the same Jesus calls us to life today…"my child, get up!" Remember the words…and who spoke them!

"Lord, it's for You – for Your coming we wait, the sky, not the grave is our goal: O trump of the angel! O voice of the Lord! Blessed hope!" (Horatio Spafford)

What was the background to Spafford's hymn words? How could he be so hopeful? How do the words of Jesus bring us hope now and in the future? How would you explain your hope to someone who does not understand?

April 4

"Take nothing for the journey…"
Luke 9:3   Key passage: Luke 9:1-9

"Be prepared." Every Scout knows the motto, but "be prepared" for what? There are known events and there are surprises. "If only I'd seen that coming," we mumble. How foolish to set out without thinking of what you might need for the journey or the task ahead. Jesus commended the virgins who came prepared with spare oil for their lamps, the builder who dug deep for foundations, the man who counted the cost before setting out on a project. The maxim is "to fail to prepare is to prepare to fail."

So why should Jesus say to his disciples, "Take nothing for the journey? Is this irresponsibility on a grand scale? Or feeding off the efforts of other people? The command of Jesus is a call to simplicity and focus in Christian discipleship. We are easily deflected from our mission focus by anxiety about daily living. Jesus commanded His disciples, "Seek first (God's) kingdom and his righteousness, and all these things will be given to you as well" (Matthew 6.33). Prepare to go today with your hand in the hand of God…

"Put your hand in the hand of the man who stilled the water…" (Anne Murray). Lord, help me to get my priorities right, to trust You for all I shall need in this day, and to walk this day with You in humble obedience.

April 5

"…shake the dust off your feet…"
Luke 9:5   Key passage: Luke 9:1-9

We once visited a premier Welsh seaside resort on a day when the wind was howling, the sea crashing over the promenade, and it was carnival week… It sticks in the memory, and we're not in a rush to return! Sometimes memories, as unfortunate as they are, define our view of a place or a person.

Jesus' instruction to His disciples concerning their behaviour on their mission is specific, not just in the positives – to preach the kingdom, heal and drive out demons – but in the negatives – to travel light and stick to the task. But then there is this warning about the reception they may receive. "If people do not welcome you, shake the dust off your feet when you leave…". Washing the feet of visitors was a sign of welcome., the opposite a sign of judgment. Paul and Barnabas did it when leaving Antioch (Acts 13.51). The dust of Gentile countries was believed to be defiled, to be removed when returning home. Israelites who reject the kingdom are no better than the Gentiles. They are to be rejected. What do you need to "dust off" today?

Lord, show me today the places and things I need to reject in order to focus on You and Your kingdom.

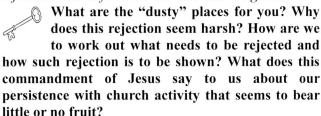 **What are the "dusty" places for you? Why does this rejection seem harsh? How are we to work out what needs to be rejected and how such rejection is to be shown? What does this commandment of Jesus say to us about our persistence with church activity that seems to bear little or no fruit?**

April 6

"You give them something to eat…"
Luke 9:13   Key passage: Luke 9:10-17

"Heavenly Father bless us and keep us all alive, there's ten of us for dinner and not enough for five…". The "grace" is amusing…and sometimes rather real! Yet what do we think when we say grace before a meal? Is this a matter of habit or honest gratitude?

The feeding of the five thousand features in all four gospels, so important is it to the gospel writers. It's about a whole lot more than a miracle with a boy's packed lunch! Jesus' challenge to the disciples to feed the people is met with protests of impossibility, but Jesus is going to feed them, and the pivotal point of this miracle is in the giving thanks. The Jewish *Hamotzi* prayer is direct: "Blessed are You, Lord our God, King of the universe, who brings forth bread from the earth". The disciples by themselves are in an impossible position. Nothing they can do will feed the people, but with Jesus the impossible becomes possible. He is the "bread that comes forth from the earth" – and He, the Bread of Life, will come forth in glorious resurrection. That's grace in action!

"Bread of heaven, feed me now and evermore" (William Williams). Thank You, Lord, for satisfying my need. Feed me Your truth and power today.

April 7

"Make them sit down…"
Luke 9:14   Key passage: Luke 9:10-17

I enjoy assembling IKEA furniture. It's something to do with the puzzle of the instructions – no words, just pictures! How many happy hours have been spent comparing illustrations working out the next step.

When you break down a task into easy stages, it goes well. When I'm tempted to ignore the instructions since I reckon I know what to do, disaster looms. Confronted by over 5000 hungry people, most hosts would have panicked, but Jesus calmly commands, "Make them sit down". This is no "food to go" exercise – it's going to be a proper meal. Each group of 50 is to be fed. Why 50? Maybe just manageable groups, but 50 also represents the coming of the Holy Spirit (at Pentecost), and 50 is the number of Jubilee, the year of deliverance and freedom from burden. Jesus is about to deliver a miracle of physical feeding, but the greater miracle of spiritual feeding comes as the Spirit of God works to bring deliverance to His people. By this miracle, Jesus proves His divine credentials. Sit down and receive from the hand of the Saviour.

"Be still, for the presence of the Lord, the Holy One is here…" (David Evans). Lord, when I'm agitated and anxious, still me in Your presence to receive from You what You wait to give me.

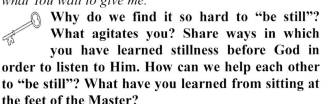 **Why do we find it so hard to "be still"? What agitates you? Share ways in which you have learned stillness before God in order to listen to Him. How can we help each other to "be still"? What have you learned from sitting at the feet of the Master?**

April 8

"Who do the crowds say I am?"
Luke 9:18   Key passage: Luke 9:18-27

As a simple country lad, I cannot forget my first visit to London. Everything seemed so big, and there were people everywhere. I felt so small and insignificant…and I was! As Samuel Johnson said "If a man is tired of London, he is tired of life". Caesarea Philippi was the "London" of Jesus' day, the city of springs, grotto, and shrines all dedicated to the Greek god Pan – the god of all things. It was a place of pagan worship, the grotto being the supposed entrance to the underworld, where religious prostitutes plied their trade. "Anything goes" was the maxim.

With this as the backdrop, Jesus asks His disciples "Who do the crowds say I am?" What chance does a peasant carpenter from Nazareth have in the face of all the seductive attractions of this place? The question remains "Who do people say Jesus is?" with so many "gods" competing for attention. How do we respond to the claims of Jesus? It's not just a matter of having an opinion on Jesus. It is, "Who is He…for you?

"Who is He that from the grave comes to heal and help and save…?" (Benjamin Hanby)

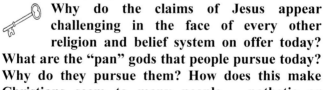 **Why do the claims of Jesus appear challenging in the face of every other religion and belief system on offer today? What are the "pan" gods that people pursue today? Why do they pursue them? How does this make Christians seem to many people – pathetic or prudent?**

April 9

"What about you? Who do you say I am?"
Luke 9:20   Key passage: Luke 9:18-27

"It could be you!" That was the slogan used to promote the UK National Lottery when it was launched in 1994 – and in only the second week the jackpot was won by a consortium from our local sheltered housing complex. That changed a few friendships – not all for the better.

None of us like "being put on the spot", especially when our opinion is unconsidered and unconvincing. We find ourselves saying what we think someone wants to hear rather than what we really think. As Jesus stands before the temple at Caesarea Philippi with His disciples, He asks the question that really matters, "What about you? Who do you say that I am?" It's the most important question we all have to answer. Either Jesus is who He claims to be, or He is the biggest fraudster the world has ever seen. If we believe the latter, we can safely ignore Him. If it's the former, then we have to consider His claims on our life. This is no lottery – we cannot take a chance on our answer. What about you? Have you got your answer?

"Who is He that from His throne rules through all the worlds alone…At His feet we humbly fall; crown Him, crown Him Lord of all" (Benjamin Hanby). Lord, I want to say again today that I declare You to be Jesus Christ, God's Son, Lord and Saviour!

 How did you hear this question from Jesus, "Who do you say I am?" and how did you respond initially? How do you respond now?

April 10

"The Son of Man must suffer many things…"
Luke 9:22   Key passage: Luke 9:18-27

The meal was good, and we sat back satisfied. Then we learned that the cook had never done the dish before – we were the guinea pigs! Is this the ultimate test of friendship – to try out something on people you trust, in the hope that it will work out OK?

Jesus' response to Peter's affirmation of His Messiahship is assertive – they are to tell no one, lest there be wholesale misunderstanding of who Jesus is. The Jews were looking for a messiah figure to overturn the hated Roman rule, but Jesus had not come to do that, but something greater. If the people see him only as that deliverer, they miss the greater truth. He is to "suffer many things". The term used is a legal one – describing examination by the court and being found not guilty or in a civil court of being found unqualified for a task. "Many things" include ridicule, disdain, disregard, disqualification, and the venom of the religious classes. Ultimately there was the cross, man's greatest injustice. God had never done this before, nor needed it again. This is God's friendship – suffering for you!

"Bearing shame and scoffing rude, in my place condemned He stood; sealed my pardon with His blood; Hallelujah! What a Saviour!" (Philipp Bliss").
Thank You, Jesus, for all You willingly suffered to win my love. I worship You.

April 11

"...he must be killed and on the third day be raised to life"
Luke 9:22   Key passage: Luke 9:18-27

You dial the number, and a recorded voice kicks in. "To speak to one of our advisers press 1, to leave a message press 2…" Options, options…and then at the end you want none of the options. Choice – the god of the 21st. century.

Jesus speaks, not of choice, but of compulsion – He "must suffer", "must be rejected", "must be killed", options none of us would choose, and certainly not the options He would choose. Never forget His prayer in Gethsemane: "Father, if it is possible, take this cup of suffering from me…". Jesus knows His task is to do the will of His Father, whatever that may entail. This is no grim resignation, but complete submission to God and His plan for salvation. Notice the conclusion of Jesus' words here – the last "must". He must "be raised to life on the third day". All that goes before finds its resolution in the resurrection. His death will be certain, His resurrection secure. In Jesus, all the "musts" of this life make sense in the light of Easter Day!

"Choose this day who you will serve – as for me and my house, we will serve the Lord!" *(Joshua 24.15). Thank you, Lord, for choosing the way of the cross to win my salvation. Help me to make the right choices today in following You.*

Why does the Christian gospel seem so hard? How do you respond to those who find the matter of the death of Jesus too difficult to understand? What does the Christian gospel without the cross of Jesus achieve?

April 12

"If anyone would come after me, he must deny himself…"
Luke 9:23   Key passage: Luke 9:18-27

"No dogs, except guide dogs" – the sign is quite clear, except I'd never realised guide dogs could read as presumably their visually-challenged owners are unable to! For every rule, there is an exception…

…except that in the kingdom of God, there is no exception. Jesus makes it clear – if you want to be a follower of His, here's the deal: deny self, daily sacrifice, devoted service. In reverse order we say we're "up for it" – we'll follow Jesus (the disciples expressed the same keenness), we're probably willing to "take up the cross" and put up with some discomfort, but as for denial of self, now that's going a bit far…

…and it all begins with that bit – the challenge to disclaim our own ambitions, needs, comforts. Haven't we got to "look after ourselves"? What good is a follower who can't do that? Remember, of the 12 disciples there was only one who would do that properly – Judas. In all decisions, it's not "what would I do?" but "what would Jesus do? Being me is not the most important thing in the world – knowing Jesus…that's what matters!

"Reign in me, sovereign Lord…captivate my heart, let Your kingdom come…" (Chris Bowater). Teach me, Lord, the art of self-denial and the grace of devoted service.

April 13

"…take up his cross daily and follow me…"
Luke 9:23   Key passage: Luke 9:18-27

We move house an average of eight times in a lifetime. Many of us have stories of the traumas connected to such events – and most of us say, "Never again!" But some people seem to spend their lives moving, and others stay just where they are.

Jesus challenges His disciples as to their understanding of discipleship. Following Jesus is not for part-timers, job-sharers or the faint-hearted. It will involve self-denial – renouncing one's priority to the lordship of Jesus. If that is not challenging enough, Jesus calls His followers to "take up (their) cross daily and follow me". The cross here is not the cross of Jesus – it's the disciple's cross. The word literally means "tent-peg". When the temptation is to stay where we are – ideologically and spiritually, if not geographically – the call is to pull up the pegs and move on. The apostle Paul speaks of this life as a tent we inhabit *en route* to the permanence of heaven. Life is one big house-moving adventure. Today is another day to pull up the pegs and move on with Jesus.

Lord, teach me today what it means to "take up the cross". Show me those areas of my life where I need to move on in obedience to You, to grow in grace and love.

 Which "tent pegs" do you need to pull up? What gives you security and comfort? What might God say to you about such "crosses"? How do you work out the things that are important and need retaining and the things that need "moving on"?

April 14

"Whoever wants to save his life will lose it…"
Luke 9:24   Key passage: Luke 9:18-27

"Look after the pennies, and the pounds will look after themselves." Remember such wise advice – but how difficult it is to make that work! Yet a little goes a long way when you are careful.

The challenge of Jesus to "save (your) life" goes beyond economics. Life is for living, and our daily challenge is to get the most out of it. That becomes so much more difficult at a time of crisis. If a person's focus is simply to find personal fulfilment, then good luck to them! But if your focus becomes something or someone else, then there's a new dimension of life to be experienced. Simply for the Christian, it's not all about "me", but Jesus. When everything around you concentrates on the present and your satisfaction, it's hard to maintain a focus on the future. As William Barclay put it "The Christian must realise that he is given life, not to keep for himself but to spend for others". Remember – a little goes a long way with Jesus!

"I would the precious time redeem, and longer live for this alone – to spend and to be spent for them who have not yet my Saviour known". (Charles Wesley)

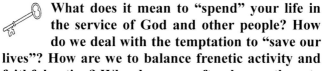
What does it mean to "spend" your life in the service of God and other people? How do we deal with the temptation to "save our lives"? How are we to balance frenetic activity and faithful action? Why do we so often leave others to do the task when there's a need for help?

April 15

"Whoever loses his life for me will save it"
Luke 9:24   Key passage: Luke 9:18-27

I once had a very strange encounter with a lady in a department store. She was obviously distressed, and told me, when I asked if I could help, that she'd just lost her husband. I swung into "pastor mode", and asked her how long since she had lost him. "About 10 minutes ago" she replied "in the bus station!"

To give one's life for the cause of Christ is the ultimate act of commitment. Not all of us will be asked to do it, but we must be willing. When Jesus said "whoever loses his life for me", He wasn't speaking figuratively! Martyrs hold a special place in God's heart. Paul speaks of martyrdom as a spiritual gift – see 1 Corinthians 13.3. The irony is it's a gift you only exercise once! It's unclear how many people are martyred for their faith – estimates vary between about 4,000 up to 80,000 annually. Today two thirds of the world's 2.3 billion Christians live in dangerous contexts. Want to follow Jesus? Be careful what you ask.

Lord, help me to be clear about the cost of following You…whatever.

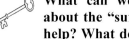 **What can we do to be better informed about the "suffering church"? How can we help? What does your church do sensitively to raise the profile of the "suffering church"? If you were in imminent danger because of your Christian faith, what do you think you would do?**

April 16

"What good is it…to gain the whole world, yet lose (your) self?"
Luke 9:25   Key passage: Luke 9:18-27

When John D. Rockefeller died, his friends asked "How much did he leave?" The family's answer was, "All of it!". You know you cannot take it with you,

To underline the point of His teaching to the disciples, Jesus told them "What good is it…to gain the whole world, yet lose (your) self?". Right now I'm not sure I'd like to "gain the whole world", but I wouldn't mind just a bit more of it! After all, I think I could cope with a bit more money, influence, importance, or recognition. But is that not the problem with the human heart – to never be satisfied? We are busy "looking for our inner selves", trying to discover who we are, and our purpose in life. What do we suppose we are going to do when we find it? Most people remain unhappy about some aspect of their life and identity – their appearance, achievements, acceptance. Jesus suggests it is in knowing Him that we find ourselves. And how much of our life does He ask? …all of it!

"Our hearts are restless until they find rest in You" (Augustine of Hippo). Lord, help me to find rest and fulfilment in knowing Jesus and being know by Him.
What gives you the greatest personal dissatisfaction? If you could change three things about yourself and your situation, what would they be? How does your Christian faith mesh with the things you wish you could change?

April 17

"O unbelieving and perverse generation…"
Luke 9:41   Key passage: Luke 9:37-45

"If you don't stand for something, you will fall for anything" (Alexander Hamilton). Many people protest their barriers to faith – suffering, injustice, war, pandemic…alongside barriers of the church and religion. You hear people say "I'm not religious…" like some kind of get-out clause from engagement with the claims of Christ. Yet often these are the same people who place their trust in vague "certainties" like politics, good deeds, neighbourliness, or in the stars and lottery numbers!

Jesus encounters the father whose son is seized in convulsions. In despair the father reveals that he has asked the disciples to do something, but they could not. In the context we are not sure to whom Jesus addresses His words, but what is clear is that Jesus despairs at the lack of faith of those involved. The father comes in faith – a faith that is imperfect, but enough for healing to flow. People marvelled at the works of Jesus, but did not see the power of God at work. The same "blindness" is spoken of by Moses: "Our God – He is the Rock, His works are perfect…but they are a warped and crooked generation…" (Deuteronomy 32.4+5)

"Is this the way you repay the Lord, O foolish and unwise people? Is he not your Father, your Creator, who made you and formed you?" (Deut. 32.6). Forgive us, Father, that we have been too ready to believe anything and everything instead of placing our trust in You, our Rock.

April 18

"Bring your son here…"
Luke 9:41   Key passage: Luke 9:37-45

"He is young, he's afraid, let him rest, heaven blessed. Bring him home" – haunting words from *Les Miserables* as Jean Valjean offers his life to God in exchange for the life of a younger man…with an equally haunting tune.

Jesus faced such a moment when confronted with the distraught father of the boy seized by a spirit. No one else could do anything – but Jesus can and does. It is clear from other healing accounts in the gospel that it was not necessary for Jesus to be physically present for the healing to occur, but Jesus wants the people to see God at work and thus honour God for His power. "Bring your son here…" It is in the faithful response of the father that Jesus heals the boy and returns him to his father and family. Faith is not just a belief of the mind and heart – it is the tangible action of response that brings the boy into the presence of Jesus. Even as the boy approaches Jesus, the possessing spirit convulses him again in rebellion to the power of Jesus. What do you need to bring to him today?

"Have we trials and temptations, is there trouble anywhere? We should never be discouraged – take it to the Lord…in prayer!" (Joseph Scriven)

How come we find it so difficult to understand faith as an action rather than just a belief? What did you have to do to become a follower of Jesus? What practical actions followed as a result of your commitment? What is Jesus asking you actually to do today as an act of faith?

April 19

"Listen carefully…"
Luke 9:44   Key passage: Luke 9:37-45

It's suggested that females speak twice as many words as a male in an average day! That's probably because men don't listen very carefully! (I think that's what I was told…)

Jesus commands His disciples "Listen carefully…". What He has to say is startling: "The Son of Man is going to be betrayed into the hands of men…" They heard the words alright, but did not understand what He meant…and worse than that, they didn't ask Him what this meant. There's a significant difference between hearing and listening. There's a sense in which the disciples could not understand, because this had never happened before – how often have you said "If someone had told me this would happen, I would never have believed them"? But listening carefully means doing just that – taking in every word and nuance, checking where we do not understand! That's why we have the Scriptures, to help us "listen carefully" and understand God's word and heart to us – and why it's important to "check out" what we do not understand. God gave us one mouth and two ears – perhaps we need to listen twice as much as we speak!

Lord, You know that I'm not very good at listening – open my ears to Your word of truth today.

 How many sermons have you heard and how many have you listened to? When does God's word "come alive" for you? What makes the difference?

April 20

"The Son of Man is going to be betrayed into the hands of men"
Luke 9:44   Key passage: Luke 9:37-45

My grandparents called their house "Anmino". Apparently when it was being built, they were always being told by the builder that it would be completed "**An**y **Mi**nute **No**w"…

Jesus tells His disciples that any minute now He will be "betrayed into the hands of men". The moment is almost here. We say that hindsight is a wonderful thing, but foresight would be so much more useful! Jesus knows His destiny on the cross is looming, and His handing over to wicked men will precede that. The disciples cannot grasp all of this – they are still in the hindsight of the transfiguration. Twice Luke records that the disciples would not speak (verses 36 and 44) – they could not understand what was "hidden from them". They would protest their ignorance, and even run away, but Jesus cannot and will not avoid His destiny. The moment has come. Jesus gives Himself willingly to redeem a lost humanity – betrayed by one who should have protected Him. Any minute now…we do not know what we might be called to face…but trust in Him who faces it with us

"I do not know what lies ahead, the way I cannot see; but One stands near to be my guide, He'll show the way to me" (Alfred Smith/Eugene Clark). Jesus, be my guide in every moment today.

April 21

"He who is least among you all – he is the greatest"
Luke 9:48   Key passage: Luke 9:46-50

A Norfolk boy was offered a choice by his grandad – a 50p or a pound coin. He chose the pound – "Mum always taught me to take the smaller part!". If only we had the same ingenuity!

We can learn so much from children. My grandchildren inevitably show me how to use my computer – sometimes their wisdom is incredible! Jesus has some quarrelsome disciples to teach – they want to know who tops the pecking order! We all strive for identity in our community, society, workplace, church… It matters where we fit – none of us want to be left at the bottom of the pile…But Jesus has some dynamic teaching on the matter of greatness - it's all down to how we regard those below us on the ladder. An important lesson for a pastor to learn is that you are not the "professional" Christian – there is much to learn from those who have been journeying simply with Jesus day by day without fanfare or recognition. For Jesus that simplicity is exemplified in a child. Which currency do you choose – humility or greatness?

"Lord of eternity dwells in humanity, kneels in humility and washes our feet…bow down and worship!" (Graham Kendrick)

 When have you learned hard lessons from children? When have you learned simple lessons from other more mature Christians? Why is it difficult to learn humility from those we regard as lesser than us?

April 22

"The Son of Man did not come to destroy men's lives, but to save them"
Luke 9:55   Key passage: Luke 9:51-56

"What have I got to give up…?" For many people there's a perception that being a Christian is a bit of an unfortunate thing, that somehow Christians are rather pathetic…I can't imagine how people get that idea…!

…except that we don't help ourselves. The disciples are unimpressed that the residents of a Samaritan village would not welcome them because of Jesus travelling on to Jerusalem. We probably know there was tension between Samaritans and Jews – and the disciples way to "fix" their aggression is to call down fire from heaven on the Samaritans – it had worked for Elijah…twice! (2 Kings 1.10+12). We easily want to pass judgment on an unbelieving world and its sinful rejection of God and His ways – as if we're the sole arbiters of justice. Not for nothing were James and John called "the sons of thunder". Jesus rebukes them and their attitude for He came to bring men to life, not to death. Perhaps we should be a bit less judgmental and bit more loving towards those who don't yet love God. Need to give up something?

"Soften my heart, Lord…from all indifference set me apart; to feel Your compassion, to weep with Your tears…" (Graham Kendrick)

How do we tend to pass judgment on unbelievers? Why do our attitudes create barriers with them? How do we show our indifference to the suffering of the world? Why do our words and prayers often sound so hollow? How can we change?

April 23

"Foxes have holes, and birds…have nests…"
Luke 9:58   Key passage: Luke 9:57-62

A friend was driving to Exeter, and his wife was navigating. Unsure of the route, they spotted a bus with "Exeter" on its destination board, and so they followed it…right into the bus station!

Following is a dodgy business and is dependent on how closely you are following. Jesus encounters a man who is obviously keen to follow Him. He has heard about Jesus, and it all sounds rather good. So the man expresses his enthusiasm – "I'll follow you wherever you go!" Really? Jesus' response is enigmatic – "Foxes have holes…" - even the creatures of the countryside have places of safety – but for Jesus there will be no such security. I wonder what you imagined when you first decided to follow Jesus? Is Christian faith an "add-on" to all the other responsibilities and privileges of life? Or is discipleship foundational to you? If you are looking for security and status in this world, then don't follow Jesus! If you need home comforts and luxuries, consider the One who had nothing to call His own. We may not be called to frugality, but we are called to follow. Don't miss the bus!

Lord Jesus, teach me to sit lightly to the security of belongings and status, and to learn what it means to follow You wherever You may lead me. I will come with You on life's journey today.

April 24

"Let the dead bury their own dead…"
Luke 9:60   Key passage: Luke 9:57-62

"Never put off till tomorrow, what you can do the day after tomorrow" (Mark Twain). It's a famous misquotation, but true for so many. It's akin to Tommy Cooper's "I used to be indecisive, but now I'm not so sure…". We often to dither.

The man who tells Jesus "I'll follow you – I just need to go and bury my father…" is possibly being disingenuous. We're not actually told that his father was dead! If he wasn't, then the man is asking for an open-ended deferral of the call to discipleship – "I'll come when I'm ready…" – and if the father is dead, then for him the need to perform the burial rites takes precedence over everything else. The man needs to decide which is the more compelling – his duties, or the call of Jesus? Jesus is clear – there are plenty of people ("the (spiritually) dead") who can see to the deceased. His call takes priority. What kind of excuses do we give for delaying our response to the claims of Jesus? How do we decide what is really important? Is it all right to be indecisive…and are we sure?

Forgive me, Lord, when I find Your call inconvenient and disruptive to my life. Help me to get my priorities right, and to seek Your kingdom first.

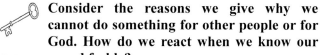 **Consider the reasons we give why we cannot do something for other people or for God. How do we react when we know our reasons sound feeble?**

April 25

"No-one who…looks back is fit for service in the kingdom…"
Luke 9:62   Key passage: Luke 9:57-62

Remember taking your driving test? What was the most important thing to do? It had been drummed into me – check your mirror! I made a great show of doing this – deliberately staring into it. I passed, but it's not a habit I have kept up with the same intensity.

Looking in the mirror is a tricky business – everything is in reverse! You need to be aware of what is behind, but you must concentrate on what is ahead. Jesus' words here would have caused consternation among the Jews, who loved their history and forebears. Looking in the "mirror" of history was fundamental to them. The irony is that if they had looked carefully they would have realised that Jesus fulfilled the prophetic word about Him. But they also failed to look forward as well – they could not grasp that the call of Jesus was for now. The men made excuses – often poor ones – wanting to follow Jesus at their own convenience. What kind of poor excuses do we make for our reluctant obedience to the call of Christ today? Take a look in the mirror.

Lord, forgive me when I find discipleship inconvenient, when there are so many other things demanding my time and attention. Help me to follow You today.

April 26

"The harvest is plentiful…the workers are few"
Luke 10:2   Key passage: Luke 10:1-16

As a pastor I discovered one thing – it's OK appealing for volunteers, but it's far better to ask people personally! People respond when invited individually.

Jesus commissions 72 workers – the figure is redolent of the number of the world's nations (Genesis 10) implying the task is global – but Jesus laments that those willing to serve are few. It would be far better to have more hands to the task – the harvest would be gathered more quickly and less would be missed, but Jesus illustrates what can be achieved with the few. He chose 12 disciples, most of whom were hardly "fit for purpose", to accompany Him on His ministry. He sends out 72 to proclaim the kingdom, and not long after they return (10.17) reporting victory in the name of Jesus. Jesus called one errant disciple, Peter, to responsibility for the church and commissions him to "feed my lambs". By the best business standards, none of these were well-fitted for the task – yet the kingdom has grown! We may protest today we're not well-suited to the task, but Jesus asks us personally…dare we refuse?

"Here I am, wholly available – as for me, I will serve the Lord" (Chris Bowater). Help me to hear your personal invitation to me today to share in the work of Your harvest. Show me one person for whom I can pray.

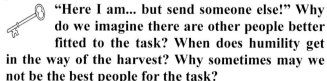 **"Here I am... but send someone else!" Why do we imagine there are other people better fitted to the task? When does humility get in the way of the harvest? Why sometimes may we not be the best people for the task?**

April 27

"I am sending you out like lambs among wolves"

Luke 10:3   Key passage: Luke 10:1-16

I must confess to being rather annoyed when colleagues refer to me as "the Reverend". I'm not sure what they are expecting me to say or do, but often I sense their embarrassment is matched by their puzzlement. Maybe you have friends or acquaintances who are equally mystified by your Christian faith.

Jesus sends out the 72 with the warning "I am sending you out like lambs among wolves". There is a vulnerability about being a follower of Jesus – you will always be at the mercy of those who do not understand, who think they know better, or who make fun of your faith. Be reassured that such a reaction is normal! However, be aware that sometimes Christians can become their own worst enemies – by being so "odd" or different, and then thinking that the reaction of others is proof of their effectiveness. "Lambs among wolves" speaks of great danger – but there's one thing lambs can do to mitigate the threat – stick together! That's why corporate worship, prayer and serving matter – and in every moment we are to rely on the grace and protection of God.

Who do you look to for spiritual support? Who can you be a support to? Thank God for those who have guided and supported you in your Christian journey.

When have you felt vulnerable as a follower of Jesus? What happened? How do we work out when to speak and when to keep silent? How can we support each other in the daily living of our faith?

April 28

"Be sure of this: the kingdom of God is near"
Luke 10:11 Key passage: Luke 10:1-16

Have you ever doubted your faith? Sometimes I meet people who tell me they've never had a doubt, and perhaps make the rest of us feel rather inadequate! There's nothing wrong with doubt – it's what you do with it that matters.

Jesus tells the disciples to be "sure of this" one thing – the nearness of the kingdom of God. This certainty is despite the doubts of those they encounter. To many people, the notion of the nearness of God is completely alien. They cannot see Him or sense Him, so why should they believe? Gagarin, the first man in space, reported "I looked and looked and looked, but I didn't see God." But what was he expecting to see? The "kingdom of God" relates to His authority. The message of Jesus is simple – the power of God is near – close at hand, there in that moment, present in the divine person of Jesus Himself. When you are tempted to ask "Where is God at this moment?" know that the answer is clear and convincing – He is near in power, presence and purpose. Be sure of this!

"He is here, He is here, and He wants to work a wonder…as we gather in His name" (Jimmy Owens). Lord, when I doubt You, come near and show me the power of Your presence.

April 29

"He who rejects me rejects him who sent me"
Luke 10:16 Key passage: Luke 10:1-16

"I had no idea…!" I love reading obituaries. That may sound morbid, but it's fascinating to discover the stories of people, what they have done and lived through. Frequently I'm surprised to find the person I knew had so much more to them…

…and there's more to Jesus than meets the eye! Jesus advises the 72 that when they are rebuffed in their mission, they must not take it personally, any more than when they are successful are they to take the credit. They are simply the mouthpieces of God, to proclaim the coming of the kingdom. "He who rejects you rejects me…". We are not responsible for saving the world, simply for telling it about Jesus! Jesus is clear that anyone who rejects the good news rejects the One who is the Good News – and in so doing they reject the One who sent the Good News, God the Father. It is vital, therefore, that we make the Good News accessible, attractive and available. We're not to strive to lure people into our churches, rather to seek to love people into the kingdom.

Lord, help me to reset my understanding of Your calling to me. Help me to be so full of Your love that others may see Jesus in me.

 Lord, help me to reset my understanding of Your calling to me. Help me to be so full of Your love that others may see Jesus in me.

April 30

"Rejoice that your names are written in heaven"
Luke 10:20 Key passage: Luke 10:17-22

"And what do you do?" It's often the question we ask any new encounter – it is easier to understand people if we know their function. An accountant friend of mine dreaded the question at social functions, and so told people "I'm a Methodist minister." The conversation stopped pretty quickly!

In the kingdom of God we are not identified by what we do or have done. Do not imagine that somehow the front row seats in heaven are occupied by the "great and good"! The 72 sent out by Jesus return sparkling with wonder – "Even the demons submit to us in your name" (10.17). They are brought down to earth with a bump by Jesus, as He points out that this has nothing to do with them and everything to do with God. They are instead to rejoice that their "names are written in heaven". God knows those who belong to Him and He is not impressed by our achievements, even if we are. When our identity rests solely in our work or qualifications, we miss the glory of knowing that we are known and love by God.

> *"It's all about You, Jesus*
> *And all this is for You*
> *For Your glory and your fame*
> *It's not about me*
> *As if You should do things my way*
> *You alone are God and I surrender*
> *To your ways"*
> *(Paul Oakley)*

MAY 1

"You have hidden these things from the wise and learned..."
Luke 10:21 Key passage: Luke 10:17-22

At a time of international crisis, be reassured – our government is "following the science" in dealing with a pandemic! Thank God for scientists working out how to resolve the problem. Our difficulty, however, is to know which "science" to follow! For every expert, there is another of different persuasion and a different solution. That's when the arguments start. We need more than "science" to get us through a crisis.

There is a great difference between knowledge and wisdom. Jesus thanks His Father that the mystery of the kingdom has not been revealed to the "wise and learned" but to "children". He does not condemn wisdom – elsewhere He urges His followers to be "wise as serpents, harmless as doves" – but the kingdom is truly to be understood by those who trust the King. If the kingdom was only understandable to those of certain intellect, then many of us would miss out! Sometimes we make Christianity too complicated. Karl Barth the theologian, when asked the greatest truth he had learned through all his study, replied "Jesus loves me, this I know!"

Lord, teach me child-like trust in You today. Thank You for minds with which to think, but help me to love You in the way in which You love me.

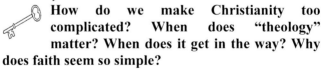 **How do we make Christianity too complicated? When does "theology" matter? When does it get in the way? Why does faith seem so simple?**

May 2

"All things have been committed to me by my Father"
Luke 10:22 Key passage: Luke 10:17-22

It may be just a trick of ageing, but there are more moments now when I feel and sound exactly like my father! The worrying thing is that I now recognise what others have been telling me for years!

Jesus makes a bold claim in this verse – to be the Son of God. This is the only time Luke records Him saying so. It was thought impossible for man to know God – flesh and spirit are separate. So when Jesus says He is the Son of God, He declares He is God in human shoes. Either He is grossly deluded, or He speaks the truth. Only a father can fully know his son, and only a son can truly know his father… and (here Jesus adds a dynamic extra) anyone to whom the son reveals that truth. If "all things have been committed to (Jesus) by (God) the Father" then it is in Jesus and Jesus alone that we can know God! When we encounter Jesus, we meet God! This takes some grasping, but without grasping it we remain in darkness. Meet the Son…and meet the Father!

"Meekness and majesty, manhood and deity in perfect harmony, the man who is God" (Graham Kendrick). Thank You, Jesus, for showing me God my Father!

May 3

"Blessed are the eyes that see what you see"
Luke 10:23 Key passage: Luke 10:21-24

It's a dangerous business being a writer – we are so dependent on proof-readers. We think we have corrected every mistake, but there's always something that escapes.

Jesus tells his disciples "Blessed are the eyes that see what you see…" Luke indicates this was a "private" word to them – literally a word to members of His household. There are some things only close family members need to know. The irony is that the disciples took some persuading of what they were sharing and seeing. Growing up, it's only when we step out into the wider world that we understand the nature of our own family and background…

…and the disciples were witnesses to all of this – the revelation of Jesus as God's Son, Lord and Messiah. They had seen the miracles, witnessed the transfiguration, heard the teaching, shared in the ministry, and would go on to be there at the crucifixion and resurrection. Little wonder that Jesus should utter these words – did they not grasp what they were seeing? We, too, are witnesses to the power of God in Jesus – read the proof and heed the truth!

"Open your eyes, see the glory of the King; lift up your voice and His praises sing! …I will proclaim: Alleluia! I bless Your name" (Carl Tuttle)

How does it make you feel to know that God has revealed His love to you in Jesus? What might be a proper response to such a revelation? Has anyone ever said to you "Why didn't you tell me?" How might that make you feel?

May 4

"Do this and you will live"
Luke 10:28 Key passage: Luke 10:25-37

Just follow the instructions! It's as simple as that...except it isn't. How often are you frustrated because something won't work, and then you discover you've omitted one simple step in the process...

Jesus encounters the "expert in the law". Surely here's a man who knows about "process". He does, which is why he tests Jesus on His understanding of the law. He asks a legal question and gets a regal answer! "How to inherit eternal life?..." Jesus replies "What does the Law say?" Well, that's easy: "Love God, love your neighbour". Yes indeed – which is why Jesus exhorts "Do this and you will live". Spoiler alert – the lawyer asks the supplementary...but has failed to grasp Jesus' answer. Jesus says to him "Do **all** this and you will live". Notice the **all** – it's only two things, but the lawyer misses the first of these: "Love God..." He's hooked up on the legal niceties of who qualifies as "neighbour". It's the first commandment that is frequently overlooked – "Love the Lord your God with all your heart..." When you truly love God, loving your neighbour becomes second nature, not second best. Just follow the instructions!

Lord, I'm so slow to follow your instructions for living. Forgive me when I fail to love God with all my heart and soul, strength and mind, and then struggle to make sense of daily living. Help me reset my priorities with You today.

May 5

"Go and do likewise"
Luke 10:37 Key passage: Luke 10:25-37

Some years ago, when cars were much simpler, I decided to go to car maintenance evening classes. There were two of us men and a dozen females. The tutor demonstrated how to set the distributor points, and invited one of us to have a go. The boys held back – we could do this! – and one of the females took over. Later, when it came to doing this on my own vehicle, I discovered that it wasn't as simple as I thought! The maxim "I hear and I forget, I see and I remember, I do and I understand" suddenly made sense!

Jesus is asked by His questioner "Who is my neighbour?". The man is quick to work this one out from Jesus' story of the mugged traveller – "the one who helped him". "Then go and do likewise" Jesus exhorts. The question wasn't difficult, the answer uncomplicated, but the enactment of it becomes the problem. How often do you hear someone say, "Why don't they do something about…?" when the answer lies very close to home! Don't ask "Why doesn't God do something about…?" – ask "What can I do…?" Get your hands dirty!

What may God be asking you to do today to live out the gospel? Where can you "get your hands dirty" in helping others?

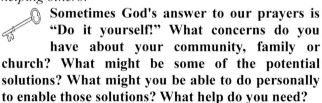 **Sometimes God's answer to our prayers is "Do it yourself!" What concerns do you have about your community, family or church? What might be some of the potential solutions? What might you be able to do personally to enable those solutions? What help do you need?**

May 6

"Only one thing is needed"
Luke 10:42 Key passage: Luke 10:38-42

It's a strange thing, but many of us are so busy being busy, that busyness becomes our business! W.H. Davies wrote "What is this life if, full of care, we have no time to stand and stare…?" Oh to have the time, we protest!

Jesus is welcome in the Bethany home of Mary and Martha. The two sisters are polar opposites – Martha the practical one, Mary the dreamer. Martha has had enough of this, demanding that Jesus tell her sister straight out this is not on! You can understand her angst – the task of running the household never ends. But Jesus gently shows Martha that there is another side to Mary's personality. Martha has lots of anxieties to service, Mary has one Lord to serve. What is more important? "Only one thing is needed…(she) has chosen what is better…". We're not told of Martha's response, or of Mary's reaction, but we do well to consider our own agendas. Martha has a mission to fulfil, and she fulfils it well. Mary has a ministry to offer, and she offers it well. The choice is simple: busyness or business? "What is this life…?"

"O Lord, Thou knowest how busy I must be this day. If I forget Thee, do not thou forget me" (Jacob Astley, 1st. Baron Astley of Reading, in a prayer before the battle of Edgehill in the English Civil War)

May 7

"Mary has chosen what is better…"
Luke 10:42 Key passage: Luke 10:38-42

Activism is an insidious enemy. We spend our lives in activity – employment, leisure, sport, family, friendships, church…the list is endless. We imagine that the more hours we spend at work the more effective we are, the more time we spend in leisure the fitter and happier we shall be, the more energy we devote to the service of others, the more meritorious this will be…

…and then a little voice says "Be still…". What? The "Martha syndrome" kicks in – so much to do, so little time to do it – and the anxiety begins to mount. What do you mean – "be still"? There's no time for dreamy reflection when there's life to live! Jesus describes Martha as being "distracted" by so many things – the word literally means being "wheeled around", being pulled in one direction then another. Distraction by one issue is one thing – distraction by multiple pressures is another. Mary has "chosen what is better…". Martha's concerns are all good, but they will be there again tomorrow and every day thereafter; Mary's concern is singular – to learn from Jesus – and that will have eternal significance. What matters most – the "good" or the "better"?

"To be in your presence, to sit at your feet when your love surrounds me and makes me complete - this is my desire, O Lord" (Noel Richards).

What are your "distractions" today? How can you fulfil your responsibilities without being ruled by them? How do you balance the "here-and-now" with the "eternal"?

May 8

When you pray say "Father..."

Luke 11:2   Key passage: Luke 11:1-13

Don't you just love it - someone rings up and starts talking without identifying themselves...especially when they've got the wrong number! It's a tricky business holding a conversation when you're not sure who's on the other end!

The disciples want some of the action, so they ask Jesus to teach them to pray as He does. What follows has shaped Christian worship ever since. *Lesson number 1: prayer isn't about technique, but trust.* "When you pray, say 'Father'". Be sure that when you pray, someone's listening! Identify yourself – and check the identity of the person you're addressing! We can be confident when we pray that God hears us, not because it's us calling, but because it's in the very nature of God to listen to His children. When we identify God as Father we acknowledge His person, power and purpose. It's the "pater" Father, not the "abba" Father. "Abba" is intimate, but "pater" is instructive – as Father He is the one from whom life comes and through whom life is sustained. If He is indeed Father, then we are indeed His children! Prayer can be confident because we can be confident in Him!

"Lord, may I know you more clearly, love you more dearly, follow you more nearly, day by day". (Richard of Chichester)

May 9

"Hallowed be your name"
Luke 11:2   Key passage: Luke 11:1-13

I shall never forget hearing the great cellist Jacqueline du Pre in concert. I am not a cellist, but she was a virtuoso – "in a league of her own". Her ability to make an instrument speak was awesome…

… when the disciples asked Jesus to teach them the music of prayer, His answer was instructive: "When you pray, say 'Father, hallowed be your name…'" We hear the tune of those words, but must listen for the melody. The longing that God's name might be "hallowed" challenges us. The word literally speaks of the name of God being "in a league of its own" as well as "separate from common condition and use". It's the word for "holy" – set apart and separate from all other earthly meaning. How to pray? ***Lesson number 2: consider the name of God.*** It's the problem Moses had – "who shall I say sent me?" – and God replies "I AM who I AM" (Exodus 3.14). We use names to define people – but the name of God does not define Him, it refines Him as the God of eternity without limit – in a league of His own. Hallowed be that name.

"Blessed be Your name in the land that is plentiful where Your streams of abundance flow, blessed be Your name" (Matt Redman). Thank God today for the glory of who He is, the God of complete holiness, "in a league of His own". Sing a song of worship to Him.

May 10

"Your kingdom come"
Luke 11:2   Key passage: Luke 11:1-13

Christmas is just one day a year, but it seems like it's always coming! The anticipation is often more exciting than the event itself, at least for children and not a few adults! In our house it was always greeted by the cry "He's been!" as children discovered presents left for them in the night…and we still say it now!

The disciples ask how to pray. "When you pray, say…Your kingdom come". ***Lesson number 3: prayer doesn't begin with asking, but with assertion*** – a statement of who God is ("Father") and why we honour Him ("hallowed be your name") based on the reality of His power ("your kingdom come"). His kingdom is not an earthly kingdom, but a heavenly one – so it is always coming in the future but here in the present – a kingdom that exists in the authority of who God is, and that authority is here already in God's activity in creating, sustaining and loving this world. Yet His authority is "coming" in His redeeming the world and bringing all things to fulfilment at the end of time. When we pray "Your kingdom come" we announce the whole gospel – "He's been!"

"Captivate my heart, let Your kingdom come, establish there Your throne, let Your will be done!" (Chris Bowater)

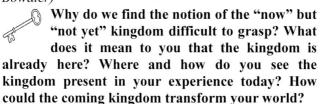 **Why do we find the notion of the "now" but "not yet" kingdom difficult to grasp? What does it mean to you that the kingdom is already here? Where and how do you see the kingdom present in your experience today? How could the coming kingdom transform your world?**

May 11

"Give us each day our daily bread"
Luke 11:3   Key passage: Luke 11:1-13

Living through a time of national crisis, "stockpiling" has become a reality. The concern about some of life's staples is understandable, but other items have disappeared off shelves with alacrity. Just what are people cooking necessitating a large quantity of toilet rolls?

Jesus teaches His disciples that when they pray they assert the authority of God in all things – so here is *lesson number 4: God can be trusted to meet your needs,* so thank Him as a matter of faith and worship. This is not a prayer for a free hand-out from the Almighty - you may have to do something about this yourself, even if that's no more than going to the supermarket or a local shop. Thank God for the provision of all that has gone into your "daily bread", including the provision of money to buy it. Remember there are so many in the world who do not have that blessing…

…but "daily bread" is all that goes to sustain life. We either think that we are responsible for everything, or we recognise the hand of God and thank Him for His goodness. Time to stockpile the gratitude!

"Bless the Lord, oh my soul, and all that is within me, bless His holy name" (Andrae Crouch). Thank God for His provision for your living today.

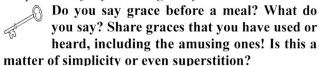 **Do you say grace before a meal? What do you say? Share graces that you have used or heard, including the amusing ones! Is this a matter of simplicity or even superstition?**

May 12

"Forgive us our sins"
Luke 11:4   Key passage: Luke 11:1-13

Politicians are noted for their inability to say "yes" or "no" to a question, but we are sinking to a new low in the use of unnecessary language – it's now popular to reply "absolutely" to every question, as if that makes the reply more assertive. Don't people realise this means "totally dissolved" or "completely overtaken"? "Absolution" is what is sought as a remedy for sin confessed – seeking a state of new perfection from the old.

Prayer lesson number 5: Jesus teaches His disciples "When you pray, say '…forgive us our sins'" This is no magic formula that suddenly somehow makes everything OK. If we feel better, we assume we've been forgiven! Somehow we have forgiven ourselves. But Jesus teaches that it is only God who can forgive, because ultimately all sin is an offence to Him. True forgiveness is not a state of mindfulness but an act of grace. Grace enables us not just to be forgiven, but to continue to live in the freedom that God's grace allows, freedom from guilt and accusation. As the saying goes "When the devil reminds you of your past, remind him of his future!" Absolutely!

"No condemnation now I dread; Jesus, and all in Him, is mine!...bold I approach the eternal throne and claim the crown through Christ, my own" (Charles Wesley)

May 13

"For we also forgive everyone who sins against us"
Luke 11:4   Key passage: Luke 11:1-13

Terms and conditions – don't you just love them? Do you just read them? Or are you just tempted to tick the box saying that you've done so, since there are pages of them in small print…? The problem is, they are conditional to your purchase, even if you think them irrelevant.

Jesus teaches the disciples "When you pray, say…'forgive us…for we also forgive everyone who sins against us'" Is this a condition or a consequence? Is God's forgiveness conditional on us forgiving others, or is forgiveness of others a consequence of God's forgiveness? *Prayer lesson number 6: the answer is "yes"! It's both/and.* Simply, if we close our heart to God, we close our heart to others – and *vice-versa*. It would be wonderful to think we are always willing and able to forgive others, but that would be far from the truth. We can let past hurts fester, and whilst saying that "we have forgiven" sometimes we have not forgotten! Remember that true forgiveness lies with God alone and is His to dispense. God has forgiven you in Christ – do the same for others. Read the small print.

Lord, open my heart to forgiveness, to give and receive in equal measure.

What do you imagine it takes for God to forgive you for your rejection of Him? Why should God forgive anyone or anything? What are some of the "hurts" from the past that still affect you? Why does their effect still linger? Who or what do you need to seek forgiveness?

May 14

"Lead us not into temptation"
Luke 11:4   Key passage: Luke 11:1-13

Some of us know the joke about elephant dust – the magic material which keeps pachyderms off our streets. "But there's no elephants around here!" you protest. Exactly…shows it works! What other proof is required?

Jesus' teaching on prayer moves from forgiveness to temptation. Clearly without temptation and our tendency to yield to it, there would be little need for forgiveness – so in giving us His pattern for prayer, Jesus urges "When you pray, say… 'lead us not into temptation'". ***Prayer lesson number 7 – God does not tempt us to prove something!*** The truth is, we tempt ourselves! James underlines the reality (James 1.13+14). Therefore do not blame God for what is not His fault! Temptation is part of normal human experience. Of itself there's nothing wrong if you are being tempted – it's the giving in to it that causes the problem. Instead of pondering on it, entertaining it and dallying over it, walk away! Just say "No!" Remember that in the struggles you face you're not alone – you have the Holy Spirit to help you prove the power of God. Face up to the "elephant in the room"!

Lord, when I am tempted by something, help me to face it and then place it in Your hands – and discover Your power to win the victory over it!

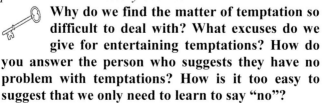 **Why do we find the matter of temptation so difficult to deal with? What excuses do we give for entertaining temptations? How do you answer the person who suggests they have no problem with temptations? How is it too easy to suggest that we only need to learn to say "no"?**

May 15

"Suppose one of you has a friend, and he goes to him at midnight"
Luke 11:5   Key passage: Luke 11:1-13

"How many friends do you have?" With social media, the answer can be in the hundreds. In truth, the number of real friends we have is considerably fewer.

   If Jesus were telling this story today, it would read "A man texts his friend late at night, who fails to answer immediately, so he resends it…" That's the thing about digital comms – we demand an immediate answer! But do friends always answer immediately? Well, not always, but that doesn't mean they are not our friends. They do answer, and when they answer, it's worth waiting for. The point is the inconvenience of the friend – to make a request when you've just gone to bed is challenging. The friend's friend has arrived after dark, and hospitality in Jesus' time was a sacred expectation – to deny it was a deep insult. Everything seems to be conspiring against the needy friend – yet he wins through by his persistence. God's friendship endures our asking, even in the direst circumstances. One true friend is enough.

"One there is, above all others, well deserves the name of friend" (John Newton). Thank You, God, for showing me what true friendship really looks like – and for enduring with me!

May 16

"Because of the man's boldness he will get up"
Luke 11:8   Key passage: Luke 11:1-13

"If you don't ask, you don't get…" In the story of the persistent friend, Jesus commends the boldness of the friend in asking at midnight when all normal people are tucked up in bed! "Bold" is probably not one of the epithets the friend would have applied to his acquaintance. Luke uses a word that means "persistence" with a hint of downright "impertinence" – the word suggests "shamelessness". Doesn't the appellant have any sense of decorum or propriety? In fact, he does, because the need to provide hospitality is a religious requirement of the good host. To deny such means being held in contempt by society at large. The man is in a real quandary, and there's only one thing for it…ask! And when you need to ask, start with a friend…!

The disciples have asked for guidance in the art of praying – and they have got more than they reckoned! Jesus knows their weakness, and urges them to learn the art of persistence in prayer. Soon some of them will prove diffident – but they need to learn boldness before God. He will answer!

"Bold I approach the eternal throne…" (Charles Wesley). "Lord, I come before Your throne of grace…what a faithful God have I!" (Robert and Dawn Critchley)

How do you feel when people go beyond the acceptable bounds of friendship to ask something of you? Do you find their boldness laudable, laughable, or irritating? How does this reflect on the openness of God to your pleading and requests?

May 17

"Ask and it will be given to you"
Luke 11:9   Key passage: Luke 11:1-13

The British love queuing. A queue usually brings out the best in many people – a sense of resignation, fair play, and not a little humour. Strangely, however, people have been getting annoyed at perceived "queue jumpers" when awaiting vaccination in a global pandemic. This is quite strange, since there's little perceived advantage in being "first in the queue", as the vaccine is only at its most effective when everyone has been inoculated.

   Similar dynamics seem to work where prayer is concerned. We may profess gladness for others when their prayers seem to be "successful", but inwardly we may well ask "What about me?" Jesus' words are simple and clear: "Ask and it will be given to you". But what is the "it" that is promised? Anything, everything? Jesus speaks here principally about the basics of life itself – the disciples are not to be anxious in following Him since God will supply all their needs. Jesus never promised a blank cheque – rather a blessed check on reality! Ask God today for His blessing and patiently join the queue!

Lord, teach me patience in waiting, persistence in asking, and pleasure in receiving from Your hand this day.

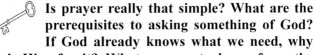 **Is prayer really that simple? What are the prerequisites to asking something of God? If God already knows what we need, why ask Him for it? What are we to learn from the process of praying?**

May 18

"Seek and you will find"
Luke 11:9   Key passage: Luke 11:1-13

We once attended a recording of the radio programme "Any Questions?" The audience were invited to submit questions, and I was one of the five people chosen. The romantic evening I'd planned with my wife was ruined as I had to sit on the front row with the other questioners. It doesn't always pay to ask questions…

…except Jesus encourages His disciples to do just that – "Seek and you will find". In teaching them about the dynamics of prayer, the lesson is ask, ask and ask again. To paraphrase: "Ask a question and you'll get an answer", "Ask more questions and you will get more answers", "Ask again and you'll definitely be answered" for it is in the nature of God to hear His children and respond. "Seek and you will find" is not a mandate for a vain searching for God in the melee of life, but an exhortation to persistence in prayer. "Seek" is literally "be on the lookout for" – miss no opportunity to find God in every situation and every solution. You will find Him – and He will find you! Now, any questions?

"You will seek me and find me when you seek me with all your heart. I will be found by you" (Jeremiah 29.13). Lord, I'm seeking You earnestly. Help me to find You today!

In what "hidden places" have you become aware of the presence of God recently? How has your faith been deepened by the discovery of God in surprising places or experiences?

May 19

"Knock and the door will be opened to you"
Luke 11:9   Key passage: Luke 11:1-13

Football is supposed to be a simple game – score more goals than your opponents, and you'll win. But some managers make it more complicated – one of my favourite characters (whose team struggles to score) summarises his players' efforts by saying. "We were knocking on the door…". The image is intriguing.

Jesus' teaching on prayer is simple; ask-seek-knock. Essentially the three actions are the same but at different levels of intensity. Here He assures the disciples and us that when we make prayer a concerted, honest, intense reality, then God will indeed hear us. God doesn't answer our prayers according to the volume of our pleading or the value of our words; He answers simply because that is in His very nature. However, His answers are not always what we would wish. A friend reckons God has at least five responses to our prayers – "yes", "no", "wait", "do it yourself", and "it's none of your business!" Sometimes we may be part of the answer to our prayer! When you knock on the door, you don't always know who's going to open it or what the welcome might be. Keep knocking!

"Call to me...and I will answer you." (Jeremiah 33L3)
Thank You, Lord God, that Your heart is always to hear the prayer of Your child. Grant me grace to accept Your answer, whatever that may be.

When have you been surprised by an answer to your prayers? When have you discovered that prayer is more powerful than you thought? When have you been part of the answer to one of your prayers?

May 20

"How much more will your Father in heaven give...?"
Luke 11:13 Key passage: Luke 11:1-13

On 13 May 1897, Marconi sent the first wireless communication over open sea. The message was transmitted over the Bristol Channel from Flat Holm Island to Lavernock Point near Cardiff, a distance of 6 kilometres (3.7 miles). It read, "Are you ready?" We're not told what the reply was or if there was a reply.

Jesus concludes His teaching on prayer with the assertion that if human fathers are able to give good gifts to their children, how much more is your heavenly father able to bless His children with good gifts? God is indeed "no man's debtor" and will not withhold anything good from His children. That does not mean all we have to do is ask Him and it's ours...remember God has more than one way of answering prayer! But here Jesus speaks about the wonder of God's giving. He says that God "gives the Holy Spirit to those who ask him!" He gives the Spirit since "the Spirit helps us in our weakness...we do not know what we ought to pray for, but the Spirit himself intercedes for us..." (Romans 8.26)

Thank you, Lord, for the gift of Your Holy Spirit the Helper. Help me to pray today in the power of Your Spirit.

May 21

"A house divided against itself will fall"
Luke 11:17 Key passage: Luke 11:14-28

"All political careers end in failure." (Enoch Powell) Those words should haunt every public servant and one can only wonder what drives men and women to pursue power and risk failure in equal measure. Every great power of the world has eventually crumbled, often from wrangling and dissent. Nothing lasts for ever.

Here Jesus faces criticism from onlookers puzzled that a mute man now speaks again – by what power has Jesus performed this deed? Is not the man speaking, they argue, a sign that the demon in him still speaks? Jesus urges that it is impossible for Him to be acting by the power of the devil, since the devil only acts to destroy good, not evil. When the devil acts, destruction follows. When Jesus acts, joy follows. Like a house of cards or dominoes, the demise of one "house" leads to the subsequent fall of another…and another. Satan's kingdom is in the process of collapse, and nothing can stop this. The "house" of God's kingdom will stand because all that God does and wills is good. Only one thing lasts for ever…

Thank You Father that You are eternal, and all You are and do will last forever. Grant me to have an eternal perspective in all I do and am this day.

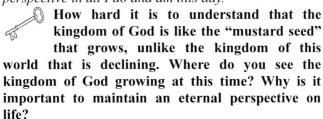

How hard it is to understand that the kingdom of God is like the "mustard seed" that grows, unlike the kingdom of this world that is declining. Where do you see the kingdom of God growing at this time? Why is it important to maintain an eternal perspective on life?

May 22

"I drive out demons by the finger of God"
Luke 11:20 Key passage: Luke 11:14-28

Diego Maradona will not quickly be forgotten for the "hand of God" incident when he bundled the ball past the England goalkeeper and knocked England out of the World Cup. Englishmen have long memories!

It is not by a hand that Jesus speaks of performing this miracle of deliverance, but by "the finger of God". In this unique reference Jesus alludes to the power of God. Elsewhere the gospel writers record Jesus speaking of "the hand of God" or "the power of God" – but "the finger"? The choice of word is deliberate. The hand is the source of the finger's power, and the finger is the source of the hand's effectiveness. Each finger has a different use. The "finger of God" is the finger of power and purpose. Some fingers work best by hanging on – others by helping out. The finger points the way, giving direction and dynamism. The finger of God cannot be ignored – the demons must obey and desert the mute. The finger of God will bring renewed speech and a revelation of the glory of God. That's the goal of the ministry of Jesus!

Lord, take the toil of my hands and the work of my fingers, and be glorified in all I do for You and others this day.

May 23

"When a strong man guards his own house, his possessions are safe"
Luke 11:21 Key passage: Luke 11:14-28

My grandmother liked pickling her own onions. She had rows of them in Kilner jars lined up in her pantry – I remember them as a child and can still taste them now! I'm not sure what kind of vinegar she used for pickling, but I recall that several of the jars' lids were rusting away with the potency of the liquid!

Preserving onions is one thing, preserving one's wealth or security is another. When Jesus is challenged how He can release the mute man from a demon, He underlines His action with a word picture of what He has just done. Imagine Satan as the "strong-man" jealously guarding his possessions – men and women under his power. There is no way out for them, and they are fooled into thinking that how life seems is all there is. They believe themselves to be "safe". How many people do you know who are apparently satisfied with their lives, unaware that Jesus offers so much more? What does it mean to be "safe" when eternity is in view? Some people are in a pickle!

"Safe in the shadow of the Lord beneath His hand and power, I trust in Him, my fortress and my tower" (Timothy Dudley-Smith)

How do non-believers think they are "safe"? Why might Christian faith seem an irrelevance when here are so many other things to worry about? How might the church address the needs of those in the later years of life?

May 24

"He takes away the armour in which he trusted"
Luke 11:22 Key passage: Luke 11:14-28

I have a friend who is a golf professional. He tells of how things were, far from the glamourous lifestyle we might imagine. He was living in a caravan behind the clubhouse, his marriage was breaking down, his golf was way "below par" and he was thoroughly miserable…"and then," he says, "I met Jesus" (at this point we'd all expect him to say that things suddenly turned around) "and things got worse!" It was only as time went on that he came to realise what it meant to follow Jesus, and how life would get better.

Jesus confronts the accusations of demonry by asserting He is far more powerful than "the strong man" of evil. It is a trick of Satan to pretend that he is strong and mighty, and that those who put their trust in the things of this world have invested well. People are in his grip. But "Satan has no authority here, powers of darkness must flee, for Christ has the victory!" The kingdom of God is not a church tea party – it is the overthrow of evil by the power of God!

"For this purpose Christ was revealed to destroy all the works of the evil one!" (Graham Kendrick). Thank God today for the release He has brought to your life, and pray for those who are still bound.

When has following Jesus been particularly tough for you? How have you been confronted by "the powers of this world"? In what situations have you had to confront "the powers of evil"? What happened?

May 25

"He who is not with me is against me"
Luke 11:23 Key passage: Luke 11:14-28

In the days before wall-to-wall entertainment, the highlight of a Sunday evening in our town was to gather at the roundabout and watch the traffic jam! The fence at the side of the road was thronged with local residents enjoying the spectacle of the police trying desperately to clear the traffic as thousands of motorists returned home from a day at the seaside. The memories seem to belong to a long-forgotten era now, but one thing is clear. Our presence probably didn't help the situation.

Jesus summarises His teaching about His ministry with this bold statement: "He who is not with me is against me". In the kingdom of God, there is no room for neutrality. As much as many would like to tick the "Don't know" box, where Jesus is concerned, that is not an option. Either you are "in the kingdom" or you are against it. The net effect of anything other than wholehearted commitment to the kingdom of God is opposition to it. As Barclay puts it "You are either on the Way or in the way". No time to sit on the fence here.

"True-hearted, whole-hearted, now and for ever. King of our lives, by Your grace we will be!" (Frances Ridley Havergal). Lord, help me to be "all-out" and "all-in" for You!

How does this teaching of Jesus sound a bit harsh? How difficult is it to be "all in" for Jesus? What pressures prevent us from such wholeheartedness? What might we do about this?

May 26

"When it arrives, it finds the house swept clean"
Luke 11:25 Key passage: Luke 11:14-28

What's not to like about housework?? As much as it's a chore, it's important for our own welfare and that of our families and friends that we keep a relatively "tidy ship".

Jesus underlines His ministry to the mute and the casting out of the evil spirit by asserting that this is a serious business. When a spirit is exorcised, it has to go somewhere – but such is the power of the kingdom of God that a man cleansed of a spirit is transformed in the same way that a house is cleaned and restored to order. A newly-cleaned property looks attractive – a glance in any estate agent's window confirms that! At this point, a delivered soul is a vulnerable soul. That is why the apostle Paul, addressing the transformation that Christ brings, urges "Do not get drunk on wine…instead, be filed with the Spirit!" (Ephesians 5.18). Jesus does not leave the man empty and vulnerable – His heart is to fill him with the grace of God. Time to get our own houses in order!

"O fill me with Your fulness Lord, until my very heart o'erflows…" (Frances Ridley Havergal)

May 27

"Blessed are those who hear the word of God and obey it"
Luke 11:28 Key passage: Luke 11:14-28

"Nice sermon, vicar!" Yes – I've heard it thousands of times, and I'm grateful…but always a bit apprehensive that it's some sort of code for "Didn't understand a word of it"! Sermons are not for listening to – they're for acting upon! It's so easy to be stirred by the energy, language and zest of the preacher, yet fail to heed the impact of the word itself. Luke uniquely records this encounter of Jesus with a woman in the crowd, who marvels at Him. She sees something in Jesus which she admires, and blesses Him by blessing His mother. How wonderful to have a son like this! Jesus does not reject her sentiments, but graciously magnifies them, asserting the importance of not just listening to His words, but obeying them.

How is the word to be heard? For the people of Jesus' day, they heard it straight from Him. That's why it's important to consider all the words of Jesus. We also hear it through the Scriptures – that's why it's important to read them! But most important is to do what they say – obey the word!

Thank You, Lord, for the possibility of hearing Your word taught and preached. Thank You for those who teach and preach it. May I be a good listener, willing to respond to what You are saying to me.

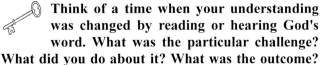 **Think of a time when your understanding was changed by reading or hearing God's word. What was the particular challenge? What did you do about it? What was the outcome? Why do we find obedience difficult?**

May 28

"One greater than Jonah is here"
Luke 11:32 Key passage: Luke 1`1:29-32

"We just need to go through a few security
questions…" It's part of life now. You've probably got
a whole notebook of passwords, security codes and
access numbers (although you're supposed to
remember them all) – all very secure!

The people keep asking Jesus for some sort of sign
as to His authenticity – the "security questions". The
one question is – will they believe Him any more even
if they are given a sign? What do they want – to be told
of compelling proof of Jesus' Messiahship so that they
might accept Him? Jesus speaks to them of the sign of
Jonah. Jonah was sent to preach to the disbelieving
men of Nineveh, was in the belly of the whale for three
days before vomited out. He then spoke God's word
with the result that the Ninevites believed and
repented. For them the sign was the person. Phillips
Brooks defined preaching as conveying "truth through
personality". Jesus is the ultimate preacher and teacher,
conveying the truth of God through who He is – one
greater than Jonah.

*Thank You, Jesus, for not just coming to bring the
message, but for being the message, bringing Your
truth through Your God-given personality.*

May 29

"No one lights a lamp and puts it in a place where it will be hidden"
Luke 11:33 Key passage: Luke 11:33-36

I had lunch with a colleague who owns a company making reading lamps reputed to be "the best reading lights in the world". He asked how I earned a living. Learning that I was a pastor, he leaned across the table and asked, "So what is life about?"

No accident that Jesus speaks about being "the light of the world"! Having encountered the disbelief of many people, Jesus asserts that "no one lights a lamp and puts it in a place where it will be hidden". God has brought the truth of His love and grace into the light of our awareness through Jesus – and we are to reveal that light where possible. We're not always very good at it – I know I fail miserably too often – but in the end you can't hide light! What's the point of covering it up – it's meant to shine. But light does not exist for its own end – it's purpose is to reveal truth and danger. What is life about?…knowing the "best light in the world"!

"Lord, I come to Your awesome presence, from the shadows into Your radiance…" (Graham Kendrick). May the light of Your presence shine in me today.

How would you answer the question, "What is life about?"

May 30

"See...that the light within you is not darkness"
Luke 11:35 Key passage: Luke 11:33-36

After living in a city for many years, we moved to a more rural location. The first time I drove out of a night time I had not realised that for years I'd been driving around town with dipped headlights, and had never needed to turn to full beam. I wondered why the road was so dark!

Sometimes we don't realise what we cannot see – and that there is so much more to encounter. Jesus is direct in His words here, suggesting that men accept what they think is "light" when really they are still in darkness. Maybe He is alluding to the "darkness" of religion that veils men's eyes to the truth about God. It is dangerous to think we have got hold of "truth" when we have only grasped a little bit of it. "See to it…that the light within you is not darkness". Pride, intellect and position all conspire to blind us to the truth of Christ in us. Beware of attitudes that shield us from knowing Jesus personally and living in the light of his grace and mercy. Time to switch to "main beam".

"Go forth and tell! Men still in darkness lie; in wealth or want, in sin they live and die" (James Seddon)

How are we so often "in the dark"? What truths about God and Jesus are fundamental and foundational to you? How much "theology" do we need to be effective believers?

May 31

"You clean the outside…but inside you are full of greed"
Luke 11:39 Key passage: Luke 11:37-54

Since the pandemic, we are all urged to "wash hands" far more. Hopefully it's a habit that might stay with us! But when Jesus accepted an invitation to lunch with a Pharisee, his host was astonished that Jesus did not "first wash before the meal". This was principally not a matter of hygiene, but of ritual. Devout Jews would wash their hands, denoting the removal of defilement of a sinful society. As important as that was, Jesus, sensing the discomfort of His host, addresses the matter with directness. One of the hearers complains that Jesus is insulting them – certainly His words are hard-hitting.

But stop and think about what Jesus is saying. We judge others by what we see, just as we want to make a good presentation. Impressions count. The Pharisees were diligent in their observance of the rules – it's just such a shame that they struggled to make the connection between right practice and right attitude. Beware of similar contradictions – enthusiastic worship and energetic service, yet egocentric selfishness and envious greed. "Stay humble, wash hearts, save lives!"

Lord, may my words be echoed by my ways in all of life this day.

JUNE 1

"Did not the one who made the outside make the inside also?"
Luke 11:40 Key passage: Luke 11:37-54

WYSIWYG – What You See Is What You Get. A useful acronym to level our expectations of people. How often can we judge people according to their appearance, accent, actions, politics, or colour.

Jesus had much to say about judging other people. His words to the Pharisees are stinging, seeming rude to the point of hurtful. That was certainly the reaction of the Pharisees here. But their response proved the point – they made a judgment about Jesus based on what they saw and heard without stopping to consider the truth of what He was saying. Sadly we live in such a febrile world at this time that so many pass judgment without stopping to consider their own situation. The media seems intent on proving that every politician or public figure is not "fit for purpose" and "celebrities" are tripping over themselves to gain publicity. What a shambolic society that sucks all this up! "Did not the one who made the outside make the inside also?" Live for Jesus "inside out" – What You Believe Is What You Give!

"Mirrored here, may our lives tell Your story – shine on me, Jesus, shine…" (Graham Kendrick)

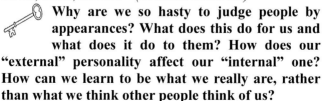 **Why are we so hasty to judge people by appearances? What does this do for us and what does it do to them? How does our "external" personality affect our "internal" one? How can we learn to be what we really are, rather than what we think other people think of us?**

June 2

"You neglect justice and the love of God"
Luke 11:42 Key passage: Luke 11:37-54

"Never mind the quality – feel the length!" – a misquote, but startlingly true with regard to sermon length. I come from a Christian tradition where the quality of the sermon is to be measured by its length. No ten-minute sermons, please – a minimum of half-an-hour is necessary! Yet I have discovered the value of the short sermon. Winston Churchill once famously said, "I am sorry to have made such a long speech – but I did not have time to prepare a shorter one".

Yet it's not sermon length for which Jesus berates the Pharisees, but their religious practice of tithing the herb stalks from their gardens. When for many Christians the issue is whether to tithe one's income before or after tax, what to do with your herb stalks seems surreal. Is God impressed with this? The irony is that the Law specifically exempts rue and other herbs from the tithe. Rather, Jesus says, they should concentrate on justice in all their dealings, and expressing their love to God in wholesome ways. What lengths do you need to go to today?

"Yes, You are a God of justice, and Your judgment surely comes: upon the nation have mercy Lord!" (Graham Kendrick)

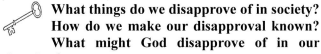

What things do we disapprove of in society? How do we make our disapproval known? What might God disapprove of in our churches?

June 3

"You love the most important seats in the synagogue"
Luke 11:43 Key passage: Luke 11:37-54

Everything comes with a price. I'd always wondered what it felt like to see your name "in print" – now I know…and it's not that exciting! As a pastor for many years, there's apparently a similar buzz from always being "out front". Any raised profile comes with a price – heightened expectations of you, with the possibility of rejection and disregard.

In His words of woe to the Pharisees, Jesus berates them for occupying "the most important seats in the synagogue". The "important seats" were the ones facing the congregation, reserved for people of status. These folk were the "pillars of the community". There's a danger in being a "pillar of the church" – by definition, pillars hold things up! We want to be well-regarded by our fellow-believers, but beware of what we may be "holding up"! Equally, beware of always occupying the back-row seats – those are usually occupied by "back-seat drivers"! It's not where we sit with God, it's where He sits with us that really matters.

Lord, help me to sit very lightly to importance and influence; may I serve instead with humility and grace in my church, community, workplace and family.

 Why are we so obsessed with "leadership" in our churches? What happened to the role of "servanthood"? Why do some of us accord our leaders such high profiles?

June 4

"You are like unmarked graves"
Luke 11:44 Key passage: Luke 11:37-54

The comedian Jim Davidson once got banned from driving for getting four speeding tickets on the same journey from London to Doncaster. His defence was that he only exceeded the speed limit once as he never slowed down in between! However, "ignorance of the law is no excuse". As harsh as that sounds, it's an absolute. It originates in Leviticus 5.17 "If a person sins and does what is forbidden in any of the Lord's commands, even though he does not know it, he is guilty and will be held responsible". There is, however, forgiveness to be found in a "guilt-offering" (Leviticus 5.18).

   Jesus criticises the Pharisees' attitudes to law-breaking with a word-picture likening them to "unmarked graves" over which men unwittingly walk. To do such a thing meant ceremonial defilement. Even today, out of respect, we will carefully walk around marked graves. But sometimes people are buried in unmarked graves. The effect of walking over them would be the same – defilement. To walk in the ways of Pharisaism equally leads to defilement. Remember "pride goes before…a fall" (Proverbs 16.18). Slow down and be careful where you "drive" today!

   "Blessed is the man who does not walk in the counsel of the wicked…for the Lord watches over the way of the righteous." (Psalm 1.1,6)

June 5

"You load people down with burdens they can hardly carry"
Luke 11:46 Key passage: Luke 11:37-54

We once owned a Mini estate. One day we collected a six-foot sofa and drove home – two thirds of it hanging out the back of the car. Not a great idea, but for those minutes it was the most comfortable Mini in town!

Jesus berates the Pharisees and teachers of the Law for their overbearing demands on the people. The problem was not just the burdensome observation of the minutiae of the Law – but as experts in the Law, they were not prepared to do anything to help the people fulfil its demands. Instead, they worked out all the ways in which they could avoid the demands of the law. Is there a difference between tax avoidance and tax evasion? If there is, then they had worked out how to "play the system"! In particular, the laws about carrying anything on the Sabbath were convoluted, but there were manifold exceptions – you just needed to be "in the loop" to understand what those were! Of course, we wouldn't burden people today, would we? Stop and consider the unwritten demands we make of each other! Be careful of creating burdens.

Lord, forgive us when we make unreal and unbiblical demands of others, especially when we exempt ourselves. Help us to follow Your Word and Your ways.

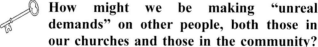 **How might we be making "unreal demands" on other people, both those in our churches and those in the community? What about the burdens of attendance at church events, commitment to causes, financial giving, expressions of membership? What about requiring people to do things our way?**

June 6

"You have taken away the key to knowledge"
Luke 11:52 Key passage: Luke 11:37-54

Here's a "definition" of an "expert"? – "ex" meaning "has-been" and "spurt" meaning "a drip"! Probably unfair, but sometimes true. I never cease to be amazed at the media's ability to sniff out an "expert" on any given topic, and you're left wondering "how did you become an expert on that?"

Jesus concludes His "woes" to the Pharisees and teachers of the law with this assessment of their capabilities – instead of helping people grasp the meaning of the Scriptures, they have made understanding impossible for people by their convoluted explanations and demands. They have made the Scriptures a closed book, only to be understood by those with special knowledge. The Scriptures are the gateway through which we know the grace and love of God, through which we now can encounter Jesus and by the Holy Spirit know Him. But you don't need a degree in theology to know God, and you don't need to be able to read Greek or Hebrew! God Himself opens His heart with the key of His Word. Know…and grow.

"All scripture is God-breathed and is useful for teaching, rebuking, correcting and training in righteousness" (2 Timothy 3.16). God, may we never be guilty of making the Scriptures so difficult that others are put off knowing You and Your grace.

To many people the Bible is a "closed book". How can we make it more accessible? How does your church to encourage the reading and sharing of the Scriptures? Why is regular Bible Study a helpful activity? How does that happen for you?

June 7

"There is nothing concealed that will not be disclosed"
Luke 12:2   Key passage: Luke 12:1-12

It's the ultimate "no-no" – a member of the Magic Circle disclosing how an illusion or trick is performed. The "magic" leaves the audience wondering "how did he do that?" There is, of course, an explanation…if only we knew it!

Jesus has a warning for His disciples about the practices of the Pharisees: beware of hypocrisy in your words and actions. Jesus warns that you can only fool others for so long – even if you continue to fool yourself. In the end, everything will come out into the open. The day is coming when God will reveal all truth – and that includes all that we have done and said that was not genuine, loving and real. It's a scary thought, and perhaps teaches us to be circumspect in our thoughts, words and deeds. The apostle James adds to this warning a special word of advice for all who "teach" – "you know that we who teach will be judged more strictly" (James 3.1). Living openly is not a matter of magic – it's a matter of trust!

"Lord, may the words of my mouth and the meditation of my heart be pleasing in Your sight…" (Psalm 19.14)

June 8

"Do not be afraid of those who kill the body…"

Luke 12:2 Key passage: Luke 12:1-12

It's been said that "you can't kill a Christian, only transfer him…" This may be tongue-in-cheek, but it's essentially true! The words of Jesus here are an encouragement to disciples who might naturally be fearful of what discipleship may entail. In the West we are immune to such realities, but for many believers today this is not so. Some 340 million Christians live in the top ten most persecuted countries in the world. For them, following Jesus means the possible loss of their families, homes, freedoms or their lives…yet they persist! Why?

Jesus Himself gives us the answer – ultimately what can a persecutor do to you? Answer: nothing! Tertullian, the second century Early Church Father, famously said "The blood of the martyrs is the seed of the church". Instead, we are to regard God Himself and fear Him – not in craven fear, but in awe of His power. As followers of Jesus, we do not ultimately answer to any earthly power – but to God alone. And one day we shall transfer from the kingdom of this world to the kingdom of eternity. So what's to fear?

"(God's) perfect love drives out fear…" Thank you, Lord for the boldness of millions of Christian brothers and sisters who today face persecution for their faith. May I be bold in my trust of You for this life and into eternity.

June 9

"Are not five sparrows sold for two pennies?"
Luke 12:6   Key passage: Luke 12:1-12

Buy One Get One Free! But if you only want one of the items, do you choose the paid one or the free one? Of course, it doesn't work like that! We regard lightly things that are "cheap" – they are expendable, of minimal regard.

Jesus reassures His disciples of their worth. "Are not five sparrows sold for two pennies?" Yet in his gospel, Matthew records that two sparrows cost one penny – so Luke suggests that in an even better deal for two pennies, an extra one is thrown in for free! Imagine what it feels like to be the "free" item…having no worth. But no individual is without value to God – "You are worth more than many sparrows". We are not told what the sparrows in question were sold for, but they represented very cheap merchandise. The lot of the sparrow was a miserable one, yet they matter to the God who created them. No individual is without worth in the eyes of Him who made them – and He knows each one personally. The gospel is indeed good news for all!

"His eye is on the sparrow and I know He watches me" (Civilla Martin). Thank You Lord that today I am known by You. Go with me in moments of joy and moments of despair.

 How do we encourage people in their gifts and abilities? How should we nurture people in the fact that they matter to God? How do we help the unbeliever understand that although God may not matter to them, they matter to Him? What is the value of "every member ministry" for the church?

June 10

"The very hairs of your head are all numbered"
Luke 12:7   Key passage: Luke 12:1-12

It is said that Donald Soper, the Methodist preacher and speaker, was appearing at Speaker's Corner, Hyde Park, London, when a man in the crowd quoted this verse and shouted out, "Mr. Soper, how many hairs in my head?" Soper replied, "You start pulling, I'll start counting!"

Jesus assures the disciples of their place in the heart of God in this pair of word pictures: the sparrows and the hairs. The followers of Jesus can take comfort that they are valued by God, and known personally and intimately by Him. Indeed, God knows more about you than you know yourself! Maybe that's not surprising, if you believe that He created you! The chef alone knows what's in the cake, the builder alone knows what's in the construction, and the inventor alone knows what's in the creation. God alone knows you inside out! And in this truth, we are meant to take comfort – since He knows what's best for us. When life is hard to shift…stop pulling – we can count on God!

"You created me in my inmost being…I praise you because I am fearfully and wonderfully made". (Psalm 139.13.14)

June 11

"Whoever acknowledges me…the Son of Man will acknowledge"
Luke 12:8   Key passage: Luke 12:1-12

"Pastor, are you alright? You look dreadful!" I hadn't seen her coming in the street and so was unprepared for the conversation. I felt fine…but it seems I didn't look it. She wasn't in the habit of holding back her anxieties…but it was good to know that I had friends who cared!

Jesus announces to His disciples that when any one of them acknowledges Him, that acknowledgment will be reciprocated in heaven. No one-sided conversations here! Rather, a warm realisation that on the day of judgment, those who own the name of Jesus will be welcomed in the presence of the Father. On the contrary, Jesus warns, those who "disown" or deny Him will be "disowned" before the angels. Be careful – for there is more than one way of "denying" Jesus. For Peter, it was a straight-out "I never knew Him". For us, maybe, it is more subtle – making light of some theological nuance, or simply by seeing Jesus as someone less than the Son of God in all His glory. Acknowledging Jesus is not a multiple-choice option - it's all or nothing.

–

"All to Jesus I surrender, all to Him I freely give…" (J. Van De Venter). Lord, may I mean what I say when I utter these words.

How can we be less than whole-hearted in our affirmation of Jesus as God's Son? How do you respond to the person who sees Jesus as a "good man" and even as God's Son, but somehow stops short of acknowledging Him personally?

June 12

"The Holy Spirit will teach you...what you should say"
Luke 12:12 Key passage: Luke 12:1-12

I'm often asked how long it takes to prepare a sermon. That's really difficult to answer. It only takes a few minutes to write the notes, but it takes the rest of the week to "live" it before it's delivered.

When the first disciples signed up to follow Jesus, they didn't receive lectures on homiletics. In fact, most of them were not particularly articulate. The gospels suggest that the most erudite of them was probably Peter – and look where that got him! In the context of reassuring His disciples in the time of trial, Jesus tells them that they are not to be anxious as to what to speak, "for the Holy Spirit will teach you...what you should say". There is, however, a world of difference between a sermon that is ill-prepared, or even one that is well prepared, and an apology for Christian faith that is Spirit inspired. Peter wrote "be prepared to give an answer to everyone who asks you to give the reason for the hope that you have within you" (1 Peter 3.15). Be prepared but don't necessarily learn the script by heart. "Live" what you give!

"May the words of my mouth and the meditation of my heart be acceptable in Your sight, O Lord, my rock and my redeemer!"

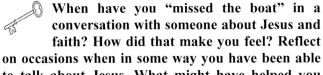 **When have you "missed the boat" in a conversation with someone about Jesus and faith? How did that make you feel? Reflect on occasions when in some way you have been able to talk about Jesus. What might have helped you with what you said? Why are actions as powerful as words?**

June 13

"Who appointed me a judge or arbiter between you?"
Luke 12:14 Key passage: Luke 12:13-21

Football is part of our national tribalism. Even if you have never been to see a match (and have no intention of doing so) it's expected you express yourself a supporter of a particular team. It identifies you.

Jesus meets a man who, seeing Jesus as a teacher in the rabbinic tradition, asks His adjudication in a family inheritance dispute. Doubtless the man is hoping Jesus will come down on his side! Why ask advice from someone if you know they will say something you don't want to hear? Jesus came to bring the spiritual blessing of God to men, not material bounty and so in the next verse He warns, "Watch out! A man's life does not consist in the abundance of his possessions". Of course, we would want to agree…except that we often intimate that what we have is some sort of "blessing from God". Be careful what you say! "God has blessed me with…" is often a mistruth. God doesn't dispense new cars, only new callings. God's "blessings" are not rewards for your endeavours – He's only on your "side" because of Jesus!

"I'm lost in wonder, I'm lost in love, I'm lost in praise forevermore, because of Jesus' unfailing love I am forgiven I am restored" (Martin Layzell). Teach me, Lord, that all that I am and have is not some kind of "reward" from You; but all I am is shaped by Your grace to me. Thank You.

June 14

"I'll pull down my barns and build bigger ones..."
Luke 12:18 Key passage: Luke 12:13-21

STOP. The sign couldn't be any clearer. It's not "Give Way" – it says STOP. Come to a halt. No more progress. Yet how many drivers see it as an invitation to keep moving, to "nip in" before the next car comes? Signs are there for a reason...

,,,and Jesus has some direct words of advice for those who can't read the signs. It's in the form of a parable, and for that is harder hitting. It's addressed to all those who think the acquisition of wealth is a one-way street. Consider the risks. The "certain man" of whom Jesus speaks is prepared to demolish what he has in order to clear the site for something bigger, but what happens if, having knocked down his barns, the new ones don't get built? Stop and think! What happens if you pour all your efforts into having plenty in this life and give no attention to what lies beyond? Notice that Jesus' parable is all about "me" and "I". Jesus does not denigrate wealth – He simply warns of its ability to blind us to eternity. Stop...and proceed with caution!

"It's all about You, Jesus, and all this is for You, for Your glory and Your fame. It's not about me, as if You should do things my way. You alone are God, and I surrender to Your ways" (Paul Oakley)

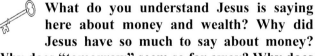
What do you understand Jesus is saying here about money and wealth? Why did Jesus have so much to say about money? Why does "tomorrow" seem so far away? Why does "today" seem so pressing?

June 15

"Take life easy; eat, drink and be merry"
Luke 12:19 Key passage: Luke 12:13-21

Some people imagine retirement as one perpetual holiday, enjoying one cruise after another…if only! Retirement is a job in its own right, to be organised and lived like any other day of life. We can only dream of no responsibilities, no pressure, and no demands on our time or resources. On the other hand, retirement can sometimes seem that the only thing that's changed is that "they've stopped paying me".

Jesus tells in parable form the story of the rich farmer who talks himself into early retirement on the basis that everything is "going his way". What could possibly go wrong? After all, what's the point of life if you can't enjoy the "fruits of your labours"? He makes the mistake of assuming that life will carry on in its own merry way for ever… "(I've) plenty of good things laid up for many years…". Little does he realise that one day "the silver cord is severed…and the dust returns to the ground it came from, and the spirit returns to God who gave it" (Ecclesiastes 12.6,7). Destination heaven – now that's proper retirement!

Lord, help me to have the right perspective in life, looking forward to the day when You will call me into Your eternal presence. May I live life to the full, but depend on You for all I need.

Why is it difficult to get a balance between living in the present, but looking to the future? Can we make people anxious about the demands of Christianity? What can we do to focus on our pastoral support of the retired and retiring?

June 16

"Do not worry about your life…"
Luke 12:22 Key passage: Luke 12:22-34

Maurice had always been a farmer, and a more gentle and unassuming man you could not wish to meet. He was also one of life's realists. He never got excited about anything. When you asked him how things were with him or on the farm, his standard answer was, "Oh, fairly." It was always "fairly". Nothing seemed to rattle him.

Jesus' disciples were very different. They seemed to react to every event with delight or despair. This is why Jesus urges them "Do not worry about your life". Worry is a great destroyer. It robs us of our peace. It nags at us to do more. It surrounds us every waking moment. It encourages us to activism without perspective. You may be one of those people who if you have nothing to worry about, it worries you. Jesus urges His disciple to look to the natural world. When did you last see a neurotic blackbird? What about a cow biting its nails in anxious brooding? Take a deep breath and smell the fresh air of God's daily provision for you! How's the Lord of creation doing for you? "Fairly." Or much better than that!

"O Lord my God, when I awesome wonder consider all the works Your hand has made…then sings my soul…How great Thou art!" (Stuart Hine)

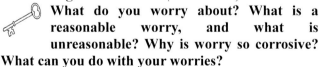 **What do you worry about? What is a reasonable worry, and what is unreasonable? Why is worry so corrosive? What can you do with your worries?**

June 17

"How much more valuable you are than birds!"
Luke12:24   Key passage: Luke 12:22-34

"A sparrow in the fist is better than a pigeon on the roof." It's a Czech saying and is comparable to "a bird in the hand is worth two in the bush."

It sounds almost as nonsensical for Jesus to suggest that each of us is more valuable than birds. Birds were cheap (no pun intended) and two sparrows could be bought for the smallest coin. Yet Jesus speaks lovingly of birds as an honoured part of God's creation. Here He speaks of the ravens (crows) which do not engage in any activity to create their own food support, yet God feeds them as much as He provides for any other part of His creation. As part of creation, they nevertheless were regarded as unclean birds (see Leviticus 11.15 – a long list of birds and other creatures regarded as "detestable" but it is not explained why). Yet God in His mercy provides for them. What a gracious God – He regards the lowly, the unclean, the weak, the sinful…and you and me!

"What is man that you are mindful of him…?" (Psalm 8.4). Thank you, Lord, that you love and care for all of your creation, the clean and unclean, the beautiful and unattractive…and me as the best part of all You have made!

June 18

"Who of you by worrying can add a single hour to his life?"
Luke 12:25 Key passage: Luke 12:22-34

A traffic jam, a long line of cars and lorries ahead. On go the brake lights, out come the maps and satnavs, off go the impatient drivers, weaving from lane to lane, trying to find a way around the bottleneck. When we do it we assure ourselves that we're making real progress, but in reality we've probably done nothing of the sort. "At least we've kept moving," we tell ourselves.

It's the same with life itself – when the bottlenecks happen, we swing into action. We've got to sort this somehow…there's got to be a way around it. Of course, we are responsible and God commends that, but Jesus here asks His disciples what they can do to extend the span of their lives by worrying about things. Worry by itself will not extend life by one second, let alone one hour. On the contrary, worry is so corrosive it's likely to shorten the span of life. The Psalmist suggests the span of our lives is known to God in any case (see Psalm 139.16). So stop worrying – get in the flow, and enjoy the ride!

Still my heart and mind today, Lord, that I may be free of undue worry about life. Help me to know that You hold me and my loved ones in Your hands.

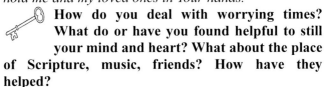 **How do you deal with worrying times? What do or have you found helpful to still your mind and heart? What about the place of Scripture, music, friends? How have they helped?**

June 19

"Consider how the lilies grow"
Luke 12:27 Key passage: Luke 12:22-34

"Beauty is only skin deep…" – words of Sir Thomas Overbury in his poem "*A wife*" written in 1613 – but the meaning has not changed in 500 years! Mind you, with over £10 billion being spent in the UK each year on cosmetics and hair products (and that's just by women), the skin is pretty deep!

Jesus has something to say about this. He's certainly not against making yourself presentable, but His point is rather different. He reassures His disciples of their worth to the Father. If any one is tempted to ask "What's the point of being a follower of Jesus?" then listen! You are loved by God and He thinks so much of you that He invites you to share in all that is His. Jesus appeals to the "lilies of the field". He probably wasn't speaking of lilies, but of flowers in general ("the grass of the field" v.28). See what wonders God has created in such beautiful flowers, which are only temporary masterpieces ("here today…"). How much more will God do in providing for you now in this life, and in the life to come!

Thank you, Father, that Your glory is revealed in all of Your creation. May Your beauty be seen in me today in all I do and am, and help me to see Your handiwork in others.

June 20

"Seek his kingdom, and these things will be given to you as well"
Luke 12:31 Key passage: Luke 12:22-34

Are you a dissectologist? That's a jigsaw enthusiast. It's a term from the nineteenth century when the first jigsaws were maps dissected into irregularly shaped pieces as educational tools. The question is – where do you start? Most people sort out the edge pieces first. It's all quite logical really…

…except that for many life is the ultimate puzzle, and how do you start to make sense of that? Jesus helpfully suggests that we start with "seeking his kingdom". Is this the frame, or the main picture? In a sense it's both! To be a follower of Jesus demands that we sit lightly to the details of the picture and concentrate on the framework. Get the framework right, and everything else fits somewhere within that. So the lessons from Jesus in this passage? Don't worry (v.22), think carefully (v.24), look insightfully (v.27) and live responsibly (v.29). Seek first His kingdom. Get the picture?

Lord, I often get in such a muddle deciding what's really important for each day. Help me today to seek Your kingdom first, remembering that my life today is set in the framework of Your eternal plan for me.

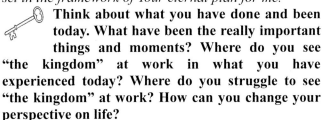 **Think about what you have done and been today. What have been the really important things and moments? Where do you see "the kingdom" at work in what you have experienced today? Where do you struggle to see "the kingdom" at work? How can you change your perspective on life?**

June 21

"Do not be afraid, little flock…"
Luke 12:32 Key passage: Luke 12:22-34

This is one of the most kaleidoscopic verses in the whole of Scripture! Read it how you will, but it contains a wonderful variety of mixed metaphors – fear, flocks, fathers, favours… - "Do not be afraid, little flock; it is your father's pleasure to give you the kingdom".

So just what is Jesus saying? At first reading, the images are a sequence of non-sequiturs. Addressed to the "little flock" – the sheep in the care of the Shepherd – He urges reassurance. They are not to fear, since they are in the presence of the One who gives protection. Sheep do not experience fear as we do. They react to present dangers, but may not perceive future threats. Sheep do not have a father, they have a "husband" tasked to manage and care for them. But this "husband" has a kingdom to pass on - and sheep don't need a kingdom, just a pasture! Confused? There is, however, a crescendo of images here, graduating from fear to favour. Quite simply, it is God's pleasure to promote us from earth to heaven, from fear to freedom, from now to eternity. What a kaleidoscope!

"The Lord's my shepherd, I'll not want…and I will trust in You alone" (Psalm 23/Stuart Townend)

June 22

"Where your treasure is, there your heart will be also"
Luke 12:34 Key passage: Luke 12:22-34

We have a tide clock hanging by our front door. It doesn't tell the time, but does tell how long it is since high tide or how long to low tide. The problem with it is it ticks very slowly and sometimes it stops without us noticing.

What makes you "tick"? The "wind-up" of daily responsibilities, the "rechargeable" power surge of position and influence, or the "counterweight" of family life? Jesus tells His disciples to get their priorities right in kingdom terms, since there is so much about daily living and its responsibilities that can get in the way of a true kingdom perspective. Concerns about income, sustainability, career, promotion, house and home, bread on the table all crowd in to crowd out an awareness of what is eternally significant – one's relationship with the living God and His promise of blessing now and hope in eternity. "Where your treasure is, there your heart will be also". What truly matters to us will power us for daily living – any chance your batteries have gone flat?

Lord, I need Your power to face life today. Help me to face my daily responsibilities, but to remember that You are with me in every decision and every difficulty. "Thou and Thou only, first in my heart, High King of heaven, my treasure Thou art."

How have you experienced God's blessing today? How has God's kingdom influenced your experience today? How do you work out what your priorities are for living each day? What do you think energizes you?

June 23

"Keep your lamps burning like men waiting for their master"
Luke 12:35 Key passage: Luke 12:35-48

"Be alert…your college needs lerts!" some wag had chalked on the lecture room board. We were never quite sure what it was we were to be alert to. Most of us spend our lives in a state of something less than alertness. We're never quite ready for the next challenge or crisis… "if only we'd seen that one coming" we protest.

Jesus urges a state of alertness for His disciples. The image has three sources – from the commands of God to His people concerning the Passover meal (to be eaten dressed and ready to depart – Exodus 12.11); from the readiness for work, with the "loins girt" (the long flowing outer garment tucked in to the inner garment to prevent it entangling); and from the image of prepared servants waiting for the master to return home (here v.36). In each context, readiness is critical to the operation. The readiness encouraged has a dual aspect – personal preparedness for the master, dressed appropriately, and practical preparedness, having "your lamps burning". Know what you are doing, and see what you are doing! Keep alert!

Lord, may I always be aware of Your promise that one day You will return in power and glory. Keep me today in that hope!

How can we be alert to the promises of God? Does the promise of Jesus' return frighten you or reassure you? Why do we try to ignore the promise of His return? Why are most of us never ready?

June 24

"You must be ready…"
Luke 12:40 Key passage: Luke 12:35-48

You pull up to the lights, and the man in the car alongside you glances across…he's not impressed with your vehicle, and has already decided that he'll beat you to the off. In gear, foot hovering over the throttle, fingers tapping on the steering wheel…the lights change to amber. He's gone…until the next set of lights, where he's sitting impatiently as you overtake him…

The "game" is anticipating the signals…and that's exactly what Jesus has in mind in urging His disciples "You must be ready, because the Son of Man will come…when you do not expect him". The master expects readiness in his servants (v.35) – what's the point of staff if they are not up to the job? The master seeks responsiveness from his servants – when he comes (v.36) they will immediately admit him to the house and welcome him in. The master rewards readiness (v.37) by reversing the household roles and serving the servants at table. Get the imagery? The irony is that whilst Jesus urges the disciples to be ready for His coming, He is already here…and they may not have grasped it. Watch the signals – and be ready!

"I believe in Jesus, I believe He is the Son of God…and I believe He's here now standing in our midst…" (Marc Nelson). Lord, help me to be ready to welcome You in every situation of my life today.

June 25

"Who is the faithful and wise manager…?
Luke 12:42 Key passage: Luke 12:35-48

There's always one…someone who asks a question when the rest of you want to finish the session and be on your way. Often they ask a question just for the sake of doing so. You'd think they could work it out for themselves…!

   …and true to form, Peter asks the question of Jesus: "Is this just for us, or for everyone?" Peter may be "slow on the uptake", but he's inquisitive. It's a good question and Jesus replies with another question causing Peter to ponder the answer. The faithful and wise manager considers a number of things: he considers the master and respects his wishes (v.43). He considers the staff and respects their welfare (v.42). He respects the property, and considers the resources (v.44,45). The image is a cameo of the kingdom and the place of servant leaders within it. Notice the term: servant leaders. In God's kingdom, all leadership is servant leadership, serving God and one another in His name.

"Teach me to dance with Your heart of compassion, teach me to trust in the word of Your promise, teach me to hope in the day of Your coming, teach me to dance to the beat of Your heart" (Graham Kendrick/Steve Thompson)

How can we best be "faithful and wise managers" of God's kingdom? What responsibilities do you carry for your family, for work, for your community, or your church? How can we be "servant leaders" in those roles?

June 26

"From everyone who has been given much, much will be demanded"
Luke 12:48 Key passage: Luke 12:35-48

"England expects…" sent by Admiral Nelson at the Battle of Trafalgar, and they did! They did their duty, and the decisive battle of the Napoleonic wars turned the tide. "Duty" comes from the Anglo-French *duete* or *doigt* – "I must…". Duty is about compulsion, and willing compulsion at that. If you don't want to do it, don't sign up to it!

Jesus warns his disciples that their responsibility is to fulfil their God-given task of doing God's will. How they, and we, struggle with that! We talk blithely about God's will as if it's something optional to be pursued at our leisure. Simply, God tells us that having given us the blessing of being part of His kingdom through the revelation of Jesus, we have a responsibility, a duty, to pursue His will in sharing the blessings of that kingdom with a disbelieving world. In 2 Corinthians 5.11-21 Paul speaks about his task of proclaiming God's work of reconciliation to all people, and reveals that he pursues this because "Christ's love compels us" (5.14). We can do no more than our "duty" to share Christ. God expects…!

Thank You, Lord, for Your love that is so powerful and personal that it drives me to live this day to Your glory. Help me to fulfil my God-given tasks today.

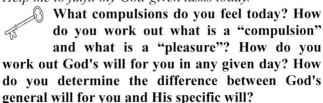 **What compulsions do you feel today? How do you work out what is a "compulsion" and what is a "pleasure"? How do you work out God's will for you in any given day? How do you determine the difference between God's general will for you and His specific will?**

June 27

"Do you think I came to bring peace on earth?"
Luke 12:51 Key passage: Luke 12:49-53

You probably haven't heard of Justus von Liebig but you will know his creation – Marmite! It is the yeast extract by-product of beer-brewing, and you either love it or hate it! "Marmite" has passed into common usage as a word denoting sharp division…

…and Jesus asked His disciples "Do you think I came to bring peace on earth?" Of course, the answer ought to be a resounding "Yes!". But Jesus' answer is an equally-resounding "No!". The point is that many will have divided opinions on Jesus. The message of the cross is divisive – Jesus Himself spoke of sheep and goats, light and darkness, Pharisees and laymen, slaves and free. All would be challenged by His claims to Messiahship. Those who cannot believe or choose not to follow will become critical of those who do – for the claims of Christ reveal the true hearts and minds of men and women. Families may be divided. I have had so many parents ask me "Where did we go wrong?" with children who have not followed in the faith. It's hard to reassure parents. Keep praying, keep loving, and keep living!

Pray today for families that are divided over Christian faith – and pray for grace to love our children whatever choices they make in life.

 How might you have experienced the divisiveness of the kingdom? What can we do for families that feel "divided" by faith?

June 28

"How is it that you don't know how to interpret this present time?"
Luke 12:56 Key passage: Luke 12:54-59

It's a national obsession…and we may not have been the first to be hooked by the weather! It matters to us what the forecast is, if for no other reason than it gives us something to talk about.

It seems that Jews were smart forecasters, and Jesus has something to say about the hypocrisy of knowing so much about the weather and interpreting the clouds, yet being unable to understand the "signs of the times" in the nation. We profess total surprise at the cataclysm of national events, yet want to be sure if we need to take an umbrella with us for a local stroll! It's no accident that the phrase "the storm clouds of war" is often used of impending international situations. Whether their lack of awareness was ignorance on their part, or a refusal to see the signs and respond to them, is uncertain, but we can all be amazingly blind to the "gathering clouds". As Christians we have a responsibility to understand what is happening in our world, and then pray for it. And always remember – the Lord reigns!

Read the world news today, and pray for one situation where there is conflict. Give thanks that God is ultimately in control, even when we have made a mess of everything.

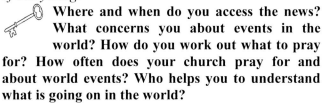 **Where and when do you access the news? What concerns you about events in the world? How do you work out what to pray for? How often does your church pray for and about world events? Who helps you to understand what is going on in the world?**

June 29

"Why don't you judge for yourselves what is right?"
Luke 12:57 Key passage: Luke 12:54-59

In football the referee is now aided by VAR – the Video Assistant Referee. Someone sitting in front of a screen miles away from the match reviews a decision or incident and advises the on-pitch referee of the appropriate decision. It was meant to make the game fairer – but has probably made matters worse. It all depends how you view it!

In Jesus' day, Palestine was subject to two parallel legal systems – Jewish and Roman. The two jurisdictions were not exactly complementary. If you didn't like the decision from one court, you could always appeal to the other for a better result! Not much changes – in our society today we seem to suffer from a similar problem…people who cannot accept the decision of a government or a popular vote, suggest that in fact the loser has won! Remember that ultimately God is the judge and arbiter of all things, and one day He will bring His justice to bear. Therefore, get right with God and have a clear conscience before Him. No more squaring the VAR sign – the cross is the ultimate symbol of justice!

Lord, may I remember today that You are judge of all, and one day You will right all the wrongs of this world. Help me today to be at peace with You in all my affairs.

June 30

"You will not get out until you have paid the last penny"
Luke 12:59 Key passage: Luke 12:54-59

Details matter. You may not like it, but sometimes the smallest omission can prevent progress…like leaving out a "dot" in an internet address. "For want of a nail the shoe was lost" demonstrates the problem…leading to a lost horse, rider, message, battle and kingdom.

Jesus warns His listeners to be careful how they conduct their lives when there is controversy. At times of crisis, be careful what you say and what you do! The media is certainly agog and full of the ill-considered opinions of so many. Words may come back to haunt you. They cannot be recalled. Take a deep breath before you engage in litigation or a war of sentiments. Read the "signs of the times" and try to understand what is going on. The penalty, Jesus warns, may be very costly. "You will not get out until you have paid the last penny". The word he uses describes the thinnest and least valuable coin. If you do not carefully consider your actions, you may be "taken to the cleaners". Words are costly - use them carefully.

"Let your conversation be always full of grace…so that you may know how to answer everyone" (Colossians 4.6)

Words are cheap. When have you regretted something you have said in an idle moment? Why do we need to be careful of our words and actions, especially in times of difficulty and crisis? When have we been guilty of silence when we should have spoken? What lead would you like to see our church leaders take in national affairs?

JULY 1

"Unless you repent, you too will all perish"
Luke 13:3   Key passage: Luke 13:1-9

The phone rings "about the accident you've had..." Another scam call. I've had so many "accidents" I'm amazed I'm still here! I'm told I'm due a small fortune in compensation...someone must be to blame!

Jesus was asked His opinion on an awful event in Jewish history – the massacre of some Galileans by the forces of Pilate. Little is known of the event, but it seems that the soldiers when restraining a protesting crowd, murdered several of them We do not know if the "mixing of blood" was literal or metaphorical, but there was heavy loss of life. Some in the crowd wanted Jesus to condemn the Galileans as "getting what they deserved". When you hear news of tragedy and deaths, how do you react? Does it make a difference who the people are? Jesus points out that death is the one certainty for each of us and it behoves us to be prepared for it. That's why He calls the crowd (and us) to repentance lest disaster befall us too. Beware of passing judgement – that is God's responsibility.

Lord, save me from a judgmental attitude to the tragedy of others. May instead I stand before You knowing Your mercy to me in Jesus and trusting in Him alone.

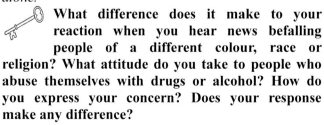 **What difference does it make to your reaction when you hear news befalling people of a different colour, race or religion? What attitude do you take to people who abuse themselves with drugs or alcohol? How do you express your concern? Does your response make any difference?**

July 2

"He went to look for fruit...but did not find any"
Luke 13:6   Key passage: Luke 13:1-9

I'm often asked by colleagues wishing to plan a meeting "Do you have a date?" "Yes," I reply "I've a diary with 365 of them in it!" Not all are available, but they're there! Dates represent opportunities, but also deadlines. How we sometimes wish that dates could be more flexible.

Jesus speaks of the coming kingdom in this parable expressing the urgency for our repentance and the reticence of God to punish. This parable emphasises something we often take for granted – that there will always be another opportunity for action, but one day it will be too late. The vineyard owner wants to take action on his unproductive fig tree, but the tenant farmer pleads for one more year of restraint. Peter sums up the truth of God's patience yet purposing to fulfil His will: "The Lord is not slow in keeping His promise (re the coming of judgment day). He is patient with you, not wanting anyone to perish, but everyone to come to repentance...But the day of the Lord will come like a thief" (2 Peter 3.9,10). Opportunity or deadline – which is it?

Lord, may I be fruitful in my life today...and challenge me to do this day what I might put off to tomorrow.

July 3

"Cut it down! Why should it use up the soil?"
Luke 13:7   Key passage: Luke 13:1-9

What have you got in your attic? Maybe you're one of the few people who have nothing there, but more probably you've put things there "just for the time being" because "they might come in handy one day". Years later you look at items and think, "Why on earth did I keep that?"

In the parable of the vineyard owner and the unproductive tree the owner is all for action now – the tree has failed to produce fruit for at least three years, so it must go. It's not doing what it should, and it's taking up space for a more productive tree. The farmer is more considerate – perhaps it should have one more chance.

We find it hard to be the vineyard owner – being decisive and ruthless. We don't want to make decisions right now. Leave it another day. Maybe we're afraid of making the wrong decision, or maybe we just don't like making decisions at all. We hear God's Word to us asking us to deal with a problem, and we vacillate. Just what have you got "in your attic" that needs dealing with now?

Lord, show me the "clutter in my attic" – unresolved issues, broken friendships, unfulfilled intentions – and give me courage to deal with them today!

What "clutter" are you harbouring? What needs dealing with and what can be disregarded and why? Why is it easy to live in the hope that "something will turn up"? What usually happens? Why do we find change in churches so difficult? What do we tend to hang onto?

July 4

"Woman, you are set free from your infirmity"
Luke 13:12 Key passage: Luke 13:10-17

Country lanes in Norfolk are a challenge – very few of them are straight! Maybe their line was determined by ancient footpaths skirting enclosures or common areas, but it is often said that the roads in Norfolk were built "according to which way the wind was blowing". Their path was rarely determined by natural features.

Jesus heals a woman "crippled by a spirit for eighteen years". We're not told what happened to the spirit which had doubled her, but we do know what happened to the Saviour who straightened her! Seeing her misery, Jesus took the initiative, called her forward and released her. Notice the sequence: Jesus prompts her (she did not come to Him seeking healing), pronounces her healing, then places his hands on her so that she "straightened up and praised God". Intriguingly, the result is one woman now upright, and a synagogue ruler doubled up under the burden of his interpretation of the sabbath rules. The woman's spine is now functioning again, the synagogue ruler's would seem to be rigid! What of the healing power of Jesus – which way is the wind blowing for you?

What do you need to ask of Jesus today – and what is the most you dare to ask Him for?

 What do you need to ask of Jesus today? What is the most you dare to ask Him for?

July 5

"Should not this woman...be set free?"
Luke 13:16 Key passage: Luke 13:10-17

Isn't that just the way of things – you take your ailing child to the doctors, and by the time you get there they've "nothing to show". They've (thankfully) got better by themselves. Fussing parents!

This woman, doubled up possibly by spondylitis for years, is healed by Jesus and restored to wholeness and her rightful place in society. You'd think that has to be good news...except that He dared to heal her on the Sabbath. There are rules, you know! The synagogue leader, mindful of his position, points out that healing is defined as work, and should be done on any other day than the Sabbath. He can't have this sort of thing happening in his synagogue.

Jesus' retort is telling – apparently it's deemed OK to untether the family ox or donkey to water it on the Sabbath, but that's different! So what about this poor woman, "tethered" by her disfigurement for years but now freed? Exactly what has Jesus done that qualifies as "work"? What matters more – conformity or deformity?

Jesus waits to heal – in order for you to have "nothing to show". That's just His way of things!

How have you known God's healing touch? Give thanks for what God has done, whether directly or through the hands or doctors or the medium of medicine.

July 6

"What is the kingdom of God like?"
Luke 13:18 Key passage: Luke 13:18-21

We swung onto the runway, the atmosphere tensed – the engines revved, we started to roll…and suddenly the engines kicked in and I was kicked back in the seat. No one could have described to me the sensation of take-off for the first time…awesome.

   We spend our lives asking "What's it like…?" when there's nothing to compare. We're desperate to understand something before experiencing it. Sometimes there's no comparison. Jesus asks "What is the kingdom of God like?" and we are given two enigmatic word pictures to consider. The mustard seed is frequently used to illustrate truths in the gospels. The tiny seed gives birth to a big plant. This one grows big enough for birds to nest in its branches. The birds represent the nations finding a home. Leaven is used to make bread. A small amount of yeast causes a large amount of flour to rise and create many loaves. The kingdom will grow. As the yeast works from the inside, so the kingdom will grow from the inside of men, not be imposed from the outside. "Your Kingdom come" – it's time for take-off!

Lord, thank You that You grow big things from small beginnings. Take the small things of my life this day and do something big with them – not for my sake but for Your glory.

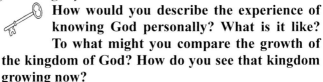 **How would you describe the experience of knowing God personally? What is it like? To what might you compare the growth of the kingdom of God? How do you see that kingdom growing now?**

July 7

"Make every effort to enter through the narrow door..."
Luke 13:24 Key passage: Luke 13:22-30

I watched in admiration as the two men removed a piano from the house. They knew exactly what they were doing. Pianos are not the lightest of things, and these two guys were not the beefiest of men, but that seemed not to matter. The secret was in the wheeled cradle onto which they lifted it. Working as one, they manoeuvred it through doorways and down steps as if it were a feather. Job done!

Jesus urges His hearers to consider the manoeuvring necessary to enter the kingdom of God. The suspicion is growing among some Jews that this kingdom is sounding rather exclusive, and they are worried they may be excluded. No one likes to think they will miss out on what they have assumed is their rightful inheritance. "Enter through the narrow door" Jesus urges. That door is narrow in breadth and in time opportunity. It means that entry is personal rather than corporate – it's just wide enough for one person to enter. at a time. Entry is pressing – it will not always be open! Make every effort now before it's too late.

Pray today for those you know who have not yet "entered in" – and those for whom time may be short.

Why does Jesus speak of a "narrow door"? What makes the doorway narrow? Who helped you to negotiate the doorway? Who might you help to enter through the same doorway?

July 8

"Many will try to enter and will not be able to"
Luke 13:24 Key passage: Luke 13:22-30

Always read the small print! How many times have you ticked the box accepting the conditions without having read them? And then you are surprised when you discover that something is not right.

Jesus warns of the many who "will try to enter and will not be able to". The words sound harsh, and at first seem incompatible with the notion of a gracious God who is always willing to be patient. He describes the plaintive knocking at the door and the refusal of the house owner to respond to their requests for entry. Their plight is simple – they assumed that because they had some association with God, everything was OK. These are the people according to verse 26 who claim "We ate and drank with you, and you taught in our streets". They had been near Jesus, even heard Him, but had not entered into faith with Him. You can sit in a garage all your life, but you'll never be a car – just as you can sit in a church for years, but remain obstinate in your spiritual ignorance. Read the small print!

Read this passage again, and pray for those who have never quite discovered a personal relationship with Jesus.

July 9

"People will come from east and west and north and south..."
Luke 13:29 Key passage: Luke 13:22-30

Always use the spell-checker! It's so easy to completely change the meaning of something with just one wrong letter or misspelling. My friend Barry reminds me that I once wrote to him and addressed him as "Dear Barmy..."

What Jesus has to say about the coming kingdom was astonishing to devout Jews – there will be people from every quarter of the globe there – a veritable United Nations. The only problem is that the very people who should be there might be absent – the Untied Nations! The promise of this multi-national kingdom means that the Gentiles will be represented. This was foretold by the prophet Isaiah: "I will bring your children from the east and gather you from the west...bring my sons from afar and my daughters from the ends of the earth" (Isaiah. 43.5,6). It will be a truly international banquet! The religious Jews thought this would be an exclusive event, and their mortification was absolute. Surely there's some mistake? But no, God means what He says and says what He means. Best to check this out!

Lord, thank You that Your kingdom is a truly international kingdom – with people of every tribe, race, nation, language, colour and tongue joining together to worship You.

Check out some facts about the worldwide Church via the internet or resource books. Where is the Church growing at a rapid rate? Why do you think that is? What can we learn in the West about the commitment of fellow believers elsewhere?

July 10

"There are those who are last who will be first…"
Luke 13:30 Key passage: Luke 13:22-30

Luton Airport – Easyjet flight to somewhere…the tannoy invites those who have paid for priority boarding to the front of the queue. The rest of us look on. Eventually we go through the gate into another waiting zone, only to discover that we're all being bussed to the plane, and the "priority boarders" get on first, only to get off the bus last and find we've already had the pick of the plane seats. Sometimes it's hard not to feel smug…

…but that's the kind of kingdom dynamic Jesus speaks of here. The mad scramble for the important places was the concern of the religious people of the day. They needed to know their "ticket" was valid. They could afford to be higher up the queue, and they made sure they were! Tough on those lower down…

…but God is ultimately the God of true justice. That's why Jesus warns of the about-turn in the kingdom. Notice in this verse He does not say that people will actually be excluded, rather that the pathetic scrambling for priority will become pointless.

Thank You, Lord, that You call us into Your kingdom not on the basis of our importance, skills or responsibilities, but on the basis of Your grace. Teach us humility to welcome others into Your kingdom!

Why do we impose earthly values on kingdom principles? How does Jesus challenge our suppositions about status, importance and influence? How does it feel to be the "last in the queue"?

July 11

"I will drive out demons and heal people today…"
Luke 13:32 Key passage: Luke 13:31-35

"I've started, so I'll finish." A Mastermind is at work! The two minutes of questioning are almost over, but there's time for just one more…which could make all the difference. As far as some of the Pharisees were concerned, Jesus' time in Jerusalem was up – there was a hint of a Herodian plot to kill Jesus. Herod knew that he had messed up with John the Baptist, and he certainly didn't want a repeat of that on his conscience – so maybe he had persuaded these Pharisees to try to frighten Jesus into going away. Jesus will have none of it, and in the only recorded instance in Scripture Jesus treats someone with contempt by calling Herod "a fox". Even when He later stood before Herod (Luke 23.8,9) Jesus' silence was deafening.

For now, Jesus' words are ringing – Jesus will continue and complete His ministry. The promise is added that "on the third day I will reach my goal". Nothing will deflect Him. The "third day" may mean either "shortly" but equally He may be speaking of the redemptive act of resurrection. He's started…so He'll finish! Hallelujah!

Praise You Lord, that You are the Lord of resurrection and purpose, and that You will fulfil Your purposes. Help us to see those purposes at work today and to rejoice in all You are doing in peoples' lives.

July 12

"How often have I longed to gather your children together…"
Luke 13:34 Key passage: Luke 13:31-35

"And all because the lady loves…" Milk Tray! The ads seem to belong to a lost age now, but they do retain their mystery in the actions of the anonymous black-clad suitor leaving a box of the chocolates somewhere surprising.

Love prompts many generous actions, and Jesus expresses His love for Jerusalem and its people in these words of lament. He is concerned for the future of Jerusalem and its people, and what it represents to the hopes and aspirations of the Jewish people. Jerusalem is the "gathering place" par excellence – the words "next year in Jerusalem" were the accepted benediction at the Passover *seder* and the *ne'ila* at Yom Kippur. Jesus longed to gather His people, but they would not respond, choosing instead to reject God's messengers and the word of calling. Contrast the attitude of the Psalmist in Psalm 57.1 when he was in turmoil – "I take refuge in the shadow of your wings until the disaster has passed". It is in the heart of Jesus to offer refuge in the shadow of trial or disaster – and all because "the Saviour loves…"

"Keep me as the apple of your eye; hide me in the shadow of your wings…" (Psalm 17.8)

 What is it you need protection from today? What does it mean to experience the protection of the Almighty?

July 13

"…but you were not willing…"
Luke 13:34 Key passage: Luke 13:31-35

"Because I can…!" None of us like being made to do things we don't want to do, especially when we can't see the reasoning. We can be very stubborn – and it's not always for the best.

Jesus' lament over Jerusalem is matched by that recorded in Luke 19.41 when on His approach to the city "he wept over it" and its impending fate. The people of Jerusalem had had every opportunity to receive God's blessing and His word but they had regularly rejected and killed His messengers and prophets (read of Manasseh – 2 Kings 21.16, Zechariah – 2 Chronicles 24.21, and Uriah – Jeremiah 26.20-23). Why? "Because we can…!" The human spirit can be awfully stubborn… "You were not willing…" God is not the God of coercion – He gives us the gift of freewill, and boy, how we like to exercise it "because we can…"! We may not always know why we choose a particular path or make a specific selection, but "because we can" we do! God remains willing to love us and accept us, but He must grieve over our selfish responses. Just "because we can" doesn't mean that we must.

Lord, teach me to bend my will to Your will. Challenge my stubbornness and change my selfishness to reflect Your will and way.

July 14

"Look your house is left to you desolate"
Luke 13:35 Key passage: Luke 13:31-35

Things, things things…we fill our lives and homes with them. Belongings of importance, memories, souvenirs…things special just to us. But to other people…? There's no sadder task than having to dispose of belongings when the owner has died, having to make agonising decisions about what to keep, what is important, and what is not. You can take a house apart, but taking a home apart is something else…

The words of Jesus here represent that agony. The "house" of Jerusalem will soon face its dismemberment, and Jesus laments its fate. If only the people could see the coming sadness. The very things that were special for them – the city, the temple, the streets and markets, the synagogues…will all be laid waste and the people sent into exile. Yet God had warned time and again of the fate of His people if they continued to ignore Him and His ways. God never promises that life will be easy, and there will always be severe trials to endure, but He will remain faithful. What of "things" today – and what of the store we place in them?

What things do you have that give you a sense of security? What would happen if you lost everything? How does your attitude to possessions need amending?

What difference would it make to your faith if you lost everything you had? What lessons can we learn from those who have little of material worth, but still honour the name of Christ?

July 15

"Is it lawful to heal on the Sabbath or not?"
Luke 14:3   Key passage: Luke 14:1-14

English is one of the hardest languages to learn – there are so many exceptions to any rules! By comparison, Spanish is easy. Maybe it's because English is such an amalgam of languages representing so many different stages of history…

...and exceptions to the rule are always an issue in any context. As Jesus dines with a prominent Pharisee, he finds Himself in the presence of a man suffering from oedema. This is an unpleasant condition and was thought to be incurable. What to do? The Pharisees are silent on the matter – surely Jesus knows the rules? But Jesus heals him, Sabbath or no Sabbath. The problem lies in the question that Jesus asked: "Is it lawful to heal on the Sabbath…?" Lawful according to which law – the law of Moses (entirely lawful) or the rabbinic interpretation of the law (only permissible when life is endangered)? They cannot answer definitively because they are confused themselves. They did not want to appear harsh or soft – so they said nothing! Silence is, however, not always golden. Jesus proves the rule of love takes precedent over the rule of law.

Why is it that rules only seem to apply to other people? How do we tend to "bend the rules" when it suits us? When is it appropriate to ignore a general rule?

July 16

"Do not take the place of honour…"
Luke 14:8   Key passage: Luke 14:1-14

Muhammad Ali claimed to be "the greatest", but who's to say that he will not be supplanted by another? The GOAT (Greatest Of All Time) debate rages in every sport, but it depends on your definition of "Greatest" – just what is being measured and compared?

Jesus watched His fellow guests arrive at the meal table, and they would routinely pick the "places of honour". They clearly had a remarkable understanding of themselves and their place in society. It's important, of course, as the apostle Paul put it (Romans 12.3) not to "think of yourself more highly than you ought…", but at the same time we persuade ourselves not to think more lowly of ourselves either! After all, one must maintain a modicum of self-respect if you're going to get anywhere in life! But what if you suddenly realise that you are "above your station"? Life is like a game of musical chairs – there may not be space for you elsewhere! As always, Jesus gives us the example of greatness wrapped in humility.

"Jesus shall take the highest honour…let's bow the knee in humble adoration" (Chris Bowater)
Thank the Lord for His great example of humility.

What gives you your identity? Why does someone's job give them their credibility? What do we look for in people we do not know well? How would we define humility? Where do we see true humility displayed?

July 17

"Everyone who exalts himself will be humbled"
Luke 14:11 Key passage: Luke 14:1-14

"Resign!" It seems to be a national obsession, seeing which of our leaders we can dismiss in disgrace. We take pleasure in setting people up then knocking them down. "Serves them right" we secretly mutter. "Who do they think they are?" Politicians, pioneers or pastors – makes no difference…we're kind of intrigued/horrified/pleased when they stumble.

Some of the loveliest people I've known have been people of impressive ability and importance. What marks them out, however, is their humility - you might never guess they were important people.

It's no accident that "humble" rhymes with "stumble". Jesus' advice is foundational to Christian behaviour – warning that the temptation to exaltation is an invitation to humbling. The higher you climb, the further there is to fall. As always, the true example of greatness wrapped in humility is found in Jesus. The apostle Paul, in his restatement of the early Christian hymn of praise (Philippians 2.5) declares "your attitude should be the same as that of Christ Jesus…who…made himself nothing…humbled himself and became obedient to death on a cross. Therefore God exalted him to the highest place…that at the name of Jesus every knee should bow…"

Lord, save me from a sense of self-satisfaction when others stumble and fall. Teach me instead what real humility looks like, and may I be humble in my relationships and responsibilities.

July 18

"Invite the poor, the crippled, the lame, the blind"
Luke 14:13 Key passage: Luke 14:1-14

God is full of surprises – none more so than those He invites into His kingdom! The fact you and I are here should be surprising enough, but there's more! I was delighted to learn recently that among the congregation in my last church is a young man who came from a very troubled family. His brother has been in prison, and he himself has had a very difficult past. Yet through his grandmother, he has come to faith and now attends church! Wow!

God's invitation to "the poor, the crippled, the lame, the blind" is not an invitation borne of desperation, but inspiration. God's not interested in the people who see religion as some kind of status statement – He is interested in those who want to know Him as Saviour. That's why the invitation to the marginalised, the moneyless, the meaningless is so important. We fret because we can't run our churches on such people. We need the able, the managers, the carers, the leaders. Jesus calls the incapable, the managed, the cared-for, the led… Yes, God is full of surprises – and that includes you and me!

Thank You, Lord, for the amazing grace that invites the unlikeliest of people into the kingdom. Show me that this includes me!

Who are the "surprise" people in your church? How are you able to welcome them and integrate them? Why does church so often seem so "middle class"? What happens to someone when they come to faith and how does life change? How is that reflected in the expectations we put upon them?

July 19

"You will be repaid at the resurrection of the righteous"
Luke 14:14 Key passage: Luke 14:1-14

Are you "risk averse"? Read the small print of every financial investment product – "warning: you may get back less than you invested". What kind of investment is that? Yet the possible return may well outstrip any loss that may be incurred.

Jesus teaches that acts of true selflessness, such as inviting "the poor, the crippled, the lame, the blind" to a banquet, will be rewarded "at the resurrection of the righteous". It's a concept that is commonplace in Judaism, and refers to the belief that meritorious actions in this life will be rewarded in the next. We see it reflected in the bestowal of the title "Righteous Among the Nations" on non-Jews who, at personal risk and with no financial or evangelistic motive, saved Jews from the genocide of the Holocaust during World War Two. "Greater love has no-one than this, that he lay down his life for his friends" (John 15.13). It's that kind of selfless dedication that Jesus commends - and which he exemplified on the cross. So what stops us getting our hands dirty – fear, faithlessness, frustration? Risk today and reward tomorrow!

May my discipleship be marked by a sense of divine "recklessness" to do Your will whatever the cost. Lord, show me what that means for today.

July 20

"Come, for everything is now ready"
Luke 14:17 Key passage: Luke 14:15-24

"Fergie time" is the extra time added onto a football match when ninety minutes have expired. The fourth official holds up his digital board indicating the number of extra minutes necessary. During this extra time the losing team often seems to find the ability to score a winner or equalizer. Sir Alex Ferguson became the master of it at Manchester United.

In biblical times, "Fergie time" was also a phenomenon. Since no one had watches, when a host put on a banquet or function, the invitations would be sent out in person. On this occasion it seems that no one declined initially. Then, when the spread was ready, a servant was sent out to call the invitees to come. A "double invitation" was commonplace, and it was courteous practice to only attend when you had been invited twice. So when the host announced "Come, for everything is now ready" it's action stations! Here we see mirrored the initial invitation of God to His people, and the sending of the "servant" Jesus with the personal call. The time is up…come, for in Jesus "everything is now ready."

"Come, now is the time to worship…" (Brian Doerksen). May I be ready to respond to God's call to worship or work when the moment arrives!

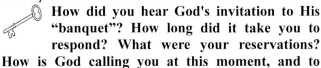 **How did you hear God's invitation to His "banquet"? How long did it take you to respond? What were your reservations? How is God calling you at this moment, and to what?**

July 21

"But they all alike began to make excuses…"
Luke 14:18 Key passage: Luke 14:15-24

Have you learned the art of excuse-giving? It's all about trying to sound convincing when you really don't want to go to that party/meeting/function. It's best to give just one reason for your non-attendance, rather than several (which suggests we're trying to convince ourselves). Guilt is a dreadful thing.

Jesus tells the parable of three men invited to a great banquet but alas they couldn't come just now. These weren't the first people to give lame excuses for non-responsiveness (see Luke 9.57-62). But in this parable they give different excuses! They represent different types of human weakness. There's the man who's just bought a field without even seeing it – he has no foresight. There's the new owner of five yoke of oxen – he has no forethought. We really can't ignore the poor chap who's just got married – he seems to have had no forewarning! Does life really surprise us at every turn? Is the call to discipleship so difficult to estimate? Is following Jesus so unattractive that we have to opt out before we've started? What's your excuse? Remember…guilt is a dreadful thing!

Teach me Lord to examine my motives when You call me to the tasks of each day. Forgive me when I try to dodge the things or people I really don't want to encounter.

July 22

"I have just bought a field…"
Luke 14:18 Key passage: Luke 14:15-24

When I was a teenager I wanted to be an estate agent. I was fascinated by land management and surveying, but not so fascinated by high-pressure sales techniques. Becoming a pastor was probably God's way of saving me from desperate customers!

When purchasing land in biblical times there was a general principle that land belonged to God and was not to be sold permanently. Land ownership was only temporary. Alongside this principle was that of Jubilee, when every seven years all debts were erased, and all property reverted to the original owner. Some of these principles still existed in New Testament times.

The excuse of this man is rather hollow – he has purchased (the right to) some land but has yet to go and see it. He needs to define the boundary, and secure the title for the relevant period. It will not be his for ever, so the urgency is not immediate – his excuse is lame. For him, the present is more important than the future. Sound familiar?

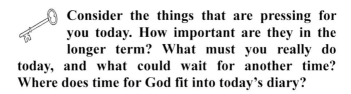 **Consider the things that are pressing for you today. How important are they in the longer term? What must you really do today, and what could wait for another time? Where does time for God fit into today's diary?**

July 23

"I have just bought five yoke of oxen…"
Luke 14:19 Key passage: Luke 14:15-24

Was this guy ever a Boy Scout? You know their motto "Be prepared!" This man was not going to be caught out. He'd just bought himself five pairs of oxen – five! What could he possibly need five for? One pair – yes. A spare pair – sensible, but five?? And it seems he'd not test-driven any of them. Was he thinking big, that he'd need them all in his industrial-scale farming activity? But he couldn't have been that smart if he'd not proved them. Socks or ox, you can only use one pair at once!

His excuse is pathetic – he must go now, but since he's already bought the creatures, surely the testing could wait until tomorrow! Just think of the excuses we make why we can't do something now because we've something we think is far more important. It's all about perspective, and this guy probably needed to go to the optician – his eyesight is rather skewed! When God comes calling with an invitation to His kingdom, a kingdom that has eternal implications, how come we feel the need to attend to temporal matters in preference? Be prepared now!

"Hear the call of the kingdom…King of Heaven we will answer the call, We will follow bringing hope to the world, Filled with passion filled with power to proclaim Salvation in Jesus' name" (Keith Getty/Stuart Townend)

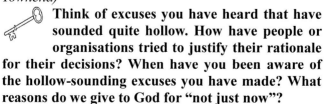 **Think of excuses you have heard that have sounded quite hollow. How have people or organisations tried to justify their rationale for their decisions? When have you been aware of the hollow-sounding excuses you have made? What reasons do we give to God for "not just now"?**

July 24

"I have just got married so I can't come"
Luke 14:20 Key passage: Luke 14:15-24

Ah…here's a man with a reasonable excuse! At least he has some sort of backing for his response. The Old Testament allows a newly-married man to stay at home for the first year of married life – "for one year he is to…bring happiness to the wife he has married" (Deuteronomy 24.5). But this chap hasn't read the small print – the exception is for exemption from military service – it's not a year's holiday! He answers Jesus as though his excuse is absolute, "I can't come."

His excuse is one of a type – suggesting that personal relationships may be a barrier to accessing the kingdom of God. Maybe you have a partner or spouse who does not share your faith, and that may create some issues. It's really important to be humble, wise and patient in living out your faith. Some spouses eventually win the other over by the grace of God. Sometimes nothing happens, and the relationship continues happily. Quite often, however, the faith of the believing partner dims. We need to be much more supportive of our relationships…lest we find ourselves making excuses.

Pray today for those you know whose partners do not share their faith – for patience and humility in their relationship, and for our churches that we might be practically supportive of all our personal relationships.

When has a personal relationship conflicted with your calling as a disciple of Jesus? How did you resolve it? Are you aware of how many people in your church have a non-believing partner? How can you best support them?

July 25

"Go out…and bring in the poor, the crippled, the blind…"
Luke 14:21 Key passage: Luke 14:15-24

It's lovely to be blessed by the generosity of a host, but you can be left feeling the need to reciprocate, and you may not be able to do so in the same way. No one wants to compare, but…

Yet at this great feast, the invited guests fail to materialise. In response, the disappointed host orders his servant to invite the less-well-heeled of the town along. Surely they will come – and they do! In fact, the host realises having such people at his table brings another benefit – their inability to reciprocate the kindness. These are the very people Jesus has just spoken of (Luke 14.13 and 14), for "although they cannot repay you, you will be repaid at the resurrection of the righteous".

The gospel is good news for all, and in particular for those who have little hope in this world. It's the ministry the writer of the letter to the Hebrews commends – "entertain(ing) strangers, for by doing so some have entertained angels without knowing it" (Hebrews 13.2).

 Who could you host in your home that you may not usually invite? Why can hospitality be such a difficult gift to exercise? How can we help each other in this?

July 26

"There is still room…"
Luke 14:22 Key passage: Luke 14:15-24

Research has shown that 85% of women regularly overfill their suitcase! Whether that's because the fairer sex tends to take more stuff than men, or because they're better at packing, we don't know. What is true is that they will always find space for one more item "just in case!" (no pun intended).

The parable of the great banquet omits one detail – the stated capacity at this great feast. Most hosts start with a maximum number in mind, dictated by the resources of the venue and the capacity of the staff. The wise hosts prioritises the invitations to ensure that the occasion is not overbooked. But this host "invited many guests". The implication is that all were welcomed and would be coming, but at the last minute they began to make their excuses. They would have come, of course, but…

"There is still room…" At the banqueting table in the kingdom of God, there's always space. No one is excluded. What about those we think least likely? What about those who don't yet know they're invited? There's still room, but there may not always be time!

Make a list of the people you know who are the unlikeliest people to become Christians or set foot inside your church…then start praying for them to know Jesus!

July 27

"Make them come in so that my house will be full"

Luke 14:23 Key passage: Luke 14:15-24

It may be hard to believe, but class warfare still rages! Look at the supermarkets in which people shop – some are more "upmarket" than others! They may sell exactly the same things, but it's the "cachet" that matters.

The parable of the great banquet represents truth at different levels, but one thing it does reveal is that class warfare is nothing new. One can only wonder if the people originally invited to the banquet would now decline if they knew the type of person who eventually would turn up, but that's exactly the issue Jesus is addressing in this parable. It's not just class, it's also ethnic status. The very idea that other groups might be invited into the "kingdom" was anathema to the religious elite. God had invited His people for generations through the prophets, and now through Jesus that invitation is renewed and widened. The invitation to Gentiles is not clarified until some time later, but here it is the poor of the under-society that are invited – and they come! They are not just invited, they are compelled…by the love of God.

What compelled you to become a follower of Jesus? What part of the gospel spoke to you most powerfully? Why is the gospel good news for different sorts of people?

What surprises do you think we might experience in heaven? Who do you imagine might be there? Why did Jesus promise "many mansions"? What is their likely purpose?

July 28

"Not one of those men who were invited will get a taste…"
Luke 14:24 Key passage: Luke 14:15-24

There's "late" and there's "late". When the bus leaves at 8.30, we can hardly complain if we turn up at 9 and find we've missed it. If we turn up at 8.31 and miss it, we may complain, but we knew the time. Some things will not wait for us for ever.

There seems to be a harsh verdict suggested by the parable of the great banquet concerning the grace of God. The master declares to his servant "not one of those men who were invited will get a taste of my banquet". This is not just a statement of fact, but also a statement of intent. The master is resolved that when the house is full, the banquet will begin, and at that moment some will miss out. That is their own decision, and the master cannot be held responsible. The urgency of responding to God's invitation is obvious – there may not always be "another chance". How many live their lives putting off or not even considering the claims of Christ? There's so much more to deal with. Don't miss the bus today!

What decisions do you need to make and act on today? What has God been saying to you recently, and what do you need to do about it today?

July 29

"Suppose one of you wants to build a tower…"
Luke 14:28 Key passage: Luke 14:25-35

Accidents don't just happen – they are the result of action or inaction on someone's part, but the consequences may not have been considered or foreseen. That's why there's a large litigation claims industry sprung up…someone's to blame!

Yet how many times have you done things without thinking of the consequences? The decision to follow Jesus may come into that category. For some, it will have been a considered and deliberate response. For others, it was an impulsive and joyous reaction. Both are valid, but both demand a serious consideration of what is being asked. That's why Jesus here talks about the cost of being a disciple of His. Discipleship is exciting but exhausting, demanding but delightful. Jesus does not want disciples who have no idea of what they have committed to. The man who decides on a whim to build a tower, but only gets as far as the foundations displays his lack of wisdom to all. The claims of Jesus demand serious consideration – "sit and estimate the cost." It's all or nothing, or in the words of the Mastermind quizmaster "I've started so I'll finish!"

"O Jesus, I have promised to serve You to the end…" (J. E. Bode). What does it mean for you to follow Jesus "to the end"?

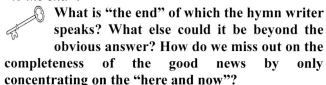 **What is "the end" of which the hymn writer speaks? What else could it be beyond the obvious answer? How do we miss out on the completeness of the good news by only concentrating on the "here and now"?**

July 30

***"Any of you who does not give up
everything…cannot be my disciple"***
Luke 14:33 Key passage: Luke 14:25-35

"Buy now…pay nothing for a year!" That sounds
great, except that you are then paying a lot for a long
time. It's all about weighing up the cost of something,
and making a considered decision.

That's exactly what Jesus is saying in these verses
about the cost of Christian discipleship. His words may
sound scary, for the simple reason that they are!
Discipleship is no soft or easy option. It's not a choice
of a comfy lifestyle. Jesus is seeking disciples who will
love Him first, last and above all…so that the human
love for family and others seems like "hatred" by
comparison (see verse 26). Such loving devotion to
Christ is not a momentary reaction, but a thought-out
commitment. It may entail a real cost (not necessarily
financial) to ambition, pride, popularity, and esteem. It
demands a willingness to persevere when the going is
tough; but it will be rewarded with the joy of knowing
Jesus and finding life in Him. Now, the call is to such
sacrifice. Forget the cheap imitations that offer comfort
for now, and a big bill later!

*Teach me Father to put loving You first beyond
everything else…and show me where I get this wrong.*

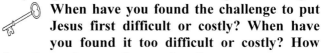 **When have you found the challenge to put
Jesus first difficult or costly? When have
you found it too difficult or costly? How
does Jesus show us the way here?**

July 31

"If (salt) loses its saltiness, how can it be made salty again?"
Luke 14:34 Key passage: Luke 14:25-35

Frank Smith started it in his north London garage in 1920. Mrs. Smith washed, cut and fried the potatoes and Frank wrapped them in greaseproof paper, adding a pinch of salt in the little blue bag, selling them from his pony and cart...

...and the rest is history. The salt makes all the difference. When the company suggested removing the blue bag, there was uproar! It's just not the same! What Jesus has to say here about discipleship is important. Following the sayings about the cost of discipleship, these words underline the necessity of incisive faith. Unless you are "sold out" for Jesus, you are ineffective.

The curious thing is that it is impossible for salt to lose its taste, unless the sodium chloride is mixed with impurities, in which case the salt literally loses its distinctive taste. It is no longer fit to preserve, enhance or flavour. "Fit for purpose" is the phrase. Jesus seeks those who are fit for the purpose of the kingdom, who will quietly and humbly enhance the lives of those around them. Crisp words indeed!

Think of someone you regard as being "the salt of the earth". What is so special about them? How can you be "salt" in your work, relationships and life? What difference can you make to other people?

AUGUST 1

"Suppose one of you has a hundred sheep and loses one…"
Luke 15:4   Key passage: Luke 15:1-7

"And….?" The question is annoying, suggesting that we are being petty. What are we going to do about it? What matters? Why are we getting so upset?

"Suppose you have a hundred sheep and lose one? It may not be sheep, it could be anything – our attitude to losing something is telling. What does it matter if it's a penny, a minute, an opportunity? There'll be another along in a moment, but the words of Jesus here reveal the true heart of God. The errant sheep is not "lost", it's just not to be "found" at that moment. It's wandered off somewhere else, is probably blissfully enjoying a different pasture and doesn't realise that it's now separated from the rest of the flock. The problem's not just with the sheep – it's with the shepherd as well. What is he to do – cut his losses and ignore the inconvenience? Or risk everything for the welfare of the one? That risk is not just to the remainder of the flock – it's also to the shepherd himself. What a picture of the Father shepherd that He should come looking for us!

"And can it be…?" that Jesus should come looking for me! What were you doing when Jesus found you? How long did He have to take to find you? How did it happen for you? Thank God for the uniqueness of your story!

August 2

"Does he not leave the ninety-nine...and go after the lost sheep"
Luke 15:4   Key passage: Luke 15:1-7

Thank God for social media! No sooner has something happened than we can express a comment on it – and all the world can read it there and then! And it all matters – it seems every opinion has merit...

I'm left wondering what the ninety-nine sheep of the flock thought about the antics of the other one sheep that wandered off. Much is rightly made in the parable of the one, and of the shepherd who goes off in lonely pursuit, but what about the ones left behind? Let's drop in on "e – Newes" (Twitter is for birds!):

"I'm appalled that one member could be so selfish as to just go off by themselves without thinking of the consequences – should be ashamed of themselves!"

"Serves them right if they've got into trouble..."

"Typical actions of a shepherd to go off as well...what kind of leaders have we got in this country...?"

"I'm angry and upset at being left to fend for myself – where's the help the government promised?"

Many of us have reacted to situations of crisis, and needed to blame someone. Does anyone have any confidence in the shepherd?

Jesus, thank You that amazingly You left everything behind in order to come and rescue me. May I be worthy of Your love today!

August 3

"...he joyfully puts it on his shoulders and goes home..."
Luke 15:5   Key passage: Luke 15:1-7

The smallest things often bring the greatest joy and for the shepherd the discovery of the errant sheep results in happiness beyond measure. Where does he take it? Home! We're not told that he went back to the remaining flock in the open fields – that could wait for another moment. There's some serious celebrating to do first!

But how does he get the wandering sheep home? He carries it! Were the sheep to find its own way back, it could get lost again! It's the shepherd who bears the burden, but he bears it "joyfully". That "joy" is more than just a big grin on the shepherd's face – it's the knowledge of the satisfactory completion of a task and duty of care and compassion. It's the same emotion the writer to the Hebrews describes of Jesus "who for the joy set before him endured the cross" (Hebrews 12.2). He shouldered the cross in order to bring his errant "flock" home, and He did this "joyfully". Where were you when He found you? Are there not others waiting to be brought home?

What amazing grace, Lord, that You came to find me, and You are in the process right now of "bringing me home". Thank You that for You this is an act of "joy". May I express that joy too in my living today!

What kind of burdens do you "shoulder"? However heavy, they do not compare with the burden Jesus shouldered at the cross. How is it possible to shoulder a burden with a sense of joy? When have you felt "carried" by Jesus? How have you experienced His shepherding care?

August 4

"Rejoice with me; I have found my lost sheep…"
Luke 15:6   Key passage: Luke 15:1-7

"A sorrow shared is a sorrow halved; a joy shared is a joy doubled" – the origin of the saying is unsure, and it all sounds rather twee…but it's true! The joy of the shepherd at finding his lost sheep is palpable, and he invites his friends and neighbours to a party to celebrate. What causes such joy?

Finding the lost sheep is the start. Did the sheep know it was lost? Probably not, or it wouldn't have wandered off. The parable teaches that the "lost" probably don't realise they are "lost" – until they are "found"! We don't know there is something better until someone tells us!

Secondly, the action of the shepherd speaks volumes of the desire of the shepherd to recover the animal. The shepherd literally goes out of his way to find it. The sheep was lost to the flock, but more importantly it was lost to the shepherd. The personal relationship was lost…until it was rekindled.

Finally the shepherd includes others in his joy. The Good Shepherd invites us to share in His joy when we come back to him.

"There is joy in heaven…" Wow! Thank You Father that You are always celebrating the return of Your lost children – help me to rejoice in the salvation of others too.

August 5

"There will be more rejoicing in heaven over one…who repents"
Luke 15:7   Key passage: Luke 15:1-7

Keys – the bane of most people's lives. When you lose them, their value becomes greater. I lost my house keys for four months and they turned up in a flower bed. It just goes to show that gardening has benefits beyond the obvious!

When we find something, the relief is enormous. The *status quo* is restored. We can feel secure again (especially if it's keys that are found!). Life can resume. The Messianic Jewish scholar Alfred Edersheim quotes a rabbinic saying that "There is joy before God when those who provoke Him perish from the world". The vindictiveness of this stands in stark contrast to the statement of Jesus here "There will be more rejoicing in heaven over one sinner who repents…" Remember 2 Peter 3.9 "God is not wanting anyone to perish, but (wanting) everyone to come to repentance". Notice that in Jesus' words, it is implied that God Himself enters into the rejoicing when one of His children turn to him. Quite simply, you have brought a smile to the face of God – how does that make you feel? Repentance is the key!

May I understand a little, Father God, of Your heart of joy when we repent and turn to You. I want to share in that sense of joy at the growth of Your kingdom. Give me a heart of delight and encouragement instead of doom and discouragement.

 What was the last party you attended? Who or what was being celebrated? How does God celebrate when one of His children turns to Him? Is this just imagination?

August 6

"...ninety-nine righteous persons who do not need to repent"
Luke 15:7   Key passage: Luke 15:1-7

Our local car parks are free from 6p.m. to 8a.m. That's great – except that they are also closed overnight. Who makes up the rules?

The words of Jesus here come with something of an edge, as He describes the actions of the shepherd in this parable. The ninety-nine sheep are left in order for the shepherd to go off seeking the one errant lamb. The shepherd has no reassurance that more of the flock will not wander off in the meantime, but given the predilection of sheep to follow each other, even when they don't have a clue where they are going or why, gives him some confidence. The sting in the tail is that the ninety-nine are described as "not need(ing) to repent". They should be OK – that's the theory! But who decides the rules? Who has decided that they do not need to repent? The implication is that they themselves have decided this is so. These are the self-righteous who see need for change. That's why for them there's no equivalent rejoicing in heaven. Where are you parked – and what rules are you following?

Lord, show me the areas of my life where I need to change my attitudes and behaviours, and then help me to seek Your forgiveness and transforming power to actually make a change!

 Why do we find the subject of repentance so difficult? How do we react when we hear a challenge to repentance? What do we see needing to change in the world around us? What do we suspect God may want to change in us?

August 7

"A woman has ten silver coins and loses one"
Luke 15:8   Key passage: Luke 15:8-10

It's amazing what you find in boxes of corn flakes! Years ago it was popular for manufacturers to include simple toys – I had a submarine and a diver which you could make to submerge with the addition of baking powder. It compromised the taste of the corn flakes, but at least it kept me amused for hours!

One day my wife lost her engagement ring. After days of futile searching, and not a few tears, we sat down one morning to breakfast and as I tipped out my corn flakes, there it was! Jesus tells a parable of the woman who lost a silver coin. It was worth the equivalent of a day's wage, a substantial sum. At marriage a woman would be presented with silver coins which she wore in a head-dress much like wearing a wedding ring. Losing one of the coins was a matter of great emotional impact. Others had given much for her to have this little. Whichever, the future has suddenly taken on a different complexion. You and I, loved by God, have been lost to Him. Who will resolve this puzzle?

"I was lost, but Jesus found me, found the sheep that went astray" (F H Rawley). Give thanks that Jesus found you when He did, and where He did!

August 8

"Does she not sweep the house and search carefully?"
Luke 15:8   Key passage: Luke 15:8-10

Memory loss is no joke - you go into a room at home and say to yourself, "What have I come in here for?" Apparently the solution is to return to the room you've just come from (if you can remember which one it was!) – the doorway acts as a prompt to a new "doorway" in our brains.

Jesus tells the parable of the woman and the lost coin to illustrate the wonder of the God who comes looking for us. What does she do when she discovers the coin is missing? She sweeps right through the house. Houses in biblical times were often small and badly lit. She had little chance of seeing it. The floor was earthen, possibly with a covering of reeds and so looking for a coin was virtually impossible. But she persists until she finds it. Perseverance literally pays off. God never gives up looking for His lost people – thank Him for the existence of persistence!

"When I was lost you came and rescued me, reached down into the pit and lifted me. Oh Lord, such love."
(Kate and Miles Simmonds)

 Share situations or people for whom you have been praying for a long time. Why persist in prayer when it seems like nothing is going to happen? Why does God sometimes take a long time to answer our prayers? What might we need to learn?

August 9

"Rejoice with me…"
Luke 15:9   Key passage: Luke 15:8-10

Everything has a price. A letter from the hospital x-ray department urged me to attend my appointment, since a missed appointment cost them £48. Sometimes you can't pay too much attention to the economics of the situation…

The woman who lost the silver coin sweeps out her house and eventually locates it. As a result she is overjoyed and invites her friends and neighbours to share in the rejoicing. We're not told what actually happened, although I'd imagine she threw something of a party to celebrate. And at the party, what shall we have – yes…cream cakes! So the woman who had lost a coin worth 50 pence spends a pound on the cakes…now that's celebrating!

What do we do when invited to share in someone's happiness? Manage a weak smile? Say something like "That's nice"? Feign gladness when inwardly we are resentful of their good fortune Or do we "push out the boat" and help organise the party? Just like the shepherd who recovers the lost sheep, the invitation is to "rejoice". That's the natural reaction of God when the lost are found…and He didn't count the cost in finding you!

Thank you Lord for the amazing generosity you show to us when You bring us "home".

Who needs you to celebrate with them? What could you do to "make someone's day"? How does being a Christian impact on the way you celebrate with others?

August 10

"There was a man who had two sons…"
Luke 15:11 Key passage: Luke 15:11-32

Clive was a good neighbour, but every conversation with him ended with the same phrase – when talking about anything he would say "They're the same, but different."

Jesus tells the story of the man with two sons. Although the story is commonly called "the prodigal son" it should really be the story of "the loving father". His sons were the same…but different. It's remarkable that two parents can produce children so different. The elder was studious and hard-working, his younger brother less so. The elder was a loner, the younger sociable. The elder was steady and predictable, the younger excitable and flirty. The elder was home-loving, the younger a traveller and adventurer. The elder was financially "careful", the younger a spendthrift.

Yet the father loved them both. You cannot treat your children equally, but you can treat them uniquely. The father is about to discover what that means, and both sons discover what that looks like. The God who uniquely comes seeking you is the God who uniquely seeks those quite unlike you – He knows you're "the same but different!"

Lord, save me from jealousy and resentment when I see my brother being blessed, and save me from a sense of superiority when I'm the one receiving the blessings.

 What amazes you about the fact that God should love you? What amazes you about some of the other people God loves? How is this possible? What does this teach us about the grace of God?

August 11

"Father, give me my share of the estate…"
Luke 15:12 Key passage: Luke 15:11-32

You used to have to wait until attaining the age of 21 before getting the key to the front door. How times change! Now you may not only own the front door, but the house as well. Waiting has become a mug's game…

…but the younger son of this parable was no mug. He'd worked out that his father was worth a fortune, and therefore his own financial future was assured – he assumed. Why have to wait until your pater is dead before enjoying it? You might have a long time to wait…so let's get on with it now. Despite the fact that he had no right to ask for his share, he dares to do so – ignoring the fact that he has no idea what the estate might be worth upon the death of his father. No matter – he wants it, and he wants it now.

How often do we ask God for something…but we want it now! We're not prepared to wait, or accept that God's answer may be "Not yet!" Will God not yet open the door of heaven and pour out His blessing?

Forgive me for my impatience, Father, when I need You to answer my prayers right away. Remind me that as my Father You know what is best for me, and Your heart is always one of love and generosity. Help me to listen to You today!

August 12

"He divided his property between them"
Luke 15:12 Key passage: Luke 15:11-32

"It's not fair!" Life isn't fair, and being the younger of two children isn't fair. Why should I always come second in the pecking order?

Cue the father of this parable, torn by his responsibilities for his two sons yet driven by his love for them. What to do in the face of the almost outrageous request from the younger boy to have his share of the family inheritance, and to have it now? To read this story with only Western eyes would cause us to miss much. This isn't about the younger boy discovering his father's dying will whilst he's still living – Jewish law permitted distribution of the father's inheritance at any time. In the first instance (by last will and inheritance) the elder of the two would receive two-thirds of the estate. But now, the father actually divides the inheritance, and in equal shares. The younger gets more...the elder less. How much more has God shared His riches with us who have no right to inheritance, nor any right to ask – what a picture of love and grace! That's a true Father for you.

"Amazing grace..." Thank you, Father God, for the breath-taking generosity of Your love to us in Jesus Your Son, when by right we were not deserving of it at all.

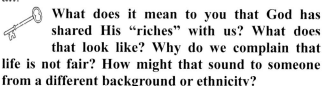 **What does it mean to you that God has shared His "riches" with us? What does that look like? Why do we complain that life is not fair? How might that sound to someone from a different background or ethnicity?**

August 13

"The younger son…squandered his wealth in wild living"
Luke 15:13 Key passage: Luke 15:11-32

Teresa May, former Prime Minister, was asked what was the naughtiest thing she had ever done. The reply? "Running through fields of wheat as a child."

Running through fields of wheat was probably the means of escape for the younger son as he left home. He was off – home was the last place he wanted to be. He needed the bright lights, the city, to live life as it should be…what's the point of money unless you spend it? He'd had enough of the humdrum of farm life, of being the younger son and keeping his place in the pecking order. Now he was number 1 – and he could please himself just as he wanted. We can only imagine what those wonderful words "squandered his wealth in wild living" really contain.

Why do we imagine the "grass is greener on the other side"? What do we imagine "wild living" is like? We may suspect it is not fulfilling, but we'd probably like the chance to find out. Or maybe we have been there, and know the truth. Life without the Father's care is not just wild, it's wanton…

Why do we often dream about "life on the wild side"? What is it about the "here-and-now" that you find restricting or unexciting? What would you really like to do…and what frightens you?

August 14

"He began to be in need"
Luke 15:14 Key passage: Luke 15:11-32

It's thought that goldfish only have a three second memory span – every time they swim round the same piece of bowl or pond, it's a new experience for them. In the goldfish bowl of his now high-octane life, the younger son of this parable discovered lots of new experiences – but not all of them were wonderful… "he began to be in need". Now that was a novelty for him. Throughout all his years back at home, where apparently life was so uneventful, had he ever been in need? Not once had he wanted for food, but now he is starving. Not once had he wanted for shelter, but now he was homeless. Not once had he ever needed to look for work, but now he was desperate. Not once had he ever wanted for company, but now he is lonely beyond words.

We may find it hard, even impossible, to share his experience. It would be easy to say, "That's his own silly fault" and often we dismiss the lot of others with a similar sentiment. Remember today those in need…but before you blame them, stop. It may not be their fault.

Pray today for those whose lifestyle has led them into desperate places…and for those in desperate need of the basics of life. Thank God for those who reach out to help people whatever the shape or source of their need.

How do we determine who needs our help and generosity, and who does not? How can we be unfairly judgmental in our responses? What do we tend to fear about the way in which others may use our resources? How might that affect our giving?

August 15

"…No one gave him anything…"
Luke 15:16 Key passage: Luke 15:11-32

Hospital chaplaincy is a great ministry. The curious thing is that when someone is in a hospital bed they could be anybody. Pyjamas are a great leveller.

The younger son of this parable found himself pursuing his dream of the hip lifestyle, funded by his inheritance from his father, and it was brilliant until the money ran out. His friends walked away and his popularity faded out. This guy who was someone to know, suddenly becomes nobody, and "no one gave him anything". Why should they? If you saw someone swilling out the pigs (a job of such low regard) you'd carry on your merry way.

He was desperate for something to eat, but no one gave him anything. He needed shelter, but no one gave him anything. He needed social contact, but no one gave him anything. He needed help, but no one gave him anything. After all, isn't the responsibility for his situation entirely in his hands? He got himself into this – he can get himself out of it. Is there no one to help?

There is a "redeemer" – that's the point of this parable – the Father who gives everything! "There is a redeemer, Jesus, God's own Son; Precious Lamb of God, Messiah, Holy One. Thank you, O my Father, for giving us Your Son, and leaving your Spirit until the work on earth is done". (Melody and Keith Green)

August 16

"He came to his senses…"
Luke 15:17 Key passage: Luke 15:11-32

"Love is blind" wrote Shakespeare in *The Merchant of Venice*. The notion comes from much earlier when the Roman god of love, Cupid, was blinded, and as a result fired his arrows randomly at whom he willed.

The younger son of this story was not in love (as far as we know) with a female, but he had fallen for something else – a love infatuation with the high-life. It was something he'd heard about and dreamed about, and now he could experience it. The problem lay in the fact that he was in some way in love with himself – he could not think beyond himself and his own satisfaction. The needs of others were subservient to the need to feed his own ego, and this was very intoxicating. Then one day "he came to his senses". What senses, you may ask? The sense that all was not well, that life was not how it ought to be, that there had to be more than this. He had reached rock-bottom – and the only way now was up. How was it for you when you heard the gentle call of God to return home?

Lord, we pray today for those who are at "rock-bottom" in their lives – the alcohol-dependants, the bankrupts, the drug-crazed, and those struggling with mental illness. Bring to them those who can reach them with real practical help, and through it all help them to know Your amazing love for them.

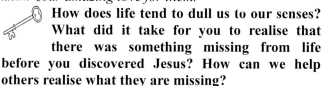 **How does life tend to dull us to our senses? What did it take for you to realise that there was something missing from life before you discovered Jesus? How can we help others realise what they are missing?**

August 17

"I will set out and go back to my father…"
Luke 15:18
Key passage: Luke 15:11-32

It's a curious phenomenon, but the return journey often seems much quicker than the outward one. Maybe you've a better idea of the distance involved, or you're just more relaxed and happy to be going home. The scenery's different, although you identify many points and discover things you didn't see on the outward leg. Home soon arrives!

The younger son knows there is only one thing for him to do in his current plight – "I will set out and go back to my father" However, this is no mere intention to buy a return ticket – his assertion "I will set out" uses the word used of resurrection – "I will rise up/stand up". Enough of this half-life of servitude and deprivation – I need to go back and start again! He knows he's been to the lowest point of life, and now needs to go back to the heights of home, of love, of acceptance, where he belongs. That place is where the father dwells, and that's where he needs to be. Each day we are called back to the loving Father – it's a shorter journey than you think!

Where is it that you need to return to? To a living relationship with God? To a personal relationship with Jesus? To renewed fellowship with your church family? To a rekindled relationship with a family member or friend?

August 18

"I have sinned against heaven and against you"
Luke 15:18 Key passage: Luke 15:11-32

"I can see clearly now the rain has gone" (Jimmy Cliff) It never rains for what it pours! So changeable is our weather, we speak of rain as the default setting; anything else is a bonus.

For the younger son in this parable it's certainly been raining pretty hard – what he thought would be a life of wall-to-wall sunshine has turned out to be days of floor-to-ceiling servitude, and misery has poured down on him.

But now comes the turning point – the realisation of what he has done. It's so easy to try to view life through our own rose-tinted spectacles and persuade ourselves our actions are of minimal consequence. For this son, that could not be. He knows he has sinned – against God, and then against his earthly father. Which part of the realisation came first we're not told. It may be that in his misery, he thinks of home, and of his father whose inheritance he has blown, and guilt overtakes him. He realises that he has wronged God in this way too. When it stops raining, the sun often shines.

Lord, may I never be guilty of wasting Your inheritance to me, the gift of Your love in Jesus Christ. Help me to be worthy of the name of Jesus in my living this day.

How do we realise when we have been wasteful of opportunities, of time? If you could start your life again, what would you do differently? How would you change? What might God be challenging you to change today?

August 19

"I am no longer worthy to be called your son"
Luke 15:19 Key passage: Luke 15:11-32

Pieces of paper – we've probably got loads of them, detailing all sorts of minutiae of life. Some are important, detailing things we've done or achieved that cannot be forgotten or altered. Certificates of examinations or degrees; birth or marriage certificates; licences enabling us to do certain things. They all matter.

For this younger son, there's something that cannot change – he will always be his father's son. That's a biological fact. It's doubtful whether he wants to be known as his father's son (remember those teenage years when you didn't want to be seen with your parents?), or whether in the light of the son's behaviour the father wants to own him as his son. The best the boy can think of is offering himself as a paid servant to his father. "I am no longer worthy…". Because of the father's response, the plaintive plea of the son is heart-rending. He knows he has failed and where does he go from here? The father loves him – just as our Father loves us. We have a piece of paper (the Scriptures) that tells us! This cannot change!

"Jesus loves me, this I know for the Bible tells me so…" (William Batchelder Bradbury). Thank God that in Jesus your status as a child of His is assured!

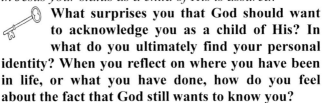 **What surprises you that God should want to acknowledge you as a child of His? In what do you ultimately find your personal identity? When you reflect on where you have been in life, or what you have done, how do you feel about the fact that God still wants to know you?**

August 20

"While he was still a long way off, his father saw him"
Luke 15:20 Key passage: Luke 15:11-32

Have you ever stood at the window waiting for someone to come? You know they won't come any quicker by you standing there, but you just hope they might! And then…

How long has this father been standing at the window, reflecting in sorrow at the departure of his youngest son in such circumstances? If things had been different, if only he'd not given him the money, if only he'd been more resolute in his advice…countless questions flood his mind. He thinks back to when his two boys were young children, and happiness had filled his home, the noise of laughter and play the soundtrack of life then…

…and then he sees something, a shadow, a figure. Are his eyes deceiving him? A figure, lonesome and lonely, making its way along the horizon. Is it? It cannot be. Yet he'd recognise that figure anywhere. His boy…his son…the one who had left so surprisingly, so suddenly, now making his way back slowly but surely. Where is he going…? No time to answer…the father is out of the door, to greet this son, his son…Welcome home!

God thought of you long before you thought of Him! Reflect on the journey you made to come home to the Father – how long did it take, who helped you on the way, what made the difference in the end? Thank God for the "welcome home" you have received!

August 21

"He ran to his son…and kissed him"
Luke 15:20 Key passage: Luke 15:11-32

Derek Redmond will be remembered for the race he never finished. At the 1992 Barcelona Olympics 400 metres semi-final, he tore his hamstring, but continued running, and with assistance from his father reached the finish line to a standing ovation. He was listed as "Did Not Finish" but the moment is etched in history as exemplifying the Olympic spirit.

Way before this another son nears the finishing line, his father running out to greet him. No one knows what will follow – will there be a showdown, a reckoning? Will the son turn away again, or be turned away? None of that – no words in that moment, just a hug and kiss of welcome, and the two men come home together, reconciled and ready.

Words are not essential in such moments – and what could be said? That can wait for later – all that matters now is the image of the family reunited. The matter with the elder son will follow soon enough, but for now the father's heart is thrilled, and the son's heart is filled. That's how the Father greets his returning children!

"How deep the Father's love for us, how vast beyond all measure, that He should give His only Son to make a wretch His treasure!" (Stuart Townend). Father, thank You for being such a wondrous Father.

How might you have expected the father of this story to react? When have you feared a reckoning and then been pleasantly surprised? What does this teach us about the nature of true fatherhood?

August 22

"Quick! Bring the best robe and put it on him…"
Luke 15:22 Key passage: Luke 15:11-32

"Rome wasn't built in a day"; it takes time to do things. How long is often a cause of frustration to us. Yet when this younger son comes back home, the father runs out to meet him, and is shocked at the appearance of his boy – barefoot, bedraggled, barely recognisable…but it's his son all right. The father immediately orders his servants into action. "Quick…!" The order is terse. "At the double!" He cannot have his son looking like this, but if the son's looks are a reflection of his inner feelings, then this is worse. He has pleaded his unworthiness and confession of wrongdoing, and the father has heard this. In this moment he wants to restore the son to the family. The best robe is a sign of restored position, and the ring a symbol of restored authority. The son is no slave but a full member of his family household. Shoes on his feet symbolise his status as free, in slavery no more. The restoration is immediate and compelling. The welcome of God to His errant child is similarly immediate and total. What a Father!

You are the God of restoration – and thank You for restoring me to Your family, restoring my life when I was lost, and restoring Your image within me. I praise you, Father.

August 23

"This son of mine was dead and is alive again"
Luke 15:24 Key passage: Luke 15:11-32

Who'd be a parent? The task of parenting is raising adults, not children! Not every parent understands that – raising adults who are interesting, caring, useful members of society. The problem is most parents uncannily see their own faults and foibles replicated in their offspring and it is not always comfortable viewing.

  The return of the younger son brings untold joy to this father. For the father, the son's earlier departure was like a bereavement…because it was. The suggestion is that the son cut himself off from family, since there were more important and enjoyable things to do. How many parents feel they have "lost" their children? So when the boy comes home, it's as if he has come back to life. The father expresses it in this powerful couplet: "dead and alive again/lost and found". The father has his son back – and the son has his family back (with the possible exception of his older brother, who has issues to resolve). No wonder, as Jesus remarked, "There is joy in heaven over one sinner who repents…" That's how the Father feels when you come to Him!

Pray today for families that are "broken" by lost relationships - for healing and wholeness to be restored between parents and children.

 What happens when we think we know better than our parents or seniors? What does it take to learn the lesson of humility? What "dies" when we turn our backs on those who love us and nurture us?

August 24

Murphy's law – what can go wrong will go wrong. Named after Edward Murphy, a USAF captain employed on a project determining the effects of crash deceleration on humans, it applies across the whole range of experience. The father in this parable certainly felt its effect.

As he is busy welcoming his errant younger son back home, the older son is out "in the field". That's where he was always to be found, and where he knew best. He was "Mr. Steady", reliable and hardworking, unlike his younger sibling. Day after day he had tended the land and produced the crops. He had tilled the land, picked the stones, planted the seeds. He had toiled at the harvest, boiled in the sun, given all for the family farm. Not for him the distraction of wine, women and song.

Ever felt like the older son? You don't particularly welcome attention, but it seems there are always others who get the acclaim…and you wonder why! You want to serve God, but it would be nice to be appreciated occasionally. Remember today those who serve "in the field" quietly yet committedly. They are not overlooked.

Think of someone you know who is quietly "out in the fields" doing their daily tasks. Don't just pray for them – find a way of encouraging them.

August 25

"The older brother became angry and refused to go in…"
Luke 15:28 Key passage: Luke 15:11-32

"Light the blue touchpaper and stand well back." It only takes a spark, but the fire that follows can be furious – this is true of gunpowder and grievance alike. While the loving father is busy seeing to his returning younger son, the older son, seeing what is happening, becomes indignant to the point of wrath, and refuses to have anything to do with it.

As in all things, it depends on your viewpoint. All the older son sees is his wasteful and wanton brother coming back home, and his wonderful father pulling out all the stops for him. Is the old man out of his mind? Who's losing the plot here? We know that there's "always two sides to the story" but we're still very ready to rush to judgment on the little that we know. It's not cool assessment that we make – we often engage in heated outbursts of ire. The older son represents in Jesus' teaching those who are already in God's heart yet who cannot believe that God is willing to seek others outside. Stand back…and take a deep breath!

Forgive me, Lord, when I rush to judgment on other people, without knowing their story. Ignorance can so easily lead to indignance. Save me from wrong emotions and help me to understand more of Your Father heart to Your children.

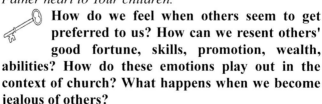 **How do we feel when others seem to get preferred to us? How can we resent others' good fortune, skills, promotion, wealth, abilities? How do these emotions play out in the context of church? What happens when we become jealous of others?**

August 26

"His father went out and pleaded with him"
Luke 15:28 Key passage: Luke 15:11-32

"If you wish to win a man over to your ideas, first make him your friend." (Abraham Lincoln) The art of persuasion is tricky, but a necessary skill to learn, and it's one that every parent has to master. The father of this parable has an impossible job to do – to reconcile his two warring sons. The request of the younger son for his share of the inheritance has been an affront to his older brother, and so it's no surprise that the older son reacts as he does upon the younger's return. He's having none of this. The father knows there is only one thing to do – to seek reconciliation…but it's not going to be easy.

The older son remains outside, sulking. He won't even be in the same house as his brother. The father can only go out to find him. This is an image of the God who has "gone out" to find the missing children and bring them home. The father pleads with the elder son to return. God not still pleading with His lost children to return.

Thank You Father that You were prepared to "go outside" the glory of heaven to reconcile us to You. Help us to find You right now as You still seek us in love.

August 27

"But…you kill the fattened calf for him…!"
Luke 15:20 Key passage: Luke 15:11-32

"You can choose your friends but you can't choose your family" (Harper Lee). There is an essential difference between the two. Friends are for a while, family are for a lifetime. By his protestations, the older son reveals that he has not understood what it means to be a son and part of this family. He suggests that he has "slaved" for his father rather than worked with him. He argues that he has never been spoiled with a party for him and his friends (but he may never have asked), and most hurtful of all, he refers to his younger brother as "this son of yours." Not only does he fail to understand what being a son means, he also fails to understand what being a father is about.

"You kill the fattened calf for him…!" Envy is a corrosive sentiment. It skews our understanding and eats away at our sense of peace. It makes us the victim instead of the victor. It places us firmly outside the family of faith and freedom. How is it today in your family – at home, at church, in your community?

Save me, Lord, from the corrosion of envy when others seem to do so well in life and I seem to struggle. Remind me that nothing can change the fact that I am a child of Yours.

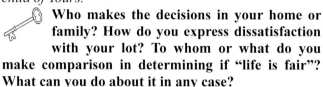 **Who makes the decisions in your home or family? How do you express dissatisfaction with your lot? To whom or what do you make comparison in determining if "life is fair"? What can you do about it in any case?**

August 28

"You are always with me…"
Luke 15:31 Key passage: Luke 15:11-32

"Listen carefully…I shall say this only once…" (Jeremy Lloyd) – a popular saying from the TV series "'Allo, 'Allo". You may hear the loving father of this parable saying these words to his older disgruntled son. The father's response to his son's outburst is careful, loving, thoughtful….and singular "You are always with me…" It's not the best translation; the phrase would be better interpreted "You are with me…all ways".

The father recognises the son's commitment to the family business. He has been an "ever present". Not a day has passed without his presence alongside the father. This son has never given his father cause for concern – no mean achievement! The son has always been aware that one day he will inherit the farm and all the responsibility, and all his life has been a preparation for that. However, this has taken over his thinking to the exclusion of the appreciation of who and what his father is. As a parable on the lot of the Jews alongside the Gentiles, it reveals their presumption of heredity and honour. "Listen carefully…" says the Lord, "Be reassured of your place in my heart"

"I will not boast in anything – no gifts, no power, no wisdom – but I will boast in Jesus Christ, His death and resurrection" (Stuart Townend)

August 29

"Everything I have is yours…"
Luke 15:31 Key passage: Luke 15:11-32

I once met a lady whose father had won the national lottery jackpot. You might think this good fortune would have given some happiness, but she was miserable – she suspected her father had spent it all! To be honest, I secretly hoped he had!

The older son feels that his younger brother has just "won the jackpot" – what with all the fuss and the killing of the fatted calf. "What about me…?" you sense him saying. Despite the father giving the younger son his share of the bequest, the older son's inheritance remains safe. As far as the father is concerned, nothing has changed. The property settlement still stands – "Everything I have is yours…" The regretful son is focussing on the wrong thing – he equally could have gone off and "squandered…" but he didn't. He remained resolute in his rectitude – never putting a foot wrong, but somehow he has missed appreciating the love of his father. His concern is really all about himself. God reassures His people that His love for them remains sure, but as Father he is also free to love His other children. Now that's a jackpot worth winning!

Lord, save me from a fixation about myself, and help me to realise that Your love is good news for other people too! May I not be judgmental of others who do things differently to me!

How do you feel about the "me" culture of today? Why is society so fixated on personal fulfilment and satisfaction? What is the key to personal happiness? Why is fulfilment so difficult to find?

August 30

"We had to celebrate and be glad…"
Luke 15:32 Key passage: Luke 15:11-32

Greetings card manufacturers have recently come up with some astonishing occasions for celebrations – including your dog's birthday, your divorce and other less proper occasions. Some people have a strange sense of propriety.

When the younger son came home he was welcomed by a father who did what any true father would do – he laid on a party! The older son was not only miffed – he was missed as he refused to attend. The father's response? "We had to celebrate." This was not only a great thing to do, it was the right thing. Martin Luther, in a different context, declared, "Here I stand, I can do no other". The compulsion to celebrate in this practical way is matched by the impulsion to "be glad" – rejoicing together. The word used speaks of a "welcome home", a greeting and expression of good health. There's no regrets or expressions of doubt, no going over the past – that is done, we are now in the present. The picture is of course a vivid illustration of the joy of the Father of heaven welcoming His errant children home. Celebration can begin!

Lord, I find it hard to think that my turning to You provoked a reaction of joy in heaven – but it's true! Help me to find that sense of joy in knowing You as Father.

August 31

"He was lost and is found"
Luke 15:32 Key passage: Luke 15:11-32

My father was a policeman. One evening, a stranger walked into the police station with some "lost property" – one of those enormous Bibles beloved of Victorian families, the kind you used to find on lecterns in most churches, and decidedly not the size you could slip in a pocket! The man had carefully removed all family details from the flyleaf, then deposited it with the Constabulary - smart thinking!

The father in this parable rejoices at the return of his younger son to the family home and circle – it's as if he has come back to life! Lost to the family and its love, he is now restored. He's not just come back physically, he has returned emotionally and spiritually. The family without him could not be the family it should – they were missing something. They are now complete – even if the older son has some issues to sort. By the gifts given to him – the robe, ring, shoes – he is restored to the family name. Unlike the Bible handed in as "lost", his name is most certainly in the flyleaf! What a picture of restoration to the family of God!

"Because of Jesus' unfailing love, I am forgiven, I am restored" (Martin Layzell). Thank You Father for receiving me into Your family as an act of grace through Jesus. May I always be "found in You"

"The sum of the whole is greater than the sum of its parts." How is this true in a family context? How is this true for the father and family in this story? How might this be true for you in your family? What about in your church? What are you together that you cannot be by yourself?

SEPTEMBER 1

"Whoever can be trusted with very little can also be trusted with much"
Luke 16:10 Key passage: Luke 16:1-15

Ever watched someone making seaside rock? Squat candy letters are assembled, wrapped in more candy, and finally s..t..r..e..t..c..h..e..d…mercilessly!... until the stick reaches the correct circumference – at which point the letters which appeared illegible suddenly make sense.

Jesus suggests that men are lettered through with their intentions and principles. These are the things that "make us tick" – often hidden, but others can "read us". The parable of the Shrewd Manager is about trustworthiness. The man who is honest will be faithful in all his dealings. He will not succumb to the temptation to cut corners, even just a bit, to benefit himself. Dishonesty is not just a temptation of those in "big business" – it's also about the "small change"… owning up when the shop assistant gives you the wrong change, when the bill in the restaurant is incorrect (but in your favour). Whoever is trustworthy in small things can be trusted in large things too. God will give more responsibility to those who can be trusted.

Lord, may I be honest and true in all my dealings with everyone, whoever they are. Give me strength to resist the temptation to profit from the mistakes of others, and may I reflect Your truth in all I do and say.

What has God trusted you with? How have you fulfilled that responsibility? Why do people "cut corners" in their responsibilities? Is that fair? How do you respond to the complaint of the Psalmist, "Why do the wicked prosper" (Psalm 37:1)?

September 2

No servant can serve two masters
Luke 16:13 Key passage: Luke 16:1-15

The Mont St. Michel in France is a stunning UNESCO World Heritage site. You can walk out to it, but it's equally enthralling to go on one of the regular shuttle buses because they can be driven from either end! Few vehicles have two steering wheels, but these do.

Jesus is clear that life offers a choice of two steering wheels, but you can't use both at once. You can't go in two different directions simultaneously! "No servant can serve two masters…" Notice the choice of language here. Jesus indicates that, whoever we are or whatever we think we are, at the end of the day we are servants of a greater power. For a lot of people that is servitude to something other than the kingdom of heaven. We may happily be servants of our own ambitions, careers, families and freedoms, but we are still servants! Jesus says you cannot be His servant as well as being a servant of every other important thing in your life. You can't drive life from both ends. Which way are you going?

"Jesus, all for Jesus, all I am and have and ever hope to be…All of my ambitions, hopes and plans I surrender these into Your hands." (Jennifer Atkinson/Robin Mark)

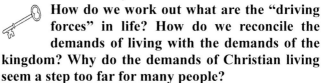 **How do we work out what are the "driving forces" in life? How do we reconcile the demands of living with the demands of the kingdom? Why do the demands of Christian living seem a step too far for many people?**

September 3

"You cannot serve God and Money"
Luke 16:13 Key passage: Luke 16:1-15

I keep my toolbox in the shed. That's where it belongs – it's not a thing of beauty or intrinsically attractive, but it is very useful. There are plenty of other things in my house that I use far less than the toolbox and its contents, but they cannot swap places with the toolbox. Everything in its place.

Jesus warns that you cannot serve both God and Money. This was a shocking thing for the Pharisees to hear – "they loved money"...for them it was an important thing. In the ancient world money was among the realities to be personalised and given the name and status of a god – the Greek god Plutus. He was the son of Demeter the goddess of fruitfulness, and was pictured as a child with a cornucopia of good things in his possession. Mammon (Money) is the Hebrew equivalent, tempting and beguiling in appeal. Jesus never condemned money of itself, and He had more to say about money than almost anything else – but He does warn of Money's allure. It's just a tool – keep it in its box!

In a world driven by money, Lord, help me to focus on something greater – the ability to see money as a tool to be used for the blessing of others and the glory of Your name!

How do you use your money? How do you decide what is essential, and what is not? What is the purpose of money? How can it be misused, and how can it be well used?

September 4

"God knows your hearts"
Luke 16:15 Key passage: Luke 16:1-15

You've probably had them – phone calls or e-mails purporting to be from someone "official" but there's something that's just not right. Beware the scammers! When my wife gets a call "about the accident you've just had" her response is "Yes, I had such a bang on the head, I've forgotten the details – tell me about it."

Jesus addresses the Pharisees who equally seem to have forgotten one thing – God not only hears our words and sees our actions, He also knows our hearts. For them, money was the issue – it was what made "the world go around". The problem was that money of itself was seductive, and the Pharisees were obsessed by opportunities to make money and to profit from the needs and misfortunes of others. There's nothing wrong with good business – Jesus commends those who are careful and wise stewards of their money to benefit others – but it's easy to err into a "grey area" to generate profit for yourself. "God knows your heart". He sees right through you to your real motives and the warning is stern – "What is highly valued by men is detestable to God". Don't forget that!

"Lord, You have searched me and you know me…You are familiar with all my ways. Before a word is on my tongue, You know it completely" (Psalm 139.1-4). So "search me O God and know my heart" (Psalm 139.23)

September 5

"It is easier for heaven and earth to disappear…"
Luke 16:17 Key passage: Luke 16:16-18

Ever used an adynaton? I thought not. It's a figure of speech describing something quite improbable, like "pigs might fly". Now you know! Jesus uses one in His encounter with the Pharisees – "it is easier for heaven and earth to disappear than for the least stroke of a pen to drop out of the Law".

Many people thought Jesus too revolutionary – they wanted someone to overturn the Roman occupation, but not someone who seemed simultaneously to overturn Judaism as well. They considered Jesus was not an advocate of the Jewish Law – the five books of Genesis to Deuteronomy, which gave the means by which God was to be known – but rather that He was undermining it by speaking of the kingdom of God. What they could not understand was that by their rigid interpretation of the Law and insistence on adherence to its demands, they were actually missing the goal of the Law…that they might know God's grace. So Jesus says something improbable – not one dot or squiggle of the Law is ignored in the kingdom… He has come to be their Christ, not their critic!

Lord, help me to see "Christ in all the Scriptures" and to know Your grace to me in Jesus.

Why does the Bible seem such a "closed book" to many people? How have we reinforced the idea that the Bible is a book of prohibition and condemnation? How can we change this perception of the Scriptures?

September 6

"Send Lazarus to cool my tongue"
Luke 16:24 Key passage: Luke 16:19-31

"Garcon!" Who'd be a waiter? Certainly not the hapless Manuel in *Fawlty Towers* who daily seemed to be in mortal danger at the hand of his boss Basil Fawlty (and actually was – in one episode he was almost knocked unconscious when John Cleese hit him over the head with a real frying pan instead of a padded prop)… but then what are staff for…?

Jesus told the story of the rich man and the beggar Lazarus. In life their lots were very different – but in death the tables are turned. In the torment of hell, the rich man is in agony, and makes a pitiful plea: "Send Lazarus to cool my tongue…" What are staff for? In his world other people exist to serve him and his needs. He knows where to go when he needs something – and people will bend to his will, won't they? Surely even Lazarus can be spared to assist him? But the usual rules of deference no longer apply. He'd missed out on knowing the Servant King who came to bring freedom and forgiveness. Out of the frying pan, into the fire?

Forgive me, Lord, when I regard others with something less than humility. Thank You for Jesus the Servant King, who shows us what real servanthood looks like.

September 7

"Between us a great chasm has been fixed"
Luke 16:26 Key passage: Luke 16:19-31

You may not have heard of Peter Lodge, but you've probably heard him! His is the voice on London Underground that announces "Mind the gap"! He was the sound engineer who generated the recording in 1968, but to save royalties he recorded his own voice.

Abraham, in response to the plaintive pleading of the rich man in torment, explains there is between heaven and hell "a great chasm" that is now unbridgeable. The word used is dramatic – "a yawning gulf". There will be no possibility of a transfer back. Some people think this teaching too final and frightening, preferring to imagine that the grace of God can reach anyone at any time and in any place or state, but that is not what Jesus had to say. Behind these words are a stark warning. "God is not willing for any to perish…" but don't play a game of "chicken" with Him! Jesus alone is the One who has bridged the chasm – it's time to get on board!

Lord, help me to know where I stand with You – forgiven, redeemed and restored to You. I pray for those close to me who have not yet "bridged the gap".

Why is "hellfire" preaching unfashionable? Is it true that there will always be another opportunity with God? How should this impact our understanding, and our living out of our faith?

September 8

"Let him warn them…"
Luke 16:28 Key passage: Luke 16:19-31

Dawn Spencer-Smith acquired a motorhome and drove off. She put the vehicle into cruise control, then climbed in the back to make a cup of tea…the resulting crash was catastrophic. "I thought it was like an autopilot…" she said. In a similar American case, the hapless owner sued Winnebago for not including a warning of this in the handbook.

Jesus' story of the rich man and Lazarus tells of the rich man pleading from hell for Lazarus to warn his five brothers of the agonies of hell. The rich man is, however, still stuck in "cruise control" thinking that Lazarus is somehow at his beck and call. It's always someone else's job to do these things. But Abraham is insistent – they have had Moses and the prophets warn them…what else do they need before they take notice? How many times do we have to be told something before we react? How willing are we to listen to the promptings of God about eternity? How long did it take you to respond to the invitation of Jesus to follow Him? Time to forsake cruise-control and get in gear!

Help us, Lord, to be clear in our preaching and teaching of the need for personal response to the claims of Christ. May I be clear today where my trust and hope is…in Jesus!

September 9

"They will not be convinced…"
Luke 16:31 Key passage: Luke 16:19-31

My maternal grandmother was convinced that man never walked on the moon, that it was all some kind of conspiracy, and what we saw on television was a mock-up in a studio. Conspiracy theories abound about all sorts of things, from moon shots to world pandemics.

It seems that some people will not examine the weight of evidence, but instead start from a conviction and seek to explain away anything to the contrary as part of the conspiracy. Abraham, after his conversation with the rich man in torment, concludes that the brothers of the rich man will not believe, even if "someone rises from the dead" to warn them. Some people will just not be told! The truth of these words is that Jesus came not to undo the work or word of the forefathers and prophets, but to fulfil it. God has spoken His truth persistently and clearly for generations, but many chose not to heed Him. When Jesus the Son came, they similarly ignored and repudiated Him…and then the reality strikes! Listen to what God has to say today – and respond to it now!

Lord, I pray for friends and family who find it hard or impossible to believe. May I help them to find You in the midst of their doubts.

What are the "conspiracies" that people believe in? How does this impact us? Why is it easier to believe a "conspiracy theory" than believe the truth? What does this tell us about the nature of the Christian gospel?

September 10

"Watch yourselves"
Luke 17:3   Key passage: Luke 17:1-10

The car slowed and the driver wound down his window: "How do I get to…?" he asked me. In youthful confidence I sent him on his way and then realised to my horror that I'd told him completely wrong! I hope he forgave me.

Jesus warns of the signals and directions we give out that may send others the wrong way. "Watch yourselves," He warns. There is a burden of responsibility on all who follow Jesus. You are not just responsible for yourself – as a follower of Jesus you are also responsible for others who look to you. Jesus speaks of "things that cause people to sin" (verse 1). The word He uses is *"skandalon"* – scandal. It is used of a trap that is set off by something wandering into it, much like a mousetrap is activated by a cheese-hungry rodent! You may think your actions are innocent enough, but they may lead others into error and danger. So beware of careless language, lazy actions and risqué suggestions that do not honour God and bring shame on you and others. Others are looking to you for direction in life – don't send them the wrong way.

Lord, may my words be echoed by my ways…and may Your way be echoed in my words.

September 11

"If you have faith as small as a mustard seed…"
Luke 17:6   Key passage: Luke 17:1-10

"I can, therefore I am" – words of the French philosopher and mystic Simone Weil (referencing the quote of Descartes "I think therefore I am"). Weil devoted her life to the support of the working classes and the improvement of their lot. For her, the simple attitude of resolution would serve her well in her mission.

Jesus teaches a similar attitude of commitment – "If you have faith as small as a mustard seed…" The disciples have got stuck in the notion that faith is affected by its quantity – if you don't have enough faith then things won't happen. Jesus teaches that what matters is quality – all you need is genuineness of heart for faith to be effective. Although the mustard seed is very small, when germinated it grows to a tree out of all proportion to its seed. Faith is like that. In the right context, it gives growth. What challenge do you face personally or in your church and where does faith figure in its resolution?

Lord, I believe; help my unbelief! Teach me the heart of faith to trust You in all things.

 What do we mean by "faith"? A belief, a system, a denomination, a religion, a code…? Which of these is Jesus talking about here? Consider the reality of who exercises the faith, but also in who or what that faith is being exercised. Why is faith by itself only part of the story? What does faith need in order to be valid?

September 12

"Go, show yourselves to the priest"
Luke 17:14 Key passage: Luke 17:11-19

"Don't just stand there…do something!" The impulse to action is strong…nothing's going to happen unless someone makes it happen. How often have you sat in a traffic jam seeing what the problem is, but no one doing anything about it? I'm out of the car to sort it out… it's amazing what some are prepared to do (or not do) to assist!

The ten lepers' encounter with Jesus is interesting – they're "stuck in the queue". Presentation before the local priest was part of the regime – they had been deemed "unclean" and put out of normal social contact, and it would only be by word of the priest that they might ever be restored. Some chance of that ever happening…! But then they met Jesus. They didn't realise then that the One they met was the Priest above all, but it was He who pronounced their healing, not in words, but in action. They must present themselves to the local priest, for in their obedience they were healed. Nine went to the priest, and one (a Samaritan) came to Jesus. What do you need from Him today? Don't just stand there…do something!

Lord, when I need to know Your healing, show me when I need to do something about it.

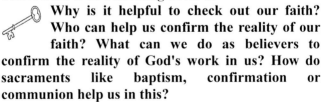 **Why is it helpful to check out our faith? Who can help us confirm the reality of our faith? What can we do as believers to confirm the reality of God's work in us? How do sacraments like baptism, confirmation or communion help us in this?**

September 13

"Where are the other nine?"
Luke 17:17 Key passage: Luke 17:11-19

What a topsy-turvy world we inhabit! We spend years teaching our children to say "thank you" and then send them out into a world where so often it's the last thing we do. It's one thing saying it, quite another meaning it!

Jesus' encounter with this group of ten lepers is dynamic. Cast out of normal society by their condition, they huddle together in misery…when Jesus comes along. They may well have heard about Jesus, but their knowledge is limited – they address him as "Master", a term used of someone who is "knowledgeable" about something. "Have pity on us!" Jesus' response is immediate and important – "Go and show yourselves to the priests!" One of the priest's responsibilities was to ensure good public health and he alone would verify the health or otherwise of an individual. In the case of a leper, this verification was visual. Nine set off, oblivious to the fact of their instant healing, but the tenth (a Samaritan at that!) doesn't wait for the "official verification" – he realises that in that moment he is healed and he returns to thank Jesus. Where are the other nine?

Lord, may I always be aware of Your power to act in the most difficult of circumstances – and may I have a heart of gratitude for all Your goodness to me.

September 14

"The kingdom of God is within you
Luke 17:21 Key passage: Luke 17:20-37

Robert Barker and Martin Lucas will never live it down…in their 1631 reprint of the King James' Bible, they unfortunately managed to omit the word "not" from the commandment "Thou shalt not commit adultery". As Royal Printers, they lost their licence and livelihood…all for the sake of one three-lettered word. Mind you, that word mattered…!

The word of Jesus to His disciples here is equally important – "the kingdom of God is within you". The critical word is "within" – "*anothen*" - meaning severally "within", "inside", "among", "around". We shall not be arrested or lose livelihoods by misinterpreting it, but we shall miss out on the glorious truth of the kingdom by passing over it. The disciples sought evidence of this kingdom around them, looking for physical evidence – land, borders, armies, palaces. They were to see none of them. They had little idea of the kingdom within them – except that they knew that Jesus had called them and was changing them from weak and disbelieving men to His disciples. The kingdom among them is being experienced in sharing in Jesus' ministry. The kingdom starts inside and works outwards. That's it…in a word!

"Reign in me, Sovereign Lord…Captivate my heart, let Your kingdom come". (Chris Bowater)

How do you experience the kingdom of God...within you? Inside you? Among you? Around you? How do these aspects relate to each other? What were the disciples looking for and what did they actually find?

September 15

"Do not go running off after them…"
Luke 17:23 Key passage: Luke 17:20-37

I once went to hear a famous preacher. He was on form
– telling stories about himself for most of the evening.
A skilled entertainer… I'm not sure we actually got to
the "preach" but he had the congregation eating out of
his hand. I sadly concluded that some people are
seeking something rather different from others of us…

Jesus similarly warned His disciples to beware of
those who thought they could confidently identify the
coming of the kingdom of God. Speaking the word of
God is an awesome responsibility, but there are always
those who listen to the preacher better than they listen
to what the preacher is actually saying! There's no
mystique in preaching – just a lot of mist sometimes!
Jesus promises that the coming of the kingdom will be
clear and unequivocal, as powerfully revealed as
lightning illuminating the sky (verse 24). The task of
the preacher is to reveal Jesus the Word, not their own
cleverness with words. Don't go running after heroes –
they've nothing real to tell you!

*Reflect on those you listen to who are preaching God's
Word. Pray for them, for their humility, obedience and
responsibility in preaching that Word.*

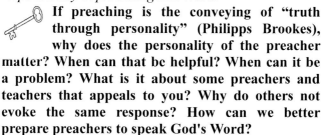 **If preaching is the conveying of "truth
through personality" (Philipps Brookes),
why does the personality of the preacher
matter? When can that be helpful? When can it be
a problem? What is it about some preachers and
teachers that appeals to you? Why do others not
evoke the same response? How can we better
prepare preachers to speak God's Word?**

September 16

"He must suffer many things and be rejected"
Luke 17:25 Key passage: Luke 17:20-37

I once worked as a packer on a food production line. The boxes came through the machine at an alarming speed and we had to pack them in crates. One box was continually rejected, and when we opened it up there was not a grain of food inside, but there was something else you wouldn't want to know about.

Rejection is always difficult, but sometimes necessary. Jesus warns that the Son of Man will suffer and be rejected. Such rejection goes beyond mere ignoring. The word used speaks of rejection after trial. The Son of Man will be given due consideration, but not accepted. He will "suffer many things" at the hands of men – scoffing, despising, accusations – then be denied the very thing He came for…the place of honour in the hearts of men. He will be rejected like the defendant in a criminal trial who goes in the dock and promises to tell the truth of what really happened…only for the jury to reject his story as unreliable and untrustworthy. But what Jesus says is truth, for He is the Truth. Reject Him at your peril!

Lord, I'm sorry that for so long I rejected You and Your truth. Help me to reject falsehood and lies, and live by the truth of Your word.

September 17

"Just as in the days of Noah, so it will be"
Luke 17:26 Key passage: Luke 17:20-37

Throughout the world pandemic, there has been much talk of "getting back to normal", whatever that means. Will "normal" life ever be possible again? Was there ever a "normal"? Certainly there was life as we used to know it, but it feels as if life is carrying on in a "parallel universe".

…and Jesus speaks of the coming of the kingdom of God in "normal" daily living. "As it was in the days of Noah…" life was carrying on as "normal" – eating, drinking, getting married. There was nothing to suggest the disaster that lurked just round the corner…indeed, it is clear that Noah probably put up with a lot of disdain for his madcap idea of building an ark, given that the sea was well over 100 miles away, that he was of some great age, and that no one could take seriously his suggestions of a flood…and then it started to rain.

In the same way the kingdom of God is coming, indeed is already here, yet few can see it. O to have the eyes of faith to see beyond the "normal"!

Lord, open my eyes to the true condition of the world in all its need, then give me grace to respond to need and to pray for Your kingdom to come!

 How has a personal or global crisis affected you? What do you do now that did you did not do before? What have you left behind? How does the reality of the kingdom of God relate to your experience of living through such times?

September 18

"Remember Lot's wife!"
Luke 17:32 Key passage: Luke 17:20-37

Have you ever walked into a lamppost? It hurts…pride as well as physically! It happened to me when I turned round to look at something else. Happily it's the kind of thing you only do once.

   Looking back can be risky. Jesus specifically warns about this concerning the coming of the kingdom on the day of judgment. Both Noah and Lot were saved from the judgment because, despite their own failings, they heeded God's prompting and took action. Lot's wife was also delivered from the doomed situation of Sodom, but made the mistake of looking back and lamenting for a moment what she was leaving behind. Jesus warns of the householder who thinks he has time to retrieve his belongings from his house, or the labourer who just wants to pop home to get something before answering the call to the kingdom…and both miss out! The immediacy of the call is reflected in the call of Jesus to His first disciples – "they left their nets…" – and the excuses given by those who couldn't "come right now…" The kingdom of God will come with a sureness and suddenness – don't be looking the wrong way!

"Hear the call of the Kingdom to reach out to the lost with the Father's compassion in the wonder of the cross, bringing peace and forgiveness and a hope yet to come let the nations put their trust in Him" (Keith Getty)

September 19

"One will be taken, the other left"
Luke 17:34,35   Key passage: Luke 17:20-37

It's games afternoon, and we are lined up to enable the captains to pick their teams. You've guessed it…were you also the last to be chosen (or "donated" to the other side)?

Jesus speaks about the domestic situations in which the call of the kingdom of God comes with suddenness, with the result that "one will be taken, the other left" – a married couple in bed, two women doing domestic chores, two work colleagues in the field together. There is a sharpness of experience here as the kingdom comes in power – with the result that separation will be experienced. Such teaching is not popular and sounds harsh, but Jesus is pointing out that you are either for Him or against Him, so the "separation" has been self-determining. Notice also that proximity to the one who is "saved" is not enough to merit salvation – you don't access the kingdom by "association". God's judgement is individual just as His salvation is individual. It's not down to others to determine whose team you are on. It's your choice alone.

"Who is on the Lord's side…?" (F. R. Havergal) Thank God for the choice you have made…and pray for those who have not yet made such a choice.

What do these words mean to you and those closest to you? Each person is responsible for making their own response to the claims of Jesus. How does that sound to you and your closest family and friends? Is there something you need to do as a result of considering this?

September 20

"Where there is a dead body, there the vultures will gather"
Luke 17:37 Key passage: Luke 17:20-37

"When seagulls follow the trawler it is because they think sardines will be thrown into the sea." Uttered by Manchester United player Eric Cantona after his 2011 court appearance for assaulting a fan with a kung-fu kick. He left counsel and reporters totally confused by the imagery.

He was not the first to say this and Jesus uttered something similar to the Pharisees when speaking of the coming of the Son of Man – "Where there is a dead body, there the vultures will gather." Not a pretty picture, but a graphic one! What did Jesus mean by this? It reads as though He is reciting some kind of proverb, but with a renewed meaning. Speaking of the coming kingdom, Jesus indicates that there will be those who miss this, through their own ignorance and stubbornness. Such people are "spiritually dead", and this cannot be ignored – they will inevitably face the judgement of God. God has appointed the time of His coming, and He will keep His promise. The warning is simple – don't be left "all at sea"!

Lord, impress on my heart those who do not yet know You personally – family and friends – that in Your timing I may be able to speak with them of the love of God in Jesus. May they never be able to say "You never told me!"

September 21

"Will not God bring justice for His chosen ones?"

Luke 18:7   Key passage: Luke 18:1-8

"I will do right to all manner of people…without fear or favour, affection or ill will." This is the Judicial Oath, taken by every serving judge and magistrate, and is a promise to "do justice" and it must be upheld. That's not always easy since, as we all know, there's "two sides to every story".

In these two parables about prayer, Jesus illustrates that God will always "do justice" in His world and for His people. Here He declares that if an unjust judge will eventually do justice, how much more can God be relied upon to do so as well? Remember that this is all about prayer! This means that God will respond to the prayers of His children, but it doesn't mean that He will always respond in the way expected or hoped for. God is just…and will do what is just for His children. In the context of the persistent widow, maybe we also learn that God will respond to the persistent prayer as well. "Successful" praying is not about a one-hit wonder…it is about persistence in asking. God has promised – He will "do right", with affection.

Thank You, Father, that You always do what is right, for You are the God of true justice. Give me insight into Your ways, to accept Your answers to my prayers knowing that You know what is best and good for me in every situation.

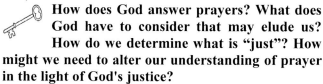 **How does God answer prayers? What does God have to consider that may elude us? How do we determine what is "just"? How might we need to alter our understanding of prayer in the light of God's justice?**

September 22

"I thank you that I am not like other men…"
Luke 18:11 Key passage: Luke 18:9-14

It's quite instructive sitting in the queue at the barbers! Not only do you hear the variety of banter between the barber and customer, but you also see the range of styles requested…and you wonder how some customers see themselves!

Jesus told this story of the Pharisee and Tax collector – men from opposite ends of the "popularity spectrum" of society. The mindset of the Pharisee in particular is fascinating. He knows who he is…and insists that others should know as well. "I'm not like other men…" since he is generous, law-abiding and religious – not bad for a Pharisee! "Other men" are greedy, criminal and evil… (oh look, just like that tax collector over there…). Not only does the Pharisee know clearly what he is, he's anxious to inform God as well, just in case the Almighty hasn't noticed! Hasn't God done well to choose a man like him?

Before rushing to judgement, look at yourself – how often does your attitude mirror this man? We may quietly look down on others, pass judgement on them and impress ourselves with our own religiosity. Time for a trim!

Lord, when I'm tempted to look down on others, help me to look up to You.

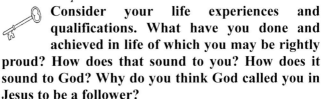 **Consider your life experiences and qualifications. What have you done and achieved in life of which you may be rightly proud? How does that sound to you? How does it sound to God? Why do you think God called you in Jesus to be a follower?**

September 23

"God have mercy on me a sinner"
Luke 18:13 Key passage: Luke 18:9-14

It's only one word, but it makes all the difference…and what a difference there is between "a" and "the" – between the indefinite and the definite article. For the two men of this parable, this is not a matter of semantics – it demonstrates the stark difference between them. The Pharisee who thought he was "the" man of the moment, and the tax collector who should have been just "a" bit-part player. But the parable turns the tables.

The tax collector knows one thing that the Pharisee does not – the truth about himself! So distraught is he with that truth, that all he can is prostrate himself before God and plead, "God, have mercy on me…the sinner!" The word used is the definite article – "the". Just as the Pharisee describes himself as not being "like other men" because of his goodness, the tax collector sees himself as not being like other men because of (the level of) his sinfulness. This is not false piety, but honesty borne of humility. God hears that with the result that "this man…went home justified". How is it – are you "a" sinner saved by grace, or "the" sinner?

God, show me the truth about myself as "the" sinner whom You have forgiven in Jesus Christ!

September 24

"Everyone who exalts himself will be humbled"
Luke 18:14 Key passage: Luke 18:9-14

A pastor colleague of mine went hospital visiting. Unable to find room anywhere, he parked in a space reserved for one of the top doctors – "It's all right" he told the attendant "I'm a heart specialist."

Jesus warns "everyone who exalts himself will be humbled" in the parable of the Pharisee and the tax collector. Self-awareness is one of the standards of living today – the need to be positive about yourself and to believe in yourself. No one gets anywhere by self-deprecation! What Jesus presents here goes way beyond reasonable assertiveness – the Pharisee is genuine and honest about himself…but just plain mistaken! He's right, but wrong. He will be humbled when the kingdom comes. By contrast the tax collector will be exalted. The Pharisee was a good man – measured by the standards of Pharisaism. The tax collector was a toe-rag and turncoat – measured by the standards of Judaism. But there is another standard to meet – the standard of heaven. How do we measure up against the One who is the "heart specialist"?

"Show me the truth concealed within Your Word…" (Mary Lathbury). Lord, may I accept the truth about myself, and serve You from a heart of humility and gratitude.

How does the Bible help us to see ourselves as we really are? What attitudes does it challenge? Why can it be difficult to be a Christian in certain contexts, e.g. in business, politics, sport, etc? How can we help followers of Jesus in those arenas?

September 25

"Let the children come to me"
Luke 18:16 Key passage: Luke 18:15-17

Remember when you could play conkers – without having to wear goggles? This was the stuff of greatest importance – especially if you had a "72'er"! Childhood then was rather different to now…but we probably weren't any the worse for the lack of "health and safety".

The disciples would have made great Health and Safety consultants. The children were coming to Jesus, but the disciples "rebuked" the parents. Out of a sense of duty, concern for Jesus or for the parents, we do not know – but they weren't having this! Jesus, however, seizes the opportunity to speak of and demonstrate the principles of the kingdom – by asking that the children be permitted to come. Seeking the blessing of a Rabbi was a tradition for parents of a child on the first birthday – and whether it was this that brought the parents with their young children we are not told, but Jesus blesses the children with these words of spiritual wisdom. Come to the kingdom in child-like trust, not child-ish truculence (like the Pharisee just spoken of). "A little child shall lead them…" was never truer. No strings attached… for anyone who can…conquers!

"In simple trust like theirs who heard beside the Syrian sea the gracious calling of the Lord, let us, like them, without a word rise up and follow…" (J. G. Whittier)

September 26

"Why do you call me good?"
Luke 18:19 Key passage: Luke 18:18-30

The phone rings – it's someone I don't recognise, but they begin by asking if I'm having a nice day! My suspicions arouse immediately – I'm not sure what my personal welfare has to do with the product they're about to pitch to me! Another graduate of the School of Meaningless Charm…!

Jesus is approached by a man who addresses him as "Good Master". The man is a "ruler" – straight and measured! He is a civic worthy, a man of local repute. His address to Jesus is earnest and flattering…he wants to know what he has to do to gain the next level of "worthiness" as a citizen. The address "good teacher" was not used by rabbis since it suggested something of divinity in the addressee, and only God could truly possess divinity – exactly! That is why Jesus questions him in the way He does. The rich young ruler has stumbled upon a truth almost by accident – in addressing Jesus the Son… and at this moment he doesn't realise it! He is honest in his assessment of religious observance, but he's missing one thing – a personal relationship with Jesus. Ring any bells?

Lord, open to me the truth of a personal relationship with you – to know You not only as Lord but as my Lord!

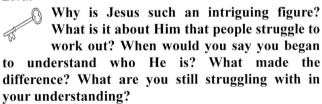**Why is Jesus such an intriguing figure? What is it about Him that people struggle to work out? When would you say you began to understand who He is? What made the difference? What are you still struggling with in your understanding?**

September 27

"You will have treasure in heaven"
Luke 18:22 Key passage: Luke 18:18-30

"Read through the whole question paper before attempting your answers." The instructions on the exam sheet couldn't be clearer…especially since the very last sentence read "All answers should be written in black pen". How many students wrote in any other colour…not having obeyed the instructions!

Jesus encounters the rich ruler. The man is earnest, exceptional and enquiring. He wants to do what is right…and he's keen to point out that so far that's what he's been doing. "All these (commandments) I have kept since I was a boy". Jesus quotes the commandments, but notice that he quotes them "out of turn" (compare Exodus 20.12-16). By quoting some of them, is He not quoting them all? Has this ruler not noticed that, despite keeping all these commandments, he has missed the first commandment "Have no other gods before me". There's the problem! Money, or the love of it, had supplanted God in his affections, negating the observance of all the other commandments…and it's not just money that gets in the way – intellect and intelligence, artistic or moral attainments, ambition…There's treasure in heaven beyond the obvious. Read the whole passage.

Consider what easily takes priority in life over your love of God – what is more important: "treasure" here and now, or "treasure" in eternity?

September 28

"It is easier for a camel…"
Luke 18:25 Key passage: Luke 18:18-30

"The difficult we do immediately. The impossible takes a little longer" – words of Charles Alexandre de Calonne, Finance Minister to Louis XVI and Marie Antoinette, when asked to supply additional money to meet debts of the Queen. Such were the demands upon him that he resorted to appeasing the Queen in such words.

Jesus similarly describes an impossible situation of the likelihood of rich men entering the kingdom. Easier to get a camel through the eye of a needle than to get a rich man into heaven…He's got to be joking, isn't He? Explanations have included the small "Needle Gate" of Jerusalem requiring laden animals to be unloaded before entering the city…or a mistranslation of the word "camel" for "cable" (of a ship's hawser dimensions) meaning it's easier to thread a great rope though a tiny needle. Both explanations are engaging, but unproven. Simply Jesus is demonstrating His mastery of hyperbole – it's not impossible for rich people to get into the kingdom, just rather difficult because of the importance they put on their wealth. "The impossible takes a little longer…" but it can happen!

Thank You, Jesus that you say it "like it is" – and Your words speak truth in all its power. Thank You that it's never impossible for anyone to never Your kingdom – just that sometimes we make it almost impossible by our attitudes and actions.

 What are the "needles" that challenge you in terms of God's kingdom? What do you find difficult, and why?

September 29

"What is impossible with men is possible with God"
Luke 18:27 Key passage: Luke 18:18-30

We love playing games with family and friends, but frequently we discover that friends play to a different set of rules. "Where did you get that from?" we ask, and the reply is either "We've always done it that way!" or more disconcertingly "That's what it says in the rules…haven't you read them?"

To the Jewish mind, material wealth was a sign of God's blessing on an individual. That was a reasonable assumption, given the hierarchical nature of society and the way religion and responsibility were intertwined. It was also a nice assumption if you were the one blessed with the wealth…! But clearly Jesus has come to turn this on its head and He identifies with the poor and needy more than any others. If this principle is true, then the wealthy have a better chance of enjoying life in the world to come as well. You know what you need to do! Jesus, however, reverses the social norm by his warning about wealth and kingdom admission. "What is impossible with men is possible with God". He alone decides on kingdom entry. Better read the rules carefully!

Thank You, Father, that it is by Your grace alone that we ever enter into Your kingdom. Challenge me when I think there are other qualifications…like church membership, notable service, responsibility and worth.

September 30

"What do you want me to do for you?"
Luke 18:41 Key passage: Luke 18:35-43

"If you don't ask, you don't get it!" (Mahatma Gandhi). He wasn't the first to say this, but he was probably the greatest example of its truth…

…apart from Jesus. Jesus stops the blind beggar in his tracks with this telling question "What do you want me to do for you?" Isn't that obvious? "Have mercy on me…" is the plaintive request. Is that all he wants – mercy? No surprise that those around Jesus order him to be quiet – Jesus has more important business than to "have mercy" on this beggar. Yet Jesus stops and asks the question that needed asking – "What do you want me to do for you?" "I want to see" is his bold request. Don't be stupid man, you're blind…! But that's it…Jesus puts the question that only He can ask…since He alone has the power to answer it! I am frequently asked to pray with and for others, and it's always worth asking "How much dare you ask God for?" Where's the extremity of your faith? God will hear and answer your plea. What do you need to say to Him today?

What is it that you would wish to ask of Jesus today? What is stopping you?

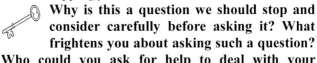 **Why is this a question we should stop and consider carefully before asking it? What frightens you about asking such a question? Who could you ask for help to deal with your reservations and fears?**

OCTOBER 1

"I must stay at your house today"
Luke 19:5   Key passage: Luke 19:1-10

It's the archetypal ending to every child's story... "and then they went home for tea." Well, that's how stories used to end! There's something homely about this story of Jesus and Zaccheus. In stark contrast to the rich young ruler, Zaccheus is someone open to God's redeeming grace despite his wealth (which he subsequently offers to correct).

Jesus' statement here might sound appealing, but it's also hortatory – "I must stay", not "I might" or "I'd like to..." There's an inevitability about it; it's going to happen! Notice that Jesus' coming is not a fleeting visit – the word used implies "staying over", a recognition that He is not just welcome for tea, but for eternity! Some people have a dalliance with Jesus and then "move on". You may know people who once professed a faith, but sadly seem to have left it behind now. Jesus' spoke elsewhere about people like seeds who grow and then wither in their faith. There's something revealing about Jesus' ministry here – He wants to be Lord in every room of the home, not just the front room!

Pray for any you know who once expressed some kind of faith but have left it behind. Pray that God would rekindle that spark within them.

Reflect on your Christian experience now, and how it was when you first came to believe. What has changed? If you did not have a recognisable moment of coming to faith (and some 80% of Christians have come by a gradual process) what have been the important moments in your spiritual experience? What would you want God to do for you now?

October 2

"Today salvation has come to this house"
Luke 19:10 Key passage: Luke 19:1-10

Remember which "house" you were in at school? It was a means of encouraging competitiveness and friendly rivalry in matters sporting and artistic…something that frequently passed me by!

When Jesus announces of Zaccheus "Today salvation has come to this house" He is declaring something quite profound. The "house" of Zaccheus was not a particularly reputable one. Zaccheus was a "chief tax collector". He didn't actually do the collecting – he was the manager! He thought that being the manager he would be "invisible" to the man in the street who resented this whole Roman tax regime and those who collected it…but he was rather more "invisible" than intended! He was short, and when it mattered, he couldn't see over the crowd, and no one was going to let him in any case! He certainly wasn't high up in the pecking order this day. Yet it is to him that Jesus gives a personal invitation. Isn't that just the way with the Saviour – seeking out the sidelined, the snubbed, the second-rate citizens? Zaccheus responds honestly, joyfully, willingly. How is it in your "house"?

Lord, I'm amazed that You welcome into Your "house" those who we wouldn't welcome in ours! Challenge me today to examine my attitude to those I don't particularly like or welcome!

October 3

"To everyone who has, more will be given"
Luke 19:26 Key passage: Luke 19:11-27

I've always hated scales…the piano sort! They were so boring, repetitive, unexciting…but without them playing never improves. Perhaps if the teacher had made them more thrilling…but then, there's no substitute for practice.

   Jesus tells the parable of the ten minas. It's not one of the "stand-out" parables, but it has an important point. It's all about commitment. The parable is similar to the parable of the talents, and both stories emphasise this truth – it's not what you've got but what you do with it that counts! That's a kingdom principle as much as a business principle. Investment is a risky business, but there will always be an outcome. The servants who invested their money were rewarded. It makes no difference that one earned more than the other – both did the right thing. The servant who didn't invest didn't risk anything, but neither did he reap anything. He ended up losing what he had. We each receive gifts and talents from the hand of God – but they are to be used to His glory and for the blessing of others. The skills are in the scales!

Help me, Lord, to practise the art of investment – in time, energy, skills and commitment to the cause of the kingdom…and amaze me with Your blessing!

What gifts and skills has God invested in you? What gifts and skills have you offered to Him? How are those gifts being used? Have others recognised your gifts? How can we encourage and affirm the gifts of other people? Why do so many gifts go unused and unrecognised?

October 4

"The Lord needs it"
Luke 19:31 Key passage: Luke 19:28-44

"I'm seeing a man about a dog," was my father's way of deflecting questions when he thought we children too inquisitive. There seemed to be an awful lot of mysterious dogs in our village!

Sometimes we are left scratching our heads thinking "what did they mean by that?" which may have been the response of the onlookers to the explanation "The Lord needs it." On one level it was a reasonable answer "The owner requires it…"; on another level they didn't quite grasp who "the Master/the Lord" might be.

The question is all about ownership. It's suggested (verse 33) that there were several co-owners of the animal. It's possible that they had already agreed Jesus' use of the animal. As an unused colt, it was suitable for a sacred purpose – and here's that moment! "The Lord needs it" for the next stage of His journey to Jerusalem.

It's also about occasion – Jesus arrives in fulfilment of the prophetic word (Zechariah 9.9) "See, your king comes to you…riding on a donkey…" to complete God's long promised work of redemption for His people…

"The Lord needs it…" That's what it means!

"The Lord has need of me, His soldier I will be; He gave Himself my life to win, and so I mean to follow Him and serve Him faithfully" (Cecil Allen)

October 5

"If they keep quiet, the stones will cry out"
Luke 19:40 Key passage: Luke 19:28-44

Look at that five-pound note in your purse or wallet. Have you wondered what it might have been used for in the past – something good and wholesome, or something cynical and dark? What stories something inanimate might tell!

As Jesus approaches Jerusalem the people come out to greet him with enthusiasm…which annoyed the Pharisees. They didn't "do" enthusiasm, let alone all this "nonsense" about Jesus being the Messiah. What are these ghastly common people thinking? Their fear was of a Roman backlash and so they ask Jesus to rebuke the people. Jesus' response is "if they keep quiet, the stones will cry out". The words reflect those of Habakkuk 2.11 where the Lord declares of the sins of the people "The stones of the wall will cry out, and the beams of the woodwork will echo it". Truth will out! The work of God in revealing His salvation through Christ will be accomplished, despite the frustrations of man. God's way is sovereign - make a note of that!

Thank You, Jesus, that the whole of creation declares that You are Lord. When I'm tempted to keep quiet, speak through my actions; when others are better at speaking of You, help me to support them and pray for them rather than resenting them.

How do you hear "the stones cry out" about the glory of God? Where does God's kingdom break into the daily round of your life? Who are the "ordinary" people you know who nevertheless exude the love and grace of God? What is it about them that speaks to you? Have you ever told them and encouraged them?

October 6

"If you had only known – but it is hidden"
Luke 19:42 Key passage: Luke 19:28-44

"I didn't see that coming!" How often are we surprised by a turn of events? When we reflect on things, perhaps we should have spotted the signs.

As the people of Jerusalem face the agony of destruction that is coming, they might hardly complain this is a surprise. Jesus comes as Messiah speaking of the coming turmoil and proclaiming the kingdom. There is a contrast in the words and actions of Jesus here that is telling. As He approaches Jerusalem, He sees the city, the beloved city of God, and He weeps over it. He sees it with present eyes in all its glory, but also with future eyes in its destruction to come, and His eyes fill with tears of agony. By contrast, the people of Jerusalem, going about their business, cannot see the future, for their eyes are blinded – "it is hidden from your eyes". They have not listened to the pleadings of God to them, to the calls of the prophets, to the urgings of Scripture…. all because "you did not recognise the time of God's coming to you". God has no surprises – just certainties!

"Open our ears, Lord, and help us to listen" (Bob Cull) to what You are saying to us about the state of our nation in these days – and give us courage to seek real change in our institutions and our homes.

October 7

"You did not recognise the time of God's coming"
Luke 19:44 Key passage: Luke 19:28-44

Most men won't stop and ask for directions, insisting that where they are heading "is somewhere round here". It seems to be an insult to male pride to ask for help and for the same reason men often won't go to the doctors, admit defeat, or ask for advice.

Yes, I'm guilty too. But what Jesus has to say to the people of Jerusalem is no laughing matter. Approaching the city, He weeps over it, knowing its coming fate at the hands of those who will destroy it. Such lament is deep since the Lord adds, "you did not recognise the time of God's coming to you." The people of Jerusalem had lost the opportunity for peace – with God as well as their enemies – and there would be consequences. In not many years the Romans would besiege Jerusalem, razing it to the ground. Such would be the destruction that it was said that a plough would be drawn across the centre of the city. They did not listen to Jesus and destruction followed. We need to listen carefully to what God has to say to our generation and when Your Word speaks directly to us and our generation, may we listen and take action,

Lord! Raise up men and women who will speak that Word with truth and power!

When have you failed to listen to advice or take action? What happened? How do you feel about that now? When have you heard God's word and failed to respond to it? What is God saying urgently to us as a nation in these days? What do we need to do?

October 8

"You have made it a den of robbers"
Luke 19:46 Key passage: Luke 19:45-48

In my childhood I attended a church that needed to raise funds and so two enterprising ladies sewed little pouches into material "money belts" to wear. The idea was that every time the sun shone, you popped a coin in one of the pouches and gave the money to the church! I seem to recall that it wasn't a particularly sunny summer that year!

Jesus is offended at what He finds in the temple courts in Jerusalem. It was accepted that worshippers should have the opportunity to make sacrifices there, and business was only allowed in Tyrian currency. What Jesus discovers is that the traders have invaded the temple court of the Gentiles (where non-Jews could pray) when they should have been outside, exacerbated by blatant profiteering. He drives them out in a public display of righteous anger…much to the annoyance of the temple authorities. "My house will be a house of prayer…". The temptation to turn worship into business is pernicious – and our churches are not immune! God is interested in prophets, not profits. What might you need to do to preserve the prayerful purpose of your church?

What does this Scripture say to you about the way your church is financed? What do we believe about giving? What do we actually do about it?

How do you determine what you give? Where does the church fit into that? What should be the purpose of giving? Why does money and its use cause so much resentment in many of us? How can we truly honour God in our giving?

October 9

"John's baptism - from heaven or from men?"
Luke 20:4   Key passage: Luke 20:1-8

"Why do you always answer my question with another question?" Some interviewers are skilled in the art of asking questions having already supplied the answer! Or worse, asking questions to which there is no answer!

Jesus encounters the chief priests, law teachers and elders who come to check out what Jesus is teaching, and His authority for what He is saying. Have they not already known, or at least suspected, the source of His authority? Jesus asks them a question in reply – and puts them on the horns of a dilemma. The issue is the matter of the baptism that John has been offering – is this divinely authentic or merely a human construct? If John's baptism is authentic, then they should have responded to his message. If merely "human" then they risk becoming even more unpopular with the people. So they say nothing!

It's the same dilemma with Jesus and His claims. Is He the Son of God or isn't He? If He is, listen to Him! If He isn't, then ignore him – but listen to those who think otherwise! The question's a good one!

Lord, we need to respond to these big questions, and we cannot remain silent. Save us from a Christianity that is all about man-made rules, and open us instead to a faith that is all about Jesus and who He is!

October 10

"What shall I do? I will send my son"
Luke 20:13 Key passage: Luke 20:9-19

Be assertive – that solves most problems! "I used to be indecisive but now I'm not so sure!" Start as you mean to continue!

Jesus tells the parable of the tenants of the vineyard who exceed their rights and reject all approaches from the owner. The application of the tale is clear. At first glance the actions of the vineyard owner seem indecisive – surely he should have "sorted out" the tenants by recourse to law… they had clearly broken all laws of contract and contact in rejecting every envoy sent to them. But the owner is a gracious man, knowing that such measures would only exacerbate the situation. He decides to send his son to reason with them. But reason is the last thing on the tenants' mind – they are motivated by blind obstinacy. They see merely instant profit for themselves and so the son is killed.

The parallels with Jesus are obvious – speaking of the graciousness of God. At His baptism, the Father declared "You are my son, whom I love" (Luke 3.22) This is the action of an assertive God – what do you say in response?

"God so loved the world that he gave his only begotten Son…" (John 3.16) Father, thank You for giving Jesus and forgiving me!

 What would you say to the person who asks, "Why do you keep talking about this Jesus?"

October 11

"The stone the builders rejected has become the capstone"
Luke 20:17 Key passage: Luke 20:9-19

My first car was a Morris Traveller. It was lovely, simple to maintain and reliable, but it's the only car I've ever sold because of woodworm! I often wonder what happened to it.

We may have things we wish we'd kept – just as much as we probably have things we wonder why we kept them! Jesus responds to the people's questioning of his parable with this powerful quotation from Psalm 118.22 "The stone the builders rejected has become the capstone". The capstone was a foundation stone set at the corner of a building to give it placement and purpose, or it was equally the keystone in an edifice which knitted the structure together and gave it security – either way the image is powerful. The builder now regrets ignoring the stone, and the building is out of kilter. It's an image that Peter returns to in his letter (1 Peter 2.7) and which Luke records in the confrontation of Peter and John before the Sanhedrin (Acts 4:11). The "stone" comes with a "health warning" – "ignore this at your own risk."

Why do people so easily ignore Jesus? What is it about His claims that they find so hard to accept? Why is it so difficult to "build your life on Him"?

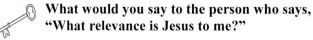 **What would you say to the person who says, "What relevance is Jesus to me?"**

October 12

"Give to Caesar what is Caesar's, give to God what is God's"
Luke 20:25 Key passage: Luke 20:20-26

"It was taken out of context!" Many politicians claim their words are being misunderstood. With the immediacy of social media, you can be in hot water before the words have hardly left your mouth.

The religious authorities are out to get Jesus, sending emissaries to trap him. Their words are so creamy and polite, but you can almost feel the threat coming! It's a question about paying monetary tribute to Rome. It's a question on everyone's lips. Is it right to support this invading power or is resistance the way forward? If Jesus says "no" then He is the ultimate revolutionary – if He says "yes" then they will accuse Him of connivance with Rome. Whatever He says someone will criticise Him…

…except that Jesus' answer is the model of probity, "Give to Caesar what is Caesar's…". The coinage of Israel had been replaced by "dirty" Roman money. If that's what Rome demands, give it to them…for one day it will be worthless. "Give to God what is God's…" for one day it will be priceless. Context is vital, content even more so.

What do you need to give to God today?

October 13

"Out of their wealth...out of her poverty"
Luke 21:4   Key passage: Luke 21:1-4

Ever been in "Poundland" and asked an assistant the price of an item? Sometimes things cost a bit more than you imagine...

...and as Jesus observes worshippers in the temple, He spots something extraordinary – a poor widow making her offering into the collecting box. Plenty of others stopped to put their contribution in, and the coins made a satisfying thud as they fell into the coffers. But for this widow, the tiny chink of two very modest coins could hardly be heard – but Jesus knew what He was hearing. For her, the coins represented her weekly income – she would be attempting to live on next-to-nothing, such was her devotion to God. The rich gave (quite a lot) but it made little difference to them – this was not giving, rather an "incidental expense". For her, this was giving par excellence. When committing an offering to God, I like to ask for God's wisdom both in the use of the money we have given, and in the use of the money we have retained – because it all belongs to Him. Knowing the "price" of giving is knowing the "price" of living!

Teach me, Lord, to give out of sense of joy and generosity rather than a sense of duty...and not to count the cost of blessing You and others!

When does giving really become giving? What about the principle of tithing. Is that realistic? How do our churches practise and model the grace of giving? What are the principles of giving that we need to follow?

October 14

"Not one stone will be left on another"
Luke 21:6   Key passage: Luke 21:5-38

I've always wondered about the plaque in church that commemorates "Those who died in the services." Is church really that boring?

Jesus' disciples are at the temple marvelling at the dedications to wealthy and worthy individuals. Jesus' words bring them up short: "the time will come when not one stone will be left on another…". The Jews loved looking backwards, to the memory of the past, and the stones of the temple were just such a trigger. The money of wealthy people had paid for these stones…and their names would be etched in the memory, if not in the stones themselves. What of tomorrow? Jesus warns of the impending destruction of Jerusalem, and what will all this mean then? "Let us now praise famous men, and our fathers that begat us" is a quotation from the Apocrypha (Ecclesiasticus 44.1) often quoted of the worthies of yesteryear. It's not the stones of yesterday that matter – they will fall. The one stone that really matters is the one that fell from the tomb to enable us to experience the resurrection of the One who died in our service!

Help us, Father God, to sit lightly to the memories of yesterday and the legacy of others – may our legacy be one that will last!

October 15

"Watch out that you are not deceived"
Luke 21:8 Key passage: Luke 21:5-38

Remember Murray Walker, the Formula 1 broadcaster, and his astonishing race descriptions? "And unless I'm very much mistaken…I am very much mistaken!" was the classic. Yet most of his commentaries were gripping and accurate…

…unlike the many commentators on world affairs in every generation. Jesus warns His disciples to be aware of those who pretend to be the Promised One – do not be "deceived". The word speaks of easy seduction into a falsehood. There will always be those who claim a special understanding of the broad sweep of world events and history – and those who believe them! Christians are not immune to this – indeed sometimes Christians are the most gullible of customers! Recent world events show that none of us really have a grasp on what is happening and in common with most politicians, the most we can do is to react to events rather than shape them. The issue is always around the genuineness of Jesus Christ – and the falsehoods peddled by imposters. Jesus' urging is simple and strategic – "keep your eyes open to the possibility of being deceived."

Teach us, Father, to weigh the claims of others against Your standards of truth and justice. Thank You that "Your word is truth" (John 17.17)

How do you decide who is telling you the truth? How does the news differ according to your perspective? Check out the headlines on a few newspapers tomorrow. How do the stories differ? What does this tell us about what we hear and believe? How does that apply to our Christian understanding?

October 16

"When you hear of wars and revolutions, do not be frightened"

Luke 21:9   Key passage: Luke 21:5-38

There have only been 26 days without war somewhere in the world since 1945! If we have never experienced war, it's impossible to imagine the fear, uncertainty, separation, deprivation, suffering, slaughter, pointlessness…

…yet Jesus urges His disciples, "When you hear of wars…do not be frightened." The words used are stronger than the translation conveys. "Wars" speaks of battling, strife, conflict, but in the context of "quarrelling" – words have turned to bitter action. How much "quarrelling" do we hear each day across nations and peoples – about everything from politics to power to passions – inciting jealousy, hatred and anger?

"Revolutions" uses the word "commotion, disorder, instability" which may be understood as "rumours of war". It speaks of a state of unsettlement. Surely it is this state in which the world perpetually exists – always "on the brink" of trouble.

"Frightened" suggests consternation, in a state of terror. That speaks of a fear the earth itself is about to collapse into chaos….

…but Jesus urges calm – "do not be afraid…I have overcome the world" (John 16.33). He should know – He is the Prince of Peace!

Reflect on what the world has been through in the last year. How have events impacted you? What changes have you had to make to your life to cope with such pressures? How has a Christian faith sustained you through these times? Thank God for His love for you in Jesus!

October 17

"Nation will rise against nation"
Luke 21:10 Key passage: Luke 21:5-38

When I was young, stamp-collecting was popular. The thing about collecting stamps is that you collect different stamps. No good collecting stamps all the same – what's the point?

Jesus warns His disciples here that at the End of the Age "nation will rise against nation". The word for "nation" is the word *ethne* – reflecting the distinctives of a people's race. Instead of observing and celebrating the things that unite us, we centre on the things that divide – colour, communication, culture, creed. There's nothing wrong about being different, but there's something very wrong about rejecting differences and insisting that our world-view is the only valid one. At the End of the Age of which Jesus speaks, nations will rise against each other – in aggression, assault, action, alarm. Today our world is "smaller" than it has ever been, yet nations are further apart than ever. Rampant nationalism divides the wealthy, rampant poverty the poor. Leaders struggle to rise above each other in power, popularity and purpose.

Against this backcloth, Jesus comes to stamp His authority with the kingdom of God!

Pray today for the leaders of nations. Whether you agree with their politics or not, pray for them and the daily decisions they have to make, that they might be wise, caring, strong and sure in the way they relate to their peoples and to the leaders of the world.

 Where are the places of war and turmoil today? Try to understand what is going on and why there is such strife, and pray for the nations.

October 18

"I will give you words and wisdom"
Luke 21:15 Key passage: Luke 21:5-38

Public speaking is easy…that's what they said at the Speakers' Club. All you have to do is stand up, open your mouth, and something will come out…! The skill is in honing what comes out!

Jesus reassures His disciples that in the febrile atmosphere of a world in turmoil, His disciples will be under the spotlight for their faith. In such circumstances they are not to worry about how to defend themselves – "I will give you the words and the wisdom…" Now this is not *carte blanche* for preachers' and speakers' lack of preparation – you can probably spot an unprepared preacher a mile off! Such dilatoriness does not commend the gospel, and people end up just being entertained instead of engaged with God's word. What Jesus is talking about here is the situation of hostility to Christians that we may well encounter. Rely on the Holy Spirit to give you words to speak in power, love and grace – and He will honour you! Notice the promise is for both words and wisdom to be given – to know what to say, how to say it, and when to be silent!

Lord, when there is opposition to You and Your truth, grant me by Your Holy Spirit words of truth and wisdom – and a peaceful heart to face the situation.

When have you faced pressure to stand up and be counted as a Christian? What happened, and how were you aware of God's help in that situation? Pray today for those who stand up for Jesus in the home, the workplace, the school or university, and the media.

October 19

"All men will hate you because of me"
Luke 21:17 Key passage: Luke 21:5-38

Phobia – the catchword of twenty-first century living. Strangely the word is now attached to every kind of malaise and especially attitudes of "hatred". The word has unfortunately become a byword for aggressive hatred, when at heart is it about "fear".

Jesus warns His disciples they will experience hatred on His account. Hatred is a very strong emotion, going beyond mere dislike or disdain. It speaks of rejection, of bitterness, of a desire to eliminate. We want to eradicate that which challenges us and exposes our own predilections. Such challenges cause us fear – fear of being found out, of being thought illogical, unacceptable, incorrect.

Jesus Himself experienced such hatred at the hands of men – because they could not understand Him. That's not because He spoke in riddles – rather they did not want to grasp what He was saying! He was too challenging to them – exposing their hypocrisy and greed. So they sought to destroy Him – and at the cross thought they had achieved this. But hatred can never win over love. To be hated as a follower of Jesus may be your experience. But thank God that love wins!

Pray today for Christians in other parts of the world who experience hatred, persecution and violence because of their faith…and pray for those whose hearts are filled with hatred because they cannot accept Jesus.

October 20

"By standing firm you will gain life"
Luke 21:19 Key passage: Luke 21:5-38

It is claimed that among other benefits, good posture can change your physical height. A straight back allows you to stand up to two inches taller, and the world looks a different place from higher up!

Jesus encourages His disciples that despite the trials of life and the challenge of the cost of discipleship, "by standing firm you will gain life". He's not talking about mere physical posture – although sometimes you can tell by people's stances what they feel about themselves! Some people give the impression that they have all the cares of the world on their shoulders – and they probably have! Jesus commends an attitude of constancy, of resolution, of faithfulness. Discipleship isn't about "sticking with it" through gritted teeth – it is about standing firm on the foundation of God's love and faithfulness in every day and in every situation. FAITH is about "Forsaking All, I Trust Him". Of course it's more than that, but it's a helpful reminder. Some of the greatest Christians I know aren't famous names, but people who model gracious constancy in their walk with Jesus – and for me they stand tall!

Lord, help me to "stand tall" today in my walk with You – to rely on the promise of Your forgiveness, peace and purpose in this day.

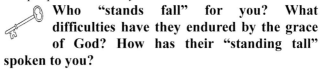 **Who "stands fall" for you? What difficulties have they endured by the grace of God? How has their "standing tall" spoken to you?**

October 21

"When you see Jerusalem…its desolation is near"
Luke 21:20 Key passage: Luke 21:5-38

Jesus speaks of the coming destruction of Jerusalem (which would happen in AD70) at the hands of the Romans. It was an event of global and catastrophic proportions. Josephus, the Roman historian, records the magnitude of this event – the capital surrounded by Roman armies and because of the resistance of the inhabitants, the city was literally taken apart stone by stone. So desperate were the citizens, being starved, that they resorted to cannibalism. Some 1.1 million people perished in the siege that followed, and over 97,000 of them were taken away into captivity.

It's hard to imagine, but in our own generation we are experiencing a global pandemic with over 2.75 million people dead from coronavirus already, with 126 million cases worldwide. The First and Second World Wars tolls are equally staggering. We cannot imagine such numbers…

So when Jesus speaks of Jerusalem, He speaks with foresight and frankness. What can we learn from these words today? Quite simply, read the signs of the times...and trust in the God who holds all history in His hands!

Lord, the numbers are beyond my comprehension, but each life is known and valued by You. Help me to "read" what is happening in the world today as I pray for this world and all whose lives are in turmoil because of disease, virus, war, hunger, hatred and death.

October 22

"Nations will be in anguish"
Luke 21:25 Key passage: Luke 21:5-38

Read this verse carefully and prayerfully. "Nations will be in anguish and perplexity at the roaring and tossing of the sea…". So what's this got to do with us right now?

The translation of the words here leaves something to be desired. "Nations" refers to the ethnic origins of the people – and right now the world is in turmoil over issues of race, colour and ethnicity. This world is uptight with tension – and it's not just over skin colour. Nations vie with each other over independence and immunisations. These nations are in "anguish" – the word speaks of "being in a state of constriction or confinement" - sound familiar? Borders are closed, the streets are empty, the towns and people besieged. Added to this, Jesus describes the nations as being in "perplexity" – the word speaks of being at a standstill, without means to survive. The leaders of nations seem stunned into inaction and uncertainty. What to do…? "Put your hand in the hand of the man who stilled the water."

In the middle of these years of global pandemic, we are in "anguish". Give wisdom to governments to make decisions that will benefit all people, to doctors to know how to treat the sick, to business leaders to know how to support their employees, to families to know how to love their children.

What has the "anguish of the nations" meant to you? How have you been impacted? What issues do the nations face today? In what have you found reassurance in these days?

October 23

"Lift up your heads...your redemption is drawing near"
Luke 21:28 Key passage: Luke 21:5-38

"The darkest hour is just before the dawn" (Thomas Fuller, 1650) is a reminder that in the most extreme of difficulties, hope should never be lost. Jesus has already spoken (verse 26) of the signs of the times at the End of the Age – "the heavenly bodies will be shaken..." Is it really true that it's always darkest just before the dawn? Scientists tell us apparently not, since the light of dawn is coming – but in that hour before sunrise, the moon has often disappeared, so the darkness seems more intense. In waking at that moment, what to do? Tempting to pull up the covers and close your eyes again...

But the word of Jesus is the opposite! "Lift up your heads..." The word used speaks of physical and spiritual lifting of the head, a call to encouragement, an urging to animation. In other words, that's the moment to rouse – it's time to get up! Why? "Because your redemption is drawing near". God has paid the price for your redemption in Christ – and at this moment, liberation for eternity is yours. It's time to wake up to reality!

Lord, when I feel overwhelmed by all the bad news and the confusion in the world, remind me that eternity is just a breath away! And in that eternity my redemption to You will be completed!

October 24

"Know that the kingdom of God is near"
Luke 21:31 Key passage: Luke 21:5-38

"Are we there yet?" Every parent knows the plaintive question emanating from the back seat of the car. Journeys can seem so long sometimes.

Jesus is aware of the questions emanating from the "back-seat" disciples concerning the coming kingdom. They couldn't understand "where" this kingdom was, let alone how it might "come". For them interpreting the times in which they lived was difficult enough – a confusion which we might share in our own generation! Jesus draws their attention to the fig tree – when leaves appear "see for yourselves…that summer is near". The fig tree was a symbol of Israel itself (see Joel 2.22) and its fruitfulness a symbol of God's blessing. When do we see God's kingdom coming? Look at the signs of the times (verses 25-27). God comes in living power in the middle of global turmoil and human terror. God comes in power and purpose, bringing healing and wholeness to broken lives and a breaking world. Are we there yet? Read the signs!

Thank God for those who have found Him in the middle of crisis and global turmoil – and thank Him for your renewed sense of God's presence with you throughout these days!

 How has your own faith developed in the last few months or years? What has helped you to grow in your knowledge of God? What does it mean to you now to be a follower of Jesus? What have you learned through tough times?

October 25

"Heaven and earth will pass away…"
Luke 21:33 Key passage: Luke 21:5-38

As a pastor I'm intrigued by the language we use to describe the fact of death and dying. That's not a morbid fascination, just a curiosity as to how many ways we can describe the brutality of death. We speak of "passing over", "going outside", "sailing over the horizon". Our Salvation Army friends speak of being "promoted to glory" – and the phrase "passing away" is commonly used.

Yet when Jesus uses this phrase, it's not in the context of dying, but in the context of divine fulfilment. "Heaven and earth will pass away…" For some these words come as something of a shock, since we imagine Scripture teaches the eternal nature of heaven – but Jesus is speaking of heaven as the celestial creation of the earth, planets and stars. They will all ultimately disappear! As vast as they are, as gigantic as the sun is, as distant as they appear, they are all on a finite path. By contrast, Jesus declares "My words will never pass away". He who is the living Word is Lord for eternity, and what He has to say stands for ever. Listen carefully!

God, the One who holds the planets, stars and galaxies in His hand as if dust, hold me in Your hand for now and for eternity. May I find security in knowing that I am your child – now and for ever!

 What does it mean to you that your future is safe in God's hand? How would you explain this hope to someone who does not know God personally?

October 26

"Be always on the watch"
Luke 21:36 Key passage: Luke 21:5-38

As a student I once had a job working 12-hour night shifts. The pay was decent – the job totally boring! About three o'clock in the morning it was difficult staying awake, especially when you had nothing to do, waiting for a colleague to tell you when to press a certain button…

Jesus urges His disciples to "be always on the watch" during days of global turmoil. What are they to "watch" for? He warns against "dissipation, drunkenness and anxieties of life". Rather a mixed bag of human experience there! "Dissipation" is debauchery or "hangover", and "drunkenness" speaks for itself. Before you protest that neither of these is a problem for you, beware! I've seen too many committed Christians fall into just such a trap. Never say "Never"! Whatever they are, "the anxieties of life" are a much more insidious temptress, easily overtaking any of us in our concern about our money, friendships, careers, possessions and responsibilities.

Be on the watch – by being alert to the greater reality of the purposes of God for you. His kingdom is near – we pray "Your kingdom come". Be awake to God's presence in you today!

Pray for those who have fallen prey to the temptress of drink – especially in an attempt to deal with their anxieties – and pray that you may never be overtaken by anxiety in such a way.

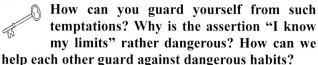 **How can you guard yourself from such temptations? Why is the assertion "I know my limits" rather dangerous? How can we help each other guard against dangerous habits?**

October 27

"Go and make preparations for the Passover…"
Luke 22:8   Key passage: Luke 22:7-23

"Christmas comes but once a year…" and it's less than two months away! You will either be prepared or panicking! Whichever, the enjoyment is in the build-up – the event is after all just one day!

Jesus tells His disciples to prepare for the Passover. The preparation is as important as the celebration. Since the Passover was quite a complicated meal, there would be much to get and prepare – meat, herbs, bones, bread, wine…The set-up of the room for the meal was vital – the meal was to be eaten reclining, so appropriate furniture would be obtained and arranged. There would be the invitations to issue, given that this was a community event – so it was not unusual for a large number, both family and friends, to gather at the table.

For Jesus' disciples, the first question was one of location, although it seems that Jesus has already made some arrangement with a host in his guest room. The Master knows His destiny, and He is anxious to share this moment with His disciples. Jesus prepares Himself for the path that will lead to Gethsemane, Calvary…and resurrection!

Lord Jesus, thank You that you were prepared for Passover, for Calvary, for resurrection and for glory! Thank You that You held me in Your heart at every moment – and that even now You are preparing me for heaven.

October 28

"A man carrying a jar of water will meet you..."
Luke 22:10 Key passage: Luke 22:7-23

Delegation is the name of the game. Jonathan Swift ("*On poetry: a Rhapsody*" 1733) originated the lines "so, nat'ralists observe, a flea hath smaller fleas that on him prey, and these have smaller yet to bite 'em, and so proceed ad infinitum…" Why do the work when you can get someone else to do it for you?

It was this principle that perhaps surprised the disciples on this day as Jesus sent them to prepare for the Passover meal in Jerusalem. "Where?" they asked. "A man carrying a jar of water will meet you…" that was the distinctive surprise – carrying water jars was women's work! Maybe Jesus had already arranged with this house-owner the use of his upper guest room, but this seems an unusual way for the disciples to identify the host. Maybe the water-bearing was symbolic of something – the man bearing an unusual burden would lead them to the place of welcome and safety. In a few hours' time, the Man bearing the burden of sin would break bread with them and lead them to the place of remembrance and sacrifice, before going to the cross.

"Bearing shame and scoffing rude, in my place condemned He stood; sealed my pardon with His blood – Hallelujah! What a Saviour!"

 What burden has Jesus taken for you – and what do you need to give Him today?

October 29

"Where is the guest room?"
Luke 22:11 Key passage: Luke 22:7-23

Pastoral visiting is a dying art. In my early years as a pastor, each afternoon was devoted to visiting. I would be shown into the visitor's "front room" – neat and tidy, formal, and often rather cold! I much preferred sitting in someone's warm kitchen.

Jesus comes to Jerusalem to celebrate the Passover with His disciples. During Passover, all accommodation in Jerusalem was free – house owners were expected to share their rooms as part of their national collective celebration. Some larger houses had a parlour above the entrance for special occasions, and this was one such occasion. Jesus has arranged the use of this particular location for the Passover meal. The term "guest room" indicates a place of temporary abode, and comes from a word concerning the place of dissolution – where the "latest meal" would be eaten before continuing on one's journey. The disciples could not have fully understood the significance of this meal, but they would with hindsight. For them, still trying to understand Jesus' destiny, this was just another Passover. For us, it becomes significant. We are now invited into that "upper room" by His sacrifice, death and resurrection.

Which room of your "house" would you invite Jesus in to…and which "rooms" would you rather avoid? Remember He invites us into His guest room.

"If Jesus came to your house..." What sort of challenge would that present to you? Why would we more gladly open up certain parts of our life than others? What about the "rooms" of our churches?

October 30

"I have eagerly desired to eat this with you"
Luke 22:15 Key passage: Luke 22:7-23

"Guess how much I love you" is a masterpiece of children's storytelling from Sam McBratney about the Nutbrown Hares trying to find a way to express the inexpressible – with the declaration "I love you right up to the moon – and back". The author's task was to write a story book using hardly any words and this was the astonishing result.

Jesus addresses His disciples using hardly any words in this Last Supper. What is telling is the introduction – "I have eagerly desired to eat this with you". Jesus twice uses the word "desire" to underline the earnestness of His longing to be with His disciples in this moment. For Him this is a pivotal moment on his journey to Calvary – the moment when He takes bread and wine in loving remembrance of God's grace to His people centuries before in the act of Passover salvation, and imbues them with new and dynamic symbolism of His coming act of Paschal salvation on the cross. We cannot underestimate the significance of this moment – this is how much God loves us!

"Now my heart's desire is to know You more…"
(Graham Kendrick)

October 31

"I will not drink again until the kingdom of God comes"
Luke 22:18 Key passage: Luke 22:7-23

When did you last see your family? For those who lived through a World War, the answer may be measured in years. For those who have lived through a global pandemic, it's probably measured in months – but either way separation is difficult…

…and for Jesus the realisation of what is to happen brings Him to this moment of intimacy with His disciples at the Passover table. The sharing of the cup symbolizes all that God's people share and have known. At the Jewish Passover meal, four cups of wine are taken. Luke refers to Jesus sharing more than one cup, but this first cup is the one of which Jesus remarks that He will not partake of this with His disciples again "until the kingdom of God comes". The cup symbolizes life, the wine the very lifeblood that gives meaning. Sharing the cup is a recognition and act of fellowship. Jesus shares His life with us as His disciples…and one day He will do so again, but in glory…with His family. Now that's a day worth waiting for!

Lord Jesus, thank You that You invited Your disciples to share that cup with You then, that You share that cup with us in the act of communion now, and one day we shall share it with You in glory. Keep us looking forward to that day!

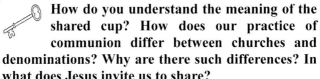 **How do you understand the meaning of the shared cup? How does our practice of communion differ between churches and denominations? Why are there such differences? In what does Jesus invite us to share?**

NOVEMBER 1

"This is my body given for you"
Luke 22:19 Key passage: Luke 22:7-23

Strange, isn't it? The very act of Jesus sharing the bread with His disciples with the words "This is my body" – the ultimate act of fellowship and the sacrament that should unite all Christian believers – has sadly become a tool of division. Some maintain the belief that the bread actually becomes the body of Jesus (transubstantiation) and can therefore only be handled by the ordained celebrant. Others suggest that this is merely symbolic and the bread remains bread. A few denominations do not share bread or wine at all. For others, it is an exclusive act, and only believers are allowed to be present…

…but read the words again! "This is my body given for you…" There is purpose in the promise. "Given for you…" Jesus is looking forwards. Passover is looking backwards. He dynamically fulfils the Passover rite and foretells the resurrection promise. Passover reminds of deliverance – Calvary reminds of destiny. Jesus gives himself in fulfilment of the prophetic word through Isaiah of the suffering servant "he poured out his life unto death…and bore the sin of many!" (Isaiah 53.12). That's Jesus – giving Himself for you!

"Broken for me, broken for you" (Colin and Janet Lunt). Thank You, Lord Jesus, that there is something so compelling in Your gift to us – and one day we shall know the full reality of resurrection expressed in that broken bread. Hallelujah!

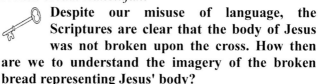 **Despite our misuse of language, the Scriptures are clear that the body of Jesus was not broken upon the cross. How then are we to understand the imagery of the broken bread representing Jesus' body?**

November 2

"Do this in remembrance of me"
Luke 22:19 Key passage: Luke 22:7-23

Dissectology – not something practiced in the biology lab or post mortem room – it's the science of jigsaws! Some people find the pastime addictive, others struggle to understand! But there's something satisfying about reassembling the picture and recreating a work of art.

When Jesus shared the Passover meal with His disciples, He shared the bread with the words "Do this in remembrance of me". The disciples may have looked at each other in puzzlement – for Jesus was still with them. Soon after He would be taken and crucified – were they to remember this moment with Him, or remember something greater?

"Remembering" can be difficult at the best of times! The action literally means "piecing back together" something that is lost or past. Some have suggested that the communion (shadowing the Last Supper) is akin to a Christian "poppy day", but since none of us were there for the original event, how can we remember? We can and do remember, for in the sacrifice of Jesus, we see and recall God's staggering love gift to a broken world. Just like the jigsaw, we have the full picture in Jesus of God's love!

"Give me a sight, my Saviour, of Your wondrous love to me, of the love that brought You down to earth to die on Calvary…" (Katherine Kelly)

 How does sharing in bread and wine help us remember Jesus and His sacrifice? What do you find helpful to think of or recall in the act of taking bread and wine?

November 3

"This is the new covenant in my blood"
Luke 22:10 Key passage: Luke 22:7-23

"Terms and conditions." The small print is what most of us pass over to get to the important stuff, but it's often in the small print that the details lie…ignore them at your peril!

Jesus shares the cup of wine with the revelation "this is the new covenant in my blood". The old accepted understanding of the Passover ritual was that God had made His covenant with His people in the blood of the lambs spread on the doorposts protecting them from the angel of death that passed over Egypt all those centuries previously. The blood acted as the guarantee of acceptability before God, the deposit that secured the contract. The "cup of salvation" shared at Passover not only looks back in thanksgiving for God's saving act, but also looks forward in triumph to God's saving act in Jesus Christ. By "drinking this cup" Jesus takes on Himself the role of Redeemer, and by our sharing this cup we receive His lifegiving power. So when you next share in communion, remember the God who remembered you: you're in the "small print"!

We are "sealed" into God's contract of salvation through the blood of Jesus. "Thank You, O my Father, for giving us Your Son!" (Keith Green)

November 4

" …which is poured out for you…"
Luke 22:20 Key passage: Luke 22:7-23

"It never rains for what it pours…" – a common saying with a most uncommon origin! It came from the Morton Salt Company of America in the early 1900's, when they started adding magnesium carbonate to make their salt pour more freely even in damp conditions.

Jesus shares the cup of salvation with His disciples at this last Passover meal before his crucifixion, knowing that "it's about to rain". As with all elements, the cup and the wine are deeply symbolic for the Jew. The cup represents life in all that it contains, the wine the lifeblood by which we live. Clearly the wine needs to be poured into the cup for it to be shared out, but the pouring is symbolic too. You will know from experience you can't get liquid back into its container once spilled…("don't cry over spilled milk"!). This wine representing the new covenant in Jesus' blood is "poured out" for each of us – it's not just "given", it's fully "poured out". He gives His all! Thank God that beyond the cross lies the empty tomb. That's why God's grace "runs freely"!

Father, it's beyond words that You should "pour out" the life of Your only Son to win forgiveness for us all. Thank You that this act of sacrifice finds its fulfilment and completion in the resurrection.

How do you react to the realisation that Jesus "poured out His life" for you whether you acknowledge Him or not? What does that teach us about the grace of God? What is a right response to such grace?

November 5

"The hand of him…is with mine on the table"
Luke 22:21 Key passage: Luke 22:7-23

1973 – Britain joins the European Economic Community and issues a commemorative fifty pence piece depicting nine hands clasped together in a circle of friendship. Whose hands they are we don't know and which is the British one is a matter of opinion. The coins, however, have become valuable as a piece of history. Once upon a time we trusted each other…

At the table of the Passover thirteen hands shared the bread and wine. Twelve of them can be identified – the thirteenth was a mystery, but Jesus declared that this hand would betray him. Inevitably there was suspicion – "Is it I, Lord?" and suspense. The words of Jesus raise the question, "Who's telling the truth?" for the act of betrayal is the ultimate lie. The words of Jesus also reveal the ultimate answer – that Jesus knows the hearts of His children. What Judas thought or felt at this moment is not revealed, the Lord knows every thought of the mind and attitude of the heart. Time to hold up your hands and grasp His trustworthy hand!

Lord, when I try hard to hide my thoughts, remind me that You know everything about me. You know my intentions, desires and ambitions. Forgive me and make me right with You!

November 6

"Woe to that man who betrays him"
Luke 22:22 Key passage: Luke 22:7-23

The story is told of the domestic servant called to account before the master of the house for an unfortunate accident. "It's not my fault, sir," the servant stammered, "I wasn't holding the tray when it hit the floor!" Blame is definitely something to be avoided…

…yet Jesus, speaking of His impending betrayal at the hands of one of His disciples, laments. "Woe to that man…". These are not words of vengeance but regret, not words of venom, but reflection. The fact is that the betrayer is responsible for his actions and their consequences. Some argue about the place of God and His will in the actions of Judas – as if Judas was some kind of automaton. How often do we "blame God" for things that have happened when the choice was entirely ours? We are an awkward jumble as human beings – wanting freedom to make our own choices, then blaming God when those choices backfire! Judas will have to bear the burden of his choice – which leads to his own miserable demise. It's all his fault – he was responsible when things hit the floor!

Lord, help me to understand that I am responsible for my actions, words and thoughts when things go wrong. I ask Your forgiveness for when I let You down and betray my lack of trust in You.

When have you tried to blame someone else for your own actions and mistakes? Think of some of the popular excuses given when things have gone wrong? Why do we try to put the blame on someone else? What does that tell us about the human mind and heart?

November 7

"You are not to be like that"
Luke 22:26 Key passage: Luke 22:24-38

You may, be aware of the game "Mornington Crescent" beloved of fans of the radio show "I'm Sorry I Haven't A Clue!" No one has ever understood the rules of "Mornington Crescent" because there aren't any! Normal rules don't apply…

Jesus answers a dispute between the disciples as to which of them might be considered the greatest. What a futile game! Jesus speaks of the way the Gentiles regard power and authority. Status and titles are everything. It's odd how people defer to you when you have a standing in society. Jesus speaks of the "kings of the Gentiles" (those who are outside God's people) as being called "Benefactors" – the word means a "well-doer", someone who has some kind of benefit conferred on them by their status. It's that kind of status the disciples, blinded by their own ambitions, seek for themselves.

"You are not to be like that," Jesus warns. The hallmark of disciples is to be humility, honesty, honour. There's no room for personal status in the kingdom – Jesus will be all in all. So think again – you do have a clue how to play the game!

Save me from a futile quest for status and regard by others, and teach me Lord what true humility looks like!

November 8

"I am among you as one who serves"
Luke 22:27 Key passage: Luke 22:24-38

I was listening to a radio discussion yesterday about the practice of tipping waiters. There was general consensus it might be better to increase prices and share the profits with all the staff since those who worked in the "backroom" were as worthy of reward as those in the public eye. In the end, it all depends on the view of the customer.

Jesus reclined at the table with His disciples for the Passover meal, and after the formalities the conversation turned to the inconsequential things – like who was the greatest of them there! In ordinary times such a matter might have been thought to be mere "man talk", but this is not an ordinary moment. Jesus has just spoken of the deeds of a betrayer among them…and they are curious to know which of them could possibly be the likeliest to do this. So, from the least to the greatest the conversation swings, and then Jesus reveals that He who is the Christ is here not to be served, but to serve. He is not engaging in mere "man talk" – He comes to serve us on the cross. What a "waiter"!

"This is our God, the servant king…" (Graham Kendrick). Thank you, Jesus for serving us in life and death, in order to bring us into the knowledge of God and the power of His forgiveness.

Why do we find the notion of "servanthood" so difficult to grasp? What is it in the human psyche that craves recognition? Why do we need constant affirmation? How do you resolve this conflict in your own life?

November 9

"You are those who have stood by me…"
Luke 22:28 Key passage: Luke 22:24-38

Supporting your local football team takes a bit of commitment. Our team is one of those "yo-yo" teams – one season we win promotion, the next we are relegated again. At least we know that each year something different will probably happen.

Jesus commends His disciples in this intimate conversation at the table, teaching them the importance of faithfulness. "You are those who have stood by me in my trials…" – if only that were completely true! Among His disciples is one, Peter, whose enthusiasm for discipleship is matched only by his uncertainty about so much of it and his denial of Jesus. Then there's James and John, the "sons of thunder" whose cure for anything was violence. Matthew was the bad boy tax collector turned good (can we trust him?), Thomas the doubter, Simon the Zealot (keen as mustard but always a bit dubious), Bartholomew who didn't do much at all…you get the picture. There was only one who achieved anything – Judas the financier. And then…

"You…have stood by me…" Gracious words from a gracious Saviour. Where do we stand? Jesus, You know my heart that I want to serve You and stand up for You in a disbelieving world. Teach me integrity – to be what I say I am, and to do what I mean to do.

November 10

"I confer on you a kingdom"
Luke 22:29 Key passage: Luke 22:24-38

Ever had a "signal moment", one of those occasions when something changed? You got the job/received your degree/passed your test…you remember where you were when it happened, when you heard.

The disciples won't or shouldn't forget this moment when Jesus announces His bequest to them – "a kingdom". What have they done to deserve this? Very little and yet Jesus entrusts the kingdom to them. They are to be what they proclaim – citizens of heaven. That's what Jesus tells them so that "you may eat and drink at my table…and sit on thrones…". Some of the disciples were thrilled at this news…without grasping what this meant. They thought they were in with something big…they were, but the kingdom comes with a price! In the very next breath, Simon Peter betrays his lack of understanding. He will never let Jesus down!

We are "heirs of this kingdom" – see Romans 8.17 where Paul also reminds us that "if…we share in his sufferings…we may also share in his glory". This is a "signal moment". God signals His gift to us. You are an heir to His kingdom!

What a gift – I am an heir to the kingdom of God! Lord, may I truly reflect Your love and grace – not just in the good times, but in the times of testing and trial.

What does it mean to you to "receive the kingdom"? How did you feel when you received some kind of accolade, reward, recognition? How does this this gift of the kingdom differ? Why does this gift last so much longer?

November 11

"Simon, Satan has asked to sift you as wheat…"
Luke 22:31 Key passage: Luke 2:24-38

You wait ages for a bus, then two come along at once. In the battle of life, troubles often don't come in pairs, they seem to come in threes! Are you struggling with a load of problems right now? Take comfort from the experience of Peter.

Jesus addresses him twice – "Simon, Simon…" There's an earnestness in Jesus' voice as He addresses him. This is really important – listen carefully! Whilst all four gospels record this matter, Luke focuses on the place of Satan in Peter's trials. "Satan has asked to sift you as wheat." Notice that Satan has no right of interference on Peter's life – it is God who allows Peter to face this trial for his own strengthening and endurance. We may struggle to understand that, but remember God's promise – He will not allow any of us to suffer beyond the level of our endurance. All the disciples will suffer – that's the way of Christian obedience – but for Peter those trials will be severe. "Sifting as wheat" indicates successive trials. Peter seems an unlikely candidate for this, but Jesus loves him deeply. Take heart in your own struggles!

Lord, when it's me struggling with testing times, I find it hard to remember that You are right there and want to strengthen me though this. I give to you the things I'm wrestling with – refine in me Your spirit of love and endurance.

November 12

"I have prayed for you…"
Luke 22:32 Key passage: Luke 22:24-38

Finishing a conversation is an acquired skill, and I know people who don't know how to do it! Saying to someone "I'll pray for you" is quite a useful tool. The problem is remembering to do it!

Jesus assures Simon Peter that He has prayed for him "that your faith may not fail". The word used speaks of "eclipsing" or "lapsing". Faith is easy when not under pressure. But when it comes to the crunch, what happens? Remember the words of the writer to the Hebrews – "faith is being sure of what we hope for and certain of what we do not see" (Hebrews 11.1). How easily faith dims under pressure, and we lose sight of the presence of God in the most difficult of times. Peter will experience great testing, but he has Jesus on His side! He has prayed for him. How awesome to know that at the cross Jesus prayed for us personally and powerfully! Instead of being eclipsed, is it not true that often faith can burn more brightly in the times of greatest darkness? When Jesus says "I'll pray for you" He means it.

Lord, I'm humbled that You pray for me each and every day – and it all started at the cross. Thank you for holding me in Your heart right now – help me to find strength in the knowledge of Your prayer for me.

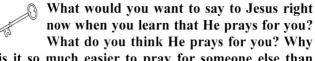 **What would you want to say to Jesus right now when you learn that He prays for you? What do you think He prays for you? Why is it so much easier to pray for someone else than for yourself?**

November 13

"When you have turned back, strengthen your brothers"
Luke 22:32 Key passage: Luke 22:24-38

Captain Mainwaring (*Dad's Army*) was delighted to learn his platoon was detailed for "special duties" on weekend exercises, but less enamoured when he discovered they were running the cookhouse!

Jesus addresses Peter in loving and unique words – "When you have turned back, strengthen your brothers". The word for turning back indicates a change of direction – it's the word used of conversion. Peter is going to face extreme testing, which will push him to the very edge of faith and trust. There will be moments when Peter will verge on forsaking Jesus – yet Jesus will not forsake him. Jesus has a special task for him in the coming kingdom and the birth of the church - a task of encouragement and strengthening. The word Jesus uses for "strengthen" is a fascinating word, indicating "setting fast", "rendering mentally steadfast", "standing immovable". This Peter, so unsure and "wobbly", will be the "rock" of the fledgling church and its source of encouragement. "Special duties" indeed! What might this steadfast God want to do through "wobbly" you?

Lord, I'm rather staggered that You have "special duties" for me! Grant me grace to see my purpose for You today in some special way – and then strength to do it with all my might!

November 14

"When I sent you…did you lack anything?"
Luke 22:35 Key passage: Luke 22:24-38

"Lord, here am I…send someone else!" Strange, isn't it, but when the call goes out for help with something, we can think of a host of reasons why it's not us that should respond. The reasoning? We don't have the time, the energy, the skills, the impulse to do it.

When Jesus tackles the disciples' wavering uncertainty about their task, He asks them whether they have ever wanted for anything in their past commitment to Him? When He sent them out to proclaim the good news of the kingdom, He deliberately sent them with meagre resources – no purse, bag or sandals (see Luke 9.3, 10.4). They were to rely on God's gracious provision mediated through the generosity of others. This was no "business trip" with attendant perks – this was kingdom business! Now they may need the very things necessary for the situation and God knows that. They needed to learn the lesson the apostle Paul learned many years later – to be content with whatever lot was his (see Philippians 4.11). God knows your needs today and He meets them!

When the clutter of life gets in the way of serving You, Lord help me to see what it is that I really need for my living today.

 What do you really need to live this day for Jesus? What are the real essentials? What are you to do with the "non-essentials"?

November 15

"He was numbered with the transgressors"
Luke 22:37 Key passage: Luke 22:24-38

"Are you normal?" How do you answer that? The good news is, "I'm the only normal one here!" We like to be accepted, to be thought of as "normal" although we also want to be a bit distinctive in some way.

In this Last Supper discourse with His disciples, Jesus reveals something unique. He uses the words of the prophet Isaiah of Himself (Isaiah 53.12) by identifying in His death with all sinners. His death is to be on behalf of all men. "He was numbered…" - He counts as "one of us". This means that Jesus stands in our place, as a substitute. Does that mean that He becomes something that He isn't? Well, yes, except that He is because He takes on Himself full humanity and carries the weight of human guilt (our guilt) all the way to the cross. This is the mystery of God incarnate – God "in human shoes". So who's the "normal" one now – you and I with our guilt, or Jesus with His atoning love? Remember – He is what we become!

What a mystery – there is a man in heaven right now, the man Christ Jesus, the Son of God, who intercedes for me before the Father, and only He can do this because He is also fully divine. Praise You, Lord, for being "numbered" with me!

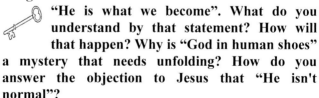 **"He is what we become". What do you understand by that statement? How will that happen? Why is "God in human shoes" a mystery that needs unfolding? How do you answer the objection to Jesus that "He isn't normal"?**

November 16

"What is written about me is reaching its fulfilment"
Luke 22:37 Key passage: Luke 22:24-38

25th June is a significant date – you're equidistant from last Christmas and the next one! Depending on your age, you look backwards with delight or perhaps forwards with despair.

Jesus is looking forwards when He speaks these words to His disciples. "The end is near" is the literal translation of His words. He sees the words of Isaiah spoken long before as now awaiting fulfilment in His coming fate. But is this the end or the beginning? To speak of "the end" evokes finality – there is nothing more beyond. But this cannot be true for Jesus, and is certainly not the Christian hope. "End" also means "purpose" or "intent". Jesus speaks of His total identification with sinners on the cross. This is His purpose, and was spoken of by prophets long ago. This is His moment, when He knows the reason He came to earth will become clear, the moment of God's anointing and appointment, the moment when the plan of salvation is fulfilled in the pain of surrender, the moment when God puts us in the centre of His will. This is a significant day!

The "end" or the "beginning"? Thank You, Lord, that Your "end" has become our "beginning" - and we may know new hope in the fulfilment of the prophetic word about You.

November 17

"That is enough"
Luke 22:38 Key passage: Luke 22:24-38

It's surprising how in a tight situation, the use of a degree of force is effective. "When in doubt, hit it with a hammer."

The disciples would have made excellent DIY experts – their solution to an issue is to exert brute force. In that, they are like most men! Not for the first time, they suggest aggression to deal with a situation. Peter carried a sword for some sort of personal protection – as the High Priest's servant discovered! Here the disciples, not quite understanding the power of Jesus' words, suggest force will deal with the situation. Jesus' retort is short and to the point "That is enough…" The words pre-echo those that will fall from His lips on the cross within hours - "It is done" literally "That is enough!" The will of God is fulfilled in this moment, and for the disciples, who think there must be another way, "that is enough". What might we need to hear from the lips of the Saviour in response to our own struggles with life – "that is enough"?

When I'm tempted to sort out the world and all my problems with brute force, teach me Lord the grace of Your way – the Lord who has done "enough"!

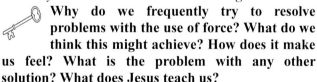 **Why do we frequently try to resolve problems with the use of force? What do we think this might achieve? How does it make us feel? What is the problem with any other solution? What does Jesus teach us?**

November 18

"Pray that you will not fall into temptation"
Luke 22:40 Key passage: Luke 22:39-46

"Lead us not into temptation…" How many times have you prayed that prayer and not quite understood what you were asking? None of us would wish to be "led into temptation", but then we may wonder if that's something God's actually in the business of doing. The prayer does go on asking God to "deliver us from evil…" – as if He's some kind of lifeboat service when we mess things up.

The prayer of Jesus here for His disciples at the Mount of Olives is profound. It's much more than a prayer that they may avoid the challenging tests and temptations that life throws up – these words are prayed in agonised realisation of what the coming crucifixion will mean and Jesus, bearing that agony and wrestling in His soul, prays that His disciples may not have to follow the same path. Thank God that because of Jesus we will not have to! We will not have to face separation from God, the wrath of His judgement, and eternity without Him. Thank God for the hope we have in Jesus.

Lord Jesus, thank You that You willingly walked that path to the cross, bearing the shame and taking the punishment that should have been mine, in order that I may never have to do that. Teach me just what it meant for You to do that and become my Saviour!

November 19

"Father if you are willing…"
Luke 22:42 Key passage: Luke 22:39-46

"Oh, what a tangled web we weave, when first we practice to deceive!" (Sir Walter Scott, 1808). How we struggle, not just with ourselves, but with God in seeking to determine His path for us through life. We talk as though the will of God is something mysterious which we must interpret without the Codebreakers Handbook. God has a will for each of us, a general will which the Scripture describes in accordance with the gracious heart of God, and a specific will unique to each of us. That doesn't mean that God has somehow "pre-programmed" us like some automaton and there is no deviation, as these words of Jesus illustrate…

"Father, if you are willing" shows that Jesus Himself struggles with His Father's will, but He does so from a clear understanding of God's divine purpose for Him. The "secret" of knowing God's will is hidden in the first word here – "Father…" Jesus' trust in the goodness, gentleness, grace and greatness of His Father is absolute, whatever the horror of the cross about to be unleashed, He trusts His Father and His divine will. There's no deceit in God.

Teach me, Father, to trust in You and Your will for me, knowing that Your heart is one of goodness and grace. If today the road is hard and rocky, go with me as in every day, and may I know Your presence in a special way.

Why did Jesus pray this prayer? Was He uncertain about God's will, or was He struggling with it? How do you react to the revealing of God's will? Is it easier to try and avoid it?

November 20

" ...take this cup from me..."
Luke 22:42 Key passage: Luke 22:39-46

We've lived in our current home for ten years, but this afternoon we discovered a new local footpath. We've walked past the end of it countless times, and wondered where it went, but now we know. That was only by accident because we saw someone disappear down it from the other end, and wondered where they were going.

We are creatures of habit – think of how you have always performed a certain task, the routes you've always travelled, the things you've always done, and never really asked "Is there another way?" That's the question Jesus asks of His Father in this moment of agony over the looming cross – "if it's possible, take this cup from me..." Find another way! The cup of salvation becomes the cup of suffering. But the cup of suffering leads to the cup of salvation! If God is to bring redemption to a broken world, it begins with a broken Saviour dying in redemptive love. Jesus could have turned His back on Calvary at that moment, but in loving obedience He walked the "path of obedience all the way to death." Now we know where it leads...!

Jesus, thank You for this reminder that the cross was no easy choice for You, but one of agony and rejection – yet You chose it in obedience. When I want to avoid the difficult and uncertain choices, grant me courage and grace to go with You.

November 21

"Yet not my will, but yours be done"
Luke 22:42 Key passage: Luke 22:39-46

I used to love pear drops – the sort they sold loose in sweet shops. I can still see them now, smell them, and remember the noise as the assistant poured them out of the big jar onto the scales and then deftly shot them into a white paper bag, twisted the ends and placed the bag on the counter.

It was when the scales tipped that I knew they were mine…I could already taste them! As Jesus prays in agony in the garden, He comes to that "scale-tipping" moment where, having laid before God His honest horror at the cross and asked if there is any other way to win salvation, He yields to God's divine will – "not my will but yours…" That takes courage, humility, honesty. How often have we asked God to reveal us His will, but followed some other preferable way? Then having followed our own way, we wonder why we are not in the place of contentment or peace. For Jesus, the scales have tipped, and the will of God is in His hands.

"He humbled himself and became obedient to death – even death on a cross!" (Philippians 2.8). Forgive me, Lord, when in my obstinacy I go on my own way, and then dare to ask where You are in the middle of my turmoil! Teach me the need to follow in the Father's footsteps.

When we pray "Your kingdom come, Your will be done" what do we imagine we are asking? What is the cost of exploring God's will?

November 22

"Why are you sleeping?"
Luke 22:46 Key passage: Luke 22:39-46

"Imposter syndrome" is not a new invention! The reality of the condition is that you are not as competent as others perceive you to be. The disciples seem to have been struck with a bout of the syndrome as they fall asleep in reaction to the grief of Jesus. Jesus should have been the one wearied by events.

Jesus challenges them, "Why are you sleeping?" At the very moment when they needed to be alert to the needs of Jesus and praying for Him, He was praying for them and they were fast asleep! It's not just they were tired – they were insensitive to the feelings of Jesus. They were unaware of what was going on around them, and all they could think of was themselves. Is that sadly reflective of our awareness too? We want to worship Jesus, but our prayers for this world and its turmoil are shallow and often non-existent. The acclaim of our worship songs is matched by the absence of our prayer. Why are we sleeping?

Wake us up, Lord, to the needs of a hurting and dying world when all we want to do is huddle in our "worship" pods and enjoy the music while the world is in discord.

November 23

"Get up and pray…"
Luke 22:46 Key passage: Luke 22:39-46

"The lights are on but no one's at home." How else do you explain the "vacant" look on someone's face? If it's us feeling vacant, we hope that no one has noticed! We don't understand what someone's talking about, or we're just not interested, or our mind is somewhere else until we're jolted into the present, and desperately try to "tune in" to what is going on.

The disciples had one of those moments – asleep at the critical moment, and then Jesus returns. He is wrestling with the consequences of the cross and God's moment of redemptive suffering for all mankind, and the disciples are having a nap! "Get up and pray…" – about what, Lord? It's not just a call to action, but to awareness and alertness. The Jewish man usually stood up to pray – Jesus has been kneeling before God in surrender. The Jew prayed with hands raised and arms outstretched – Jesus is about to pray for them and us in the same way, hands raised and arms outstretched, but on a cross. He calls us to pray too for a vacant world needing a Saviour.

Lord, I'm so lazy at praying sometimes. Shake me "awake" to the needs of this world and those around me.

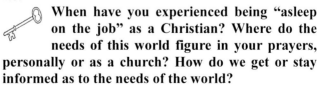 **When have you experienced being "asleep on the job" as a Christian? Where do the needs of this world figure in your prayers, personally or as a church? How do we get or stay informed as to the needs of the world?**

November 24

"No more of this!"
Luke 22:51 Key passage: Luke 22:47-53

Some people's enthusiasm is infectious…and others create more problems than they solve! We need enthusiasts, but sometimes they need a bit of taming. Peter certainly comes in that category. This was all Jesus needed at this moment – a High Priest's servant minus his ear. To be fair, Luke doesn't actually specify Peter as aggressor…but it was certainly in the spirit of Peter to do such a thing. No one's going to get the better of our Jesus in this situation…

The words of Jesus here are difficult to translate – they differ from His earlier words (verse 38) when the disciples, feeling the threatening atmosphere, produce two swords. What is clear is that Jesus asserts that there should be no fighting or aggression – all this is counter-productive to His purpose. He demonstrates His intention by healing the man. The way of Jesus is a different way to that of the world. So often our responses to issues and perceived threats do not honour God and His principles, but reflect our own brokenness and faulty humanity. "No more of this!" What might you do today that is different in honouring God?

Christians are called to be distinctive in their communities. That's different to just being "odd"! When the world "squeezes us into its mould", how can you be different and distinctive as a follower of Jesus today?

November 25

"Am I leading a rebellion…?"
Luke 22:52 Key passage: Luke 22:47-53

My wife used to work in a bank. Among the customers was a famous wrestler who often appeared on television. He was enormous (in excess of 25 stone) and would come in the bank with his pet chihuahua which he placed carefully on the counter! He was the epitome of a gentle giant.

The authorities felt threatened by Jesus, and came for him in force. The chief priests bore authority for their role, and their presence lends gravitas to the arrest, as does the presence of "officers of the temple guard" (kind of senior police officers) and "elders" (from the Sanhedrin, the local religious council). They were taking no chances with this Jesus…

…but Jesus comes "lowly", and responds to this show of force with the disarming question, "Am I leading a rebellion?" He has no weapon but love, no agenda but salvation, no soldiers but a motley band of disciples, no rallying cry except "Father, forgive!" This is no rebellion, but it is a revolution! They don't know how to cope with this. Oh the folly of believing that everything in this world can be sorted by force!

"See, your king comes to you…gentle, and riding on a donkey…" (Zechariah 9.9). How can we be "gentle" yet strong as followers of Jesus?

November 26

"This is your hour when darkness reigns"
Luke 22:53 Key passage: Luke 22:47-53

History records King Canute thinking he could hold back the tide, but the reality of the story is rather different. His courtiers thought Canute all-powerful, but he knew the truth. Demonstrating this, Canute set his throne by the sea-shore at Bosham, West Sussex, and commanded the incoming tide to halt. Yet "continuing to rise as usual [the tide] dashed over his feet and legs without respect to his royal person. The king leapt backwards, saying: 'Let all men know how empty and worthless is the power of kings, for there is none worthy of the name, but He whom heaven, earth, and sea obey by eternal laws.'" He then hung his gold crown on a crucifix, and never wore it again "to the honour of God the almighty King".

The truth will out. Jesus declares of the Jewish authorities, "This is your hour". The tide of public hatred washes in, but Jesus will not resist it. The powers of this world are "empty and worthless" as Jesus the "crowned king" hangs on a cross "to the honour of God the almighty King". The tide has truly turned!

"The head that once was crowned with thorns is crowned with glory now; a royal diadem adorns the mighty victor's brow". (Thomas Kelly)

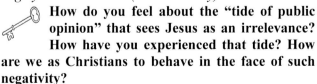 **How do you feel about the "tide of public opinion" that sees Jesus as an irrelevance? How have you experienced that tide? How are we as Christians to behave in the face of such negativity?**

November 27

"The Lord turned and looked straight at Peter"
Luke 22:61 Key passage: Luke 22:54-62

Wilhelm Rontgen's discovery is one of those "happy" accidents of history – the discovery of the X-ray. On the 8th. November 1895 Rontgen was experimenting with cathode rays passing through glass when he noticed something else - the invisible became visible.

"The Lord turned and looked straight at Peter…". Jesus didn't need to say anything – the look was enough. Peter knew that too. All his words, his enthusiasm, his ideas, his encouragement, his gushing, his longing – all counted for nothing in that moment. He knew that the loyalty he had just proclaimed to Jesus, the horror at the suggestion of Jesus' betrayal, the profession of undying commitment all sounded so hollow, because the Galilean accent that had just betrayed him to the servant girl was betraying him to his Master.

Yet "the Lord turned and looked straight" at him. That's what Jesus does – deals with people straight. No pretence, no "beating about the bush". He does what Peter is fond of doing – saying it like it is, except that with Jesus we know it's the heartfelt truth. The invisible becomes visible!

Lord, You know everything about me, even the bits that I don't want to recognise myself. Help me to face up to the truth, knowing that You still love me and want me to find fulfilment in following You.

November 28

Peter remembered the word the Lord had spoken "You will disown me…"
Luke 22:61 Key passage: Luke 22:54-62

One night whilst living in London, my wife and I got lost in the back streets of Soho. We had been to see the Christmas lights in the West End, and took a turning hoping to find the road back home. We ended up down a one-way street, with the road ahead "closed", and the turnings to left and right indicating "No Entry".

Peter must have felt in this moment a worse sense of confusion, regret, puzzlement and shame. He didn't know which way to turn. He would never have dreamed of letting Jesus down in this way, of denying any knowledge of him and forsaking Him at the moment of His greatest need, yet somehow he'd taken a "wrong turning" and was now faced with a real conundrum…and he "remembered the word the Lord had spoken". It's strange what the memory forgets – and what it suddenly recalls. Yet these words come from the lips of Jesus, who remembered Peter and loved him despite all his faults. This Jesus remembers you too…and loves you.

Thank You, Lord, that You loved Peter despite all his faults. I'm so much like him…yet You love me too. When I'm in a fix, remind me, Lord, that You only want the best for me.

 When and in what situations have you been tempted to hide your faith? How did you feel about that? How do you imagine Jesus feels about that?

November 29

"If I tell you, you will not believe me"
Luke 22:67
Key passage: Luke 22:66-71

"Truth is stranger than fiction, because fiction is obliged to stick to probability, and truth ain't." (Mark Twain). It's astonishing the things people will believe – even when they are patently in the realm of the fanciful. When that truth concerns the person of Jesus, then people's credulity finds itself stretched.

The problem here is that although Jesus is "in the dock", it's really the Sanhedrin who are on trial. They want a quick answer to satisfy their legal obligations before deciding what to do with Jesus. It's like asking a defendant if they plead guilty before even stating the charge. Is it the individual or the system that's in trouble? The issue, however, is the matter of Messiahship. For the Sanhedrin, Jesus cannot possibly be the Messiah, and therefore He is guilty of blasphemy. For Jesus, Messiahship is about rather more than personal identity – it is about divine identity. So they try to get Jesus to self-incriminate. Jesus understands that whatever He says at this moment, the Sanhedrin will not believe Him, their mind is made up. Truth stranger than fiction? Or is truth stronger than fiction?

"Who is He that from His throne rules through all the world alone?" (Benjamin Hanby)

November 30

"You are right in saying that I am"
Luke 22:70 Key passage: Luke 22:66-71

US President Bill Clinton, facing a Grand Jury investigation into his affair with Monica Lewinsky, said, "It depends on what the meaning of the word "is" is…" The reason for the statement should not worry us, but the fact that he could play with the word indicates the difficulty of making any kind of assertion and being generally understood!

Jesus faced a similar quandary before the Sanhedrin when asked, "Are you then the Son of God?" He knows He is, but they cannot bring themselves to think He is, and their understanding of the question differs so essentially from that of Jesus that it renders the question almost ineffective. That is why Jesus replies, "You are right in saying that I am". They have got the answer, but cannot understand what the answer means, simply because they have not really understood the question! For them, they have heard enough – He is guilty!

But listen to the question. If Jesus is the Son of God, Messiah, then what follows matters most of all. It matters to them individually, just as it matters to us!

"He is the Lord!" Help me, God, to understand what it means to assert that Jesus is Messiah.

 Why is it not enough just to "believe" in Jesus? Where does affirmation of His lordship lead you? How have you made that affirmation? What did that mean to you?

DECEMBER 1

"It is as you say"
Luke 23:3   Key passage: Luke 23:1-25

"Rearranging deckchairs on the Titanic" was a phrase first used in 1969 describing a futile action in the face of a much bigger crisis. Pilate may well have experienced such a sensation when confronted with these troublesome Jews wanting to prosecute one of their number over some issue of blasphemy (which was not a capital offence in Roman law), but he knew that he needed to keep these subject people "onside". There was only one thing for it – "Are you the king of the Jews?" Pilate thought he was being confronted with some kind of resistance fighter – but the reality was so different.

We're not told how Pilate asked this question – as a matter of fact or of incredulity – but the answer was unsettling: "It is as you say". Jesus was King of the Jews, but Pilate's understanding was different. That's why Pilate could only assert, "I find no basis for a charge against this man". History may not serve Pilate well, but we should understand his vacillation. It's a question every person has to answer of Jesus – "Who is He?" Jesus Himself has told us!

Is Jesus king? How do you answer that question? What does it mean to acknowledge Jesus as king? What does it mean for you? What might it mean for other people?

December 2

"Do not weep for me, weep for yourselves and your children"
Luke 23:28 Key passage: Luke 23:26-43

Eva Peron's name is etched in history – even if you know little of her, you'll probably know the musical about her. The wife of Argentine dictator Juan Peron, she is buried in La Recoleta Cemetery, Buenos Aires, with the enigmatic inscription "Don't cry for me Argentina – I remain quite near to you".

Of all the gospel writers, it is Luke who records these words of Jesus as He is led out to crucifixion. The numbers of those who clamoured for his execution were relatively small, but their voices prevailed. A larger number of sympathizers were unheard, but it was to them that Jesus addressed these words. The women onlookers were of particular interest to Luke, for he is concerned that their voice might never be heard. Jesus speaks to them as city dwellers, urging them to repent in the face of the coming judgment. Whatever is about to happen on the cross will be mirrored in the events in Jerusalem in coming days – the judgment of God will come upon them. Jesus says to them and us, "Don't cry for me…I remain very near to you."

"Yes, You are a God of justice, and Your judgement surely comes: upon the nation…have mercy, Lord!" (Graham Kendrick). When we live through times of trial, remind us, Lord, that You are very near.

 How is Jesus near to you right now? How have you experienced that nearness? What has that meant to you? What would you pray for those who cannot sense His nearness?

December 3

"If men do these things…what will happen when it is dry?"
Luke 23:31 Key passage: Luke 23:26-43

The Gospel of Luke is unique in the New Testament. Among other things, Luke writes with an intensity as a medical doctor and an interest in the physicality of life, plus a concern to provide us with a comprehensive insight into the life of Jesus. He records more of the actual words of Jesus than any other gospel writer, and has a special interest in the place of the marginalised and despised of society – and that includes women. These words of Jesus spoken to some of the women of Jerusalem are tender and instructive. The gospels never record a woman physically despising Jesus, but only attending to Him in love and service. Jesus' heart for these women is clear – He laments for them in the coming tribulation. Alfred Edersheim, himself a Jew, reflected, "If Israel has put such flame to its 'green tree' how terribly would the Divine judgment burn among the dry wood of an apostate and rebellious people, that had so delivered up its Divine King, and pronounced sentence upon itself by pronouncing it upon Him!" Consider Jesus carefully…then worship Him.

When we fail to understand that by rejecting Jesus we bring rejection upon ourselves, show us Lord the folly of our ways – and help us to worship Him as Lord!

December 4

"Father forgive them"
Luke 23:34 Key passage: Luke 23:26-43

We live in an age of offence – personal, political, racial…You can hardly move for fear of causing distress to someone by words and actions or lack of them! By contrast, you rarely hear people saying, "I've forgiven them…" yet these are the words on the lips of Jesus on the cross, "Father, forgive them."

Forgiving is tough. It challenges us at our deepest level. We think that we might forgive, but we can never forget…and the trouble is our inability to forget drags up all the emotions of the past. The prayer of Jesus is profound in its request – seeking the forgiveness of His executioners. However, we are unsure of the identity of the "them" for whom Jesus prays. It may be the Jews at whose hands He is now on the cross, or the Romans who have carried out this gruesome punishment. Could it also be that He prays for the two who hang with Him – who are just as "lost" as the onlookers? And where are we in this story? How many times have we "crucified" Jesus in ignorance and shame…yet God in His mercy is willing to forgive!

Lord, I'm humbled by the mercy You showed on that cross in announcing forgiveness – and whoever it was that You were praying for, I believe You prayed for me too. I confess that I didn't know what I was doing in rejecting You for so long. Help me to experience the real joy of forgiveness right now!

When and how have you experienced forgiveness, from another person, or from God Himself? How did it change you? How did it change your understanding of God's action in Jesus? Who or what do you need to forgive right now?

December 5

"Father, they do not know what they are doing"
Luke 23:34 Key passage: Luke 23:26-43

"Ignorance is bliss" – words first penned by Thomas Gray in 1768 in his *"Ode on a distant prospect of Eton College"*. Not having been to Eton, I'm not sure what he was blissfully ignorant of, but there is a difference between ignorance and insensitivity. We may not be held responsible for ignorance – since what you do not know you cannot answer for – but we are surely responsible for insensitivity.

The cry of Jesus from the cross echoes around Calvary – "they do not know what they are doing". The Romans knew very well what they were doing – it was one of the ways they maintained law and order especially among subject people. The Jews knew very well what they were doing – rejecting the claims of Jesus to be the Messiah and seeking to silence Him. They all knew what they were doing…but they didn't. They all lacked the spiritual insight that would have opened their eyes to the greater truth. The question for each of us is, "What will you do with Jesus?" Ignorance is never bliss…but the way to a lost eternity!

Open our eyes, Lord, to know what we are doing in acknowledging You as Lord – and forgive us for so much that demonstrates our ignorance of Your ways.

December 6

"Today you will be with me in paradise"
Luke 23:43 Key passage: Luke 23:26-43

With the death of a family member, I'm busy sorting out all kinds of legal issues. Ultimately there is the administration of the will. In this case, there are several beneficiaries, most of whom know nothing about it at this moment. The sadness at losing a loved relation will be matched eventually with gratitude at having been remembered in the will.

Jesus encounters the penitent thief next to him on his cross. This man, although being punished for his unspecified crimes, has some kind of heart of understanding and compassion. He is not totally hard-bitten. He even rebukes the third criminal for his hardness of heart. He recognises in Jesus something genuine, heart-warming, attractive – "remember me…" There were plenty of people who remembered him already, but for all the wrong reasons. Jesus remembers him for the right reason. The promise given is of immediate blessing – the penitent sought some blessing in the future…Jesus blessed Him in the immediate. Isn't that just like the Saviour? In the darkest moment, Jesus comes with reassurance of His presence now!

Thank You Jesus that we don't have to wait to receive Your mercy, but it is given right now. Come in this moment and bring the blessing of Your presence in the turmoil of daily life.

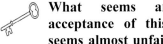 **What seems amazing about Jesus' acceptance of this penitent thief? What seems almost unfair? What do you imagine the thief saw in Jesus? What did Jesus see in him?**

December 7

"Father into your hands I commit my spirit"
Luke 23:46 Key passage: Luke 23:44-49

"I told you I was ill" is Spike Milligan's epitaph in Irish on his gravestone in Winchelsea, reflecting his love of the surreal, ridiculous and crazy. Famous last words indeed!

There are last words and famous last words, but none can match the humility and tenderness of these words of Jesus on the cross. Quoting Psalm 31.5, Luke records these words in contrast to the other gospel writers who record the words of dereliction "My God…why have you forsaken me? (Matthew 27.46, Mark 15.34), or the word of fulfilment recorded by John "It is finished" (John 19.30). For Luke, there is no contradiction in these accounts – he understands that in this moment Jesus is at one with His Father, and His last utterance is one of unbounded trust in the goodness and trustworthiness of God. Luke's record tells us loudly and clearly that death is not the end, but a moment of transition from earth to heaven, from the physical to the spiritual, from grief to glory. If Jesus could utter these words of hope in the face of death, then we may have hope in Him too!

Lord, when my final moment comes, may I commit my spirit into Your hands in trust and reassurance.

December 8

"What are you discussing?"
Luke 24:17 Key passage: Luke 24:13-35

I once had an office that was located on a street corner. It was instructive overhearing snippets of conversation from people outside, but you wondered what the rest of the discussion had been about!

As the two friends walk the road from Jerusalem down to Emmaus, they are joined by another traveller. The weather is not a topic of conversation, nor the latest sports scores…they are animatedly talking politics! "What are you discussing?" asks the stranger. – "they stood still, their faces downcast". How could this traveller from Jerusalem know nothing of the tumultuous events of the last few days? Did they really have to recount it all for him? They do…and what follows is a model summary of the Christian gospel. If you ever need to explain the Good News to someone, forget the 12-part Evangelism Course! It's all here…except that they had not yet made the connection and believed for themselves. What are you discussing with your friends and neighbours…?

Pray today for your friends, family and neighbours – especially those who do not yet know Jesus personally. Remember – someone told you once about Jesus. Pray that if the opportunity arises you may have the simple words to discuss with them the question of who Jesus is….and if the opportunity does not arise, then at least keep on praying for them!

December 9

"What things?"
Luke 24:19 Key passage: Luke 24:13-35

"I wanna tell you a story" was a favourite line of Max Bygraves. Some people are born storytellers, but others take a long time to get to the point. It's really difficult listening to someone recounting a tale and you are trying to look interested when the story becomes tiresome. The best conversationalists know exactly what questions to ask and when.

Jesus asks something very simple – "What things?" The Greek is just one word – "What?" It's the equivalent of a verbal ?, a raising of the eyebrows and tilt of the shoulders. It is the invitation to tell the story of Jesus to Jesus…and reveal their own understanding. They see Him as a prophet fulfilling a dynamic spiritual role. They see Him as a possible Saviour for Israel. They are puzzled by the disappearance of His body from the tomb, and are prepared to listen to the word of the women with whom they obviously have some kind of contact. They have heard that He may be alive…and they are at this cliff-edge of faith. Have you stood there too, armed with all the facts, but needing a personal encounter with Jesus? This could be your story…!

Jesus it's one thing knowing all about You, something else knowing You personally. If I've ever been in doubt as to a personal encounter with You, then come to me right now and help me to know beyond doubt that You are alive.

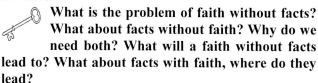 **What is the problem of faith without facts? What about facts without faith? Why do we need both? What will a faith without facts lead to? What about facts with faith, where do they lead?**

December 10

"He explained what was said in all the Scriptures"
Luke 24:27 Key passage: Luke 24:13-35

Can you feel those hairs on the back of your neck? Every felt them stand up? It's not just in moments of fear, but also moments of awe that something happens to the minor muscles at the root of our hairs. Adrenaline causes them to pull the hairs upright and you get that sensation of "being alive"!

What did these two feel at this moment? As far as they understood, this stranger had an amazing grasp of the Hebrew Scriptures and the span of Jewish history. He explained to them from the Books of the Law onwards through the Prophets all the allusions to the Messiah and the fulfilment of those words. I'd love to have listened in! What a mind to know the Scriptures (he had obviously been well schooled from a young age by excellent teachers) and then to be able to apply it to the current national situation! What a heart to understand the purposes of God as revealed in the Scriptures which find their fulfilment in the cross and the overwhelming love of God for His people! What a Saviour! Hair-raising stuff indeed…

Speak to me, Lord, the truth "in all the Scriptures" of who Jesus is. Give me a hunger for that Word, not just to read and understand, but to know the Christ of the Scriptures.

December 11

"How foolish you are, and how slow of heart..."
Luke 24:25 Key passage: Luke 24:13-35

There's a difference between the truth and the whole truth, and that's not just in a court of law! The problem is that it's so easy to get hold of a piece of truth and think you've got the whole truth. Christians are very good at that!

They're not alone! It happens across all faiths, and across all political persuasions. It happens in business and commerce, international relations and medicine. Beware of being so assertive that you exclude new truth! The two on the Emmaus Road have got all the facts at their fingertips, they recount all the events in Jerusalem, and they've just listened to a masterclass in biblical exegesis, but they still haven't made the connection. Jesus' words may sound less than complimentary, but they invite the taking of one more step. They had grasped the Scriptures about the Messiah but they hadn't grasped the things about the cross. One without the other is meaningless. We often hear preaching today about the love of God, but not so much about God's judgement and remedy for sin – that seems a bit unpopular! Truth or whole truth...what's your choice?

Help me, Lord, to grasp the whole truth of who You are – including the meaning of the cross in all its shame and agony.

When has the Christian Church mishandled "truth"? What has been the outcome? Why has much modern preaching tended to focus so much on the love of God? Why is it hard to speak of the judgment of God?

December 12

"Did not the Christ have to suffer...and enter his glory?"
Luke 24:26 Key passage: Luke 24:13-35

It is said that the psychoanalyst Carl Jung invented the phrase "the wounded healer" to reflect the possibility that the counsellor can only best help the patient by addressing their own hurts. Yet the phrase may belong elsewhere! Jesus sits at table with the Emmaus Road two and asks this telling question, "Did not the Christ have to suffer?"

We'd like the think the answer has to be "no". Why should this be necessary? Could God not send His Messiah and rescue His people there and then? Is God being cruel? The Emmaus Two knew the prophecies about the Messiah, but they focused only on the coming glory of the Messiah. Jesus points them to "all" the words of the prophets. The suffering of the Promised One was indeed necessary – He "had to suffer" in order that God's salvation might be declared. Hebrews 9.22 echoing Leviticus 17.11 declares that "without the shedding of blood there is no forgiveness". It is through suffering that Christ enters into His glory. Jesus is The Wounded Healer *par excellence* – for "by his wounds we are healed" (Isaiah 53.3).

"Upon that cross of Jesus my eye at times can see the very dying form of One who suffered there for me; and from my stricken heart, with tears, two wonders I confess – the wonders of redeeming love, and my own worthlessness" (Elizabeth Clephane)

December 13

"He took bread and gave thanks"
Luke 24:30 Key passage: Luke 24:13-35

Isn't that just the way of things…something extraordinary happens at the most unexpected of moments. If we'd known that was going to happen, we'd have been better prepared – we'd have got dressed up, had a haircut, had the camera ready…

…but we hadn't! It just happened and the event is eternally implanted in the memory. For the Emmaus Two it was one of those moments. They'd invited this travelling companion to stay overnight as it was now dark and dangerous out on the road, and before bed they shared some supper. In line with conventional Jewish tradition, a small prayer of thanks was said as bread was broken in a token of thanksgiving and shared together before the main food was eaten. They invited the visitor to say the prayer of thanks…and it was then that this thing happened! We're not told why, but "their eyes were opened"! Did they see the nail marks on His hands, was it something in the way He spoke, or was it simply God's moment of revelation? Sometimes God does that.

"Open your eyes, see the glory of the King…" (Carl Tuttle). When has God just revealed something to you without warning or preparation? How did you come to meet Jesus personally? Thank Him for the wonder of His revelation!

Reflect on a moment when your "eyes were opened" to some truth about Jesus. How did your understanding or behaviour change? Has there been a moment when you encountered Jesus in a situation of trial, difficulty, illness, or sadness? What happened?

December 14

"Peace be with you"
Luke 24:36 Key passage: Luke 24:36-49

Having experienced periods of national lockdown because of the global virus crisis, we can appreciate that sometimes it's difficult to distinguish one day from another! When the highlight of the week is remembering to put the dustbin out, you know that things have become pretty mundane!

The appearance of Jesus to the disciples was anything but mundane – this would be remembered all their lives. The Emmaus Two return to Jerusalem and find the Eleven disciples huddled together wondering what to do next, and as they excitedly share news of the appearance of the risen Christ to Simon and then to them in their home, something happens. Jesus Himself is there and greets them with the everyday "Shalom!" – "Peace be with you!" Not all gospel writers record these words. Whether they thought this too mundane to record, we do not know. What we do know is that Jesus' greeting is anything but mundane. When the Lord comes, there is hope and joy! In the middle of turmoil, Jesus comes to bring peace – He did it on a storm-tossed Galilee, He did it on a seashore, and He does it now.

Lord, speak that word of "peace" to me and to this troubled world today. When all is in disarray and confusion, help us to know Your astonishing peace!

December 15

"Why do doubts arise in your minds?"
Luke 24:38 Key passage: Luke 24:36-49

"I used to be a sceptic, but now I don't believe it!" The world is strangely divided – between those who seem to believe anything ("it's on the internet so it must be true") and those who don't believe anything (consider those who "deny" things like the Holocaust, global warming, a round earth or vaccine effectiveness).

Jesus' disciples would seem to belong in the latter category – they were finding it hard to believe in this moment that Jesus was really there – "they were startled and frightened, thinking they saw a ghost..." Well, wouldn't you be astonished? Jesus moves to reassure them. Look at the evidence before you. He appeals to the physical evidence – He shows them His hands and His feet, the marks of the nails and the crucifixion. Not only can they look, they are invited to touch and feel. Although Jesus appears in a glorified resurrection body, it obviously has some physicality to it. He asks for food, and eats it in front of them – all proof of His physical reality. So why doubt? Because it's easier to doubt than to believe? Now that I can't believe!

Lord, forgive me – I'm so full of doubts about all sorts of things, and doubt becomes a normal part of life. Teach me the certainty of Your resurrection!

 Why is it easier to doubt than to believe? How does belief challenge our certainty about ourselves?

December 16

"Look at my hands and feet. It is I myself."
Luke 24:39 Key passage: Luke 24:36-49

Semantics – the science of meaning, especially applied to words. If a "word" is "the expression of a thought", then the meaning behind the thought becomes important. "Semantics" means "significance" and so when interpreting a word, we must ask "what exactly did the speaker of this word intend to convey?"

When Jesus appeared to the disciples, He challenged them, "Look at my hands and feet." There's a world of difference between seeing and looking, just as there is between hearing and listening! Always ask, "What does that mean?" Luke records this incident using the word *"orao"* for "look". It has a deeper meaning than merely "seeing". The disciples are to look at His hands and feet...and see what? The imprint of the nails through the hands? The mark of the nail through the ankles? Is there another level of understanding beyond that? Are they to see the mark of love in those wounds, the love that took him to the cross? Do they see the purpose of God in those hands? Do they see the hand of God in that purpose...? Look carefully at the Word!

"Open my eyes that I may see wonderful things..."
(Psalm 119.18)

December 17

"Do you have anything to eat?"
Luke 24:41 Key passage: Luke 24:36-49

"The proof of the pudding is in the eating" is uttered by Cervantes in *Don Quixote*. The real test of something is not its appearance, but its acceptance. The request of Jesus to His disciples needs careful reflection because there's more to this than is obvious.

Was Jesus hungry? Possibly, but He appears to the disciples in a glorified body, one that shares some characteristics with our mortal bodies. Is hunger one of those? Is hunger merely a physical reaction or an emotional sensation?

Why does Jesus eat? To show to the disciples He is no mere ghostly apparition – since ghosts neither eat nor need to. He ate it "before their very eyes". Luke uses the word of eating and drinking suggesting "like any other human soul." He ate like you and me!

What does this show? "The pudding is the proof…" that what the disciples experienced was not some dream – there were enough disciples present to verify that. This was not some "apparition" that faded as quickly as it happened – Jesus stays with them. The Risen Jesus stands with us too – you are proof of His living presence!

Lord, when I'm consumed by doubt, show me the proof of Your living presence right now.

December 30

"I will be his God and he will be my son"
Revelation 21:7   Key passage: Revelation 21:1-8

The humble handshake has been having a rough time recently – since contact is one of the ways in which disease and virus are spread. Replaced by fist bumps (or worse, elbow prods) we have lost friendly welcome and contact. Conceived in distant times as a reassurance that our hand contained no offensive weapon, the handshake has undergone all sorts of interpretations…

…as an illustration of agreement to friendship between two parties. It's what God had done for His people centuries ago in the "new covenant": "I will be your God and you will be my people" (Jeremiah 31.33) – a commitment to His people despite their constant ignoring of His ways. God had never "gone soft" on sin, and neither had He vowed vengeance. He had promised that nothing could change the nature of His nature – He would always be the God of truth, justice, and love. That promise still holds good for you today! In Jesus He extends His nail-pierced hand in welcome to His family.

"Loved with everlasting love…But while God and I shall be, I am His and He is mine" (George Robinson)

December 31

"I am...the bright Morning Star"
Revelation 22:16   Key passage: Revelation 22:16-21

"And the winner is…" Tension mounts, expectation increases, excitement is high…the name is revealed. Then the arguments start. Social media is ablaze with disgruntled people expressing their disagreement. Arguments ensue about what should have been. If this sounds farfetched, then consider what happens at national level when new leaders are elected. Strangely, the loser often claims to be the real victor!

In the Roman world victory was regarded as the gift of the gods, and preeminent among those gods was Venus. She was honoured by generals and emperors alike and her image was carried by legions into battle. Venus was the Morning Star, shining bright out of the darkness. What the world needed in terms of power, guidance and leadership was to be found in the might of Rome. That might became corrupted, repugnant and repressive. The true dawn of righteousness and renewal is found in the One who comes, not in might but in meekness, whose promise is of hope, not hopelessness. It's often darkest before the dawn – and in the darkness of a lost world, the "I am" comes.

"One kingdom only is divine, one banner triumphs still; Its King? A peasant – and it's sign? A cross upon a hill!" (anon.)

 How has "A Word with Jesus" helped you grow as a Christian through this year? Why not start the journey again tomorrow?